KILDARE PLACE

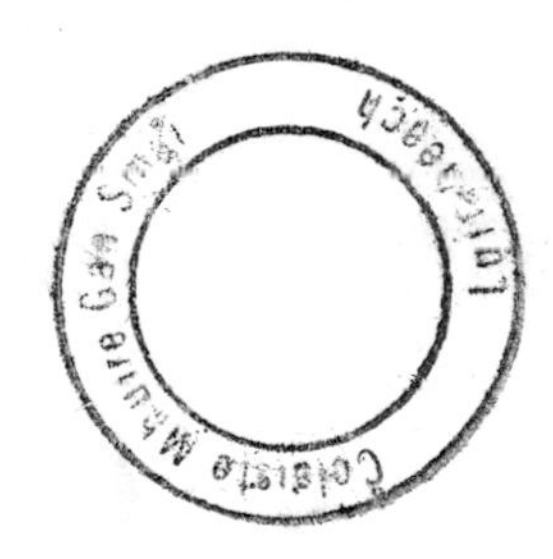
Coláiste Mhuire Gan Smál
Luimneach

KILDARE PLACE

The history of the Church of Ireland Training College 1811-1969

SUSAN M. PARKES

Foreword by Dr. Kenneth Milne,
Principal,
Church of Ireland College of Education

CICE

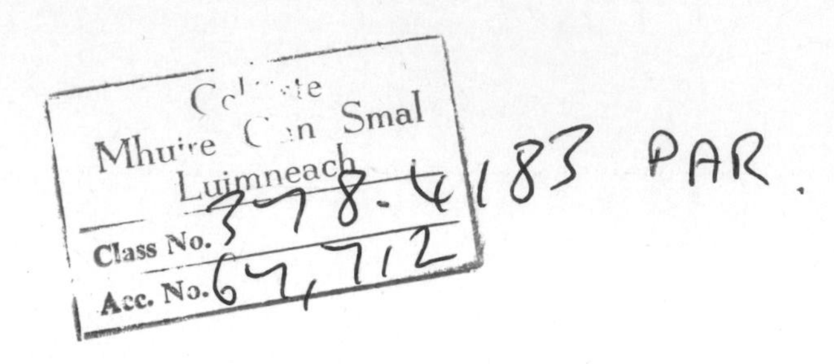

ISBN 0 9509289 0 9

Text set in 10pt. Times New Roman.

Designed by Charlotte Westbrook.

Printed in the Republic of Ireland by the Leinster Leader, Naas, Co. Kildare.

Published by the Church of Ireland College of Education,
Rathmines, Dublin 6, Ireland.

Acknowledgments: Illustrations 1—15 are reproduced by kind permission of the Governors of the Church of Ireland College of Education and illustration 16 by kind permission of the owner.

Thanks are due to the Photographic Centre, Trinity College, Dublin, for its assistance.

CONTENTS

ABBREVIATIONS

CNEI	Commissioners of National Education in Ireland
CITC	Church of Ireland Training College
TCD	Trinity College, Dublin
INTO	Irish National Teachers' Organization

LIST OF ILLUSTRATIONS

DEDICATION

To the staff and students of the Church of Ireland Training College, past and present

FOREWORD

When several years ago the College decided to have its history written it can scarcely have envisaged the emergence of a book such as Miss Susan Parkes has produced, that not only does the College proud both in scholarship and presentation, but also provides for a wider readership a contribution to our understanding of important aspects of Irish educational development over two centuries. By treating her subject consistently in the context not only of changes in teacher education, but also against the broader background of advances in elementary education, Miss Parkes has written the first detailed history of primary teacher training in this country.

What is more, the social historian is presented with a treatment of a Church of Ireland institution as it passed through the political and cultural changes of the nineteenth and twentieth centuries. Little enough of a scholarly nature has been written on these lines heretofore. Now we are presented with a case study of Anglican attitudes and reactions all the more interestingly portrayed because the author has no axe to grind other than to trace the response of an institution and its leaders, thrust by political forces into turbulent and uncharted waters.

Yet however meticulously Susan Parkes has researched and analysed her subject, we have to remember that we are dealing with history, not mathematics, and so no graph appears to help us plot the future. What we are left with, nonetheless, is a record of dedicated and professional service, and we can but hope that we in our generation may prove as resourceful as our forebears were in the face of challenges that are likely to be every bit as demanding.

KENNETH MILNE

PREFACE

At the invitation of the principal, Dr. K. Milne, I began work in 1977 on the archives of the Church of Ireland Training College which had been transferred from Kildare Place to Rathmines in 1969. These archives which since have been sorted and listed, contain the records of the Society for Promoting the Education of the Poor in Ireland (The Kildare Place Society) as well as those of the Church of Ireland Training College itself. This history of the college is based on my work and my interest in the archives and has been a pleasure and privilege to write.

To the governors of the Church of Ireland College of Education I am indebted for the invitation to write the history and for permission to consult archives. To the principal, Dr. Milne, the vice-principal, Miss G. Allen, and to the staff of the college I am most grateful for constant encouragement and warm hospitality over five years. No book is the product of the author alone and it is particularly true of this one. To Bishop G. O. Simms, secretary and chaplain of the college, 1943–52; to Miss E. F. Pearson, lady-registrar, 1933–67; to Dr. W. F. Pyle, governor of the college since 1954; and to Canon A. E. Stokes, member of staff, 1948–79, I am indebted for advice and information.

Many past students gave of their time and shared their reminiscences with me: the late Mrs. L. M. Coath (1915–17); Mr. G. W. Skillen (1916–18); Mrs. Elliott (1916–18); Miss E. E. Gillespie (1917–19); Mrs. A. Briggs (1918–20); Miss V. Hazelton (1918–20); Mrs. E. Spearman (1923–25); Mrs. K. Dennison (1923–25); Rev. W. J. Whittaker (1923–25); Mrs. A. Phillips (1931–33); Mr. R. W. J. Smyth (1931–33); Mr. F. T. Peters (1937–39); and Mr. J. Williams, pupil at the Kildare Place Model School (1949–53).

I wish to thank Miss Carol Revington for permission to use material from her M.Ed. paper 'Developments within the Church of Ireland Training College in the 1950s and 1960s'; Miss G. Willis of the Representative Church Body Library for assistance with the records of the Church Education Society; Professor T. D. Spearman, F.T.C.D. for details of his father, Mr. Thomas Spearman; Professor Joan D. Browne, formerly principal of Coventry College of Education, for details of Miss Annie Lloyd Evans; the Record Keeper, Greater London Record Office for material on Miss A. Lloyd Evans; Miss E. Cholmondeley for details of Miss F. C. A. Williams and Charlotte Mason College; Major J. B. Condon of Surrey for a copy of a scroll addressed to Miss F. C. A. Williams; Mrs. D. Mollan for material on her aunt, Miss M. J. Smith; Mr. F. O'Dwyer for advice on the architecture of Sir T. N. and Sir T. M. Deane; and to Dr. Áine Hyland of Carysfort College, Blackrock for relevant source material.

To Mr. T. Power of Trinity College who has been responsible for the calendar of the Kildare Place Society archives; to Mr. H. Hislop, keeper of the research area at the Church of Ireland College of Education; to Mrs. V. Coghlan, librarian of the college; and to Miss R. Bourne, secretary of the college, I am most grateful for ready assistance.

I wish to thank the Board of Trinity College for permission to quote material from the Board Registers and from the J. H. Bernard correspondence; also the Educational Studies Association of Ireland for permission to use material from my article 'The foundation of a denominational training college—The Church of Ireland Training College, 1878–1884', published in the *Proceedings of the 5th Annual Education Conference of the ESAI* (Limerick 1980).

Bishop G. O. Simms and Dr. K. Milne read the draft typescript and to them I am deeply indebted for advice and pertinent comment. Mrs. Jill Adams carefully typed the manuscript and corrected my mistakes. Charlotte Westbrook skilfully designed the layout and Mr. Kane guided the book through the press. My family and colleagues have supported and encouraged me throughout and to all I am most grateful. The remaining errors and shortcomings are mine alone.

Previous work on the history of CITC had been done by the first principal, Canon H. Kingsmill Moore, D.D., who in 1904 published *An Unwritten Chapter in the History of Education* which remains the standard work on the history of the Kildare Place Society. In 1911 he wrote *The Centenary of the Church of Ireland Training*

College, 1811–1911, which recorded the achievements of the college to that date. In 1942 Miss J. Beattie, lady superintendent of the college (1918–33), wrote *Brief History of Kildare Place Training College, 1811–1921* which was based on Kingsmill Moore's works. I wish to acknowledge my debt to their research and writing.

In 1984 the Church of Ireland College of Education celebrates the centenary of its establishment as a denominational training college for national school teachers, and for a hundred years it has trained Protestant primary teachers to teach in the national schools of Ireland. This history has been written to mark this achievement and is dedicated to the staff and students of the college, past and present.

Trinity College, Dublin
1983

SUSAN M. PARKES

INTRODUCTION

The Church of Ireland College of Education stands today in spacious grounds in Rathmines, Dublin 6. The students take a three year course leading to the B.Ed. degree from the University of Dublin. Its teachers serve the Protestant community in the Republic of Ireland, working in urban and rural national schools throughout the country. The college moved in 1969 to Rathmines from its old premises in Kildare Place in the centre of Dublin where it had functioned for 150 years.

The history of CITC dates from the Kildare Place Training Institution founded in 1811. This institution run by the Society for Promoting Education of the Poor in Ireland pioneered teacher training in the country and introduced the monitorial system to schools all over the island. Its successor was the Church Education Society college founded in the 1850s to train Anglican students for church schools and which offered a thorough education in religious and pious service. In 1878 the Church Education Society college was taken over by the General Synod of the Church of Ireland to be run as a training college for the Anglican community, and in 1884 the Church of Ireland Training College became a recognised denominational college for training national school teachers and receiving state aid.

As a national teacher training college CITC flourished and by 1922 had over 130 students in residence. However, following the political partition of Ireland into the Irish Free State and Northern Ireland, CITC lost two thirds of its students and shrank to a small college serving the Protestant minority in the south of Ireland only. Forced into a policy of retrenchment, the college had to adapt to meet the demands of the new education system in the Free State and had to become bilingual in Irish and English. It seemed at times that the college might not survive but due to the courage and determination of its governors and staff it continued to work and emerged in the 1960s an expanding and vigorous institution once again, and in 1969 moved to new premises in Rathmines. The name of the college was changed to the 'Church of Ireland College of Education' in line with other training colleges, and in the 1970s the students began to take the three year B.Ed. degree of Trinity College, Dublin. Today it is an open co-educational community in which the students participate in university life as well as receiving a thorough professional training.

The history of the Kildare Place college covers the development of formal teacher training from the humble beginnings of the monitorial system in the early nineteenth century to the emergence of a fully qualified graduate profession by the mid-twentieth century. It sees teacher training change from the simple recruitment of senior primary school children, drilled in the mechanics of classroom management, to a carefully selected secondary educated student body taking a three year degree course in general and professional studies. The primary school itself has changed from a place where rote learning and formal instruction were the order of the day to a place where spontaneous activity, individualised learning and creative handicraft play as important a part in the education of the child as the basic skills of literacy and numeracy. The professional status of the primary teacher has changed from that of a humble, dutiful, obedient servant to that of a confident, respected and well-paid professional. The training colleges have contributed to these developments by giving their students the necessary education and skills to undertake their difficult task, and by leading the way in educational development and reform. Primary teaching in Ireland was a lay calling and therefore the churches took a particular interest in the formation of primary teachers. The school was seen as an extension of the church and the teacher an important instrument in the religious education of the child. The partnership between church and state which developed within the national school system contributed to the success of the denominational training colleges which for a hundred years have produced teachers acceptable to both powers.

The history of the college also reflects the attitudes of the Church of Ireland to the state system of education. When the national school system was established in 1831 the Church of Ireland refused to support it as it was unable to accept the rules which required that religious instruction should be taught separately from secular and moral instruction. The established church maintained, as did other churches, that religion was central to the education of a child and should not be excluded from other knowledge. However, the Church of Ireland, unlike the other churches which entered the national system and attempted successfully to modify its rules, decided to opt out of the system and being the established church had sufficient funds to maintain its own voluntary schools. The Church Education Society was founded in 1839 to support anglican schools and until the disestablishment of the Church of Ireland in 1871 it was able to do this. However, shortage of funds eventually forced the Church of Ireland to bring its schools into the national system and accept state aid. The decision in 1884 to place the Church of Ireland Training College in connexion with the National Board was a major one in the history of the Church of Ireland. It marked the acceptance of the state school system by the Church and enabled separate Protestant primary schools to survive. Denominational education was strengthened within the national system and the rights of clerical management were upheld by the Church of Ireland school managers as well as by those of the Roman Catholic Church. The first principal of CITC, Rev. Canon H. Kingsmill Moore, played an important role in the negotiations with the government leading to the Balfour 'Free Home' scheme in the 1890s which gave the denominational training colleges financial security, and he remained an active advocate of the training colleges' interests throughout his long career as principal.

In 1922 when the Church of Ireland was faced with the political partition of Ireland it attempted to retain a joint system of teacher training whereby CITC would train teachers for schools both north and south of the border. This proved impossible due to pressure from both sides so CITC had to accept the harsh reality of becoming a much smaller college serving the religious minority in the south of Ireland only. Despite the difficulties, the college strove to meet the demands of the education system of the Free State, and the success of CITC in providing fully qualified national school teachers for the Protestant primary schools contributed much to the survival of the southern Protestant community and to its harmonious integration into the new state. Along with the preparatory college, Coláiste Moibhí, CITC produced teachers fluent in Irish who could teach the language in schools and a knowledge of Irish ceased to be a sectarian barrier. The confidence and loyalty of the Protestant minority was earned by the Free State government; and the generous support of Protestant national schools and of the training college contributed to this.

Thus the Kildare Place College over 150 years has been part of the development of education in Ireland. From the pioneer non-denominational training institution of the 1820s to the university-linked Church of Ireland college of the 1980s, it has reflected the changes and vicissitudes of the educational system of the country and has earned its place in history.

I

The Kildare Place Society Training Institution, 1811–1855

The Society for Promoting the Education of the Poor in Ireland was founded in 1811 by a group of philanthropic Dublin business men. It became popularly known as the 'Kildare Place Society' because of the location of its headquarters. The aim of the Society was to provide elementary education for the poor in Ireland and its leading principle was 'to afford the same facilities for Education to all classes of professing Christians without any attempt to interfere with the peculiar religious opinions of any'.[1]

From the outset the Society regarded teacher training as one of its main functions. At the opening meeting in December 1811 the founder members were present, including Samuel Bewley of the Quaker family, Mr. William L. Guinness, Mr. John David La Touche, the banker, and Mr. Joseph Devonsher Jackson, an eminent barrister. The fourth resolution passed contained the phrase 'to give information and assistance to local Associations for the fitting up of school houses upon a suitable plan and for providing Teachers properly qualified'. The Society was much influenced by the government commission on education which had been set up in 1806 to examine the state of education of the poor in Ireland and which had recommended that any system of providing education for the poor must attempt to unite the religious denominations in Ireland, and protect children against the danger of proselytism:

> We are convinced this to be of essential importance in any new establishments of Education of the lower classes in Ireland and we venture to express our unanimous opinion, that no such plan however wisely and unexceptionable in other respects can be carried into effectual execution in this country, unless it be explicitly avowed, and clearly understood as its leading principle, that no attempt shall be made to influence or disturb the peculiar religious interests of any Sect or descriptions of Christians.[2]

The report also declared that:

> a more essential service could not be rendered to the state than by carrying into effect a practical mode of supplying a succession of well-qualified Instructors for the children of the lower classes.[3]

Therefore it was to such purposes that the Kildare Place Society turned its attention. The leading principle of the Society was that in all schools under its auspices the Bible was to be read to the children 'without note or comment' and no other religious instruction was allowed. It attempted to separate religious from secular and moral instruction, and to maintain a strictly non-denominational principle in all its activities. At first the Society had plenty of support and in 1815 it received a generous parliamentary grant and its work grew in size and influence. By 1825 it was supporting 1,490 schools which contained about 100,000 pupils, and 207 teachers had been trained.

However, the Kildare Place Society ran into serious difficulties in the 1820s because of its fundamental rule on bible reading. While the practice of reading the scriptures 'without note or comment' was generally acceptable to Protestants it was not acceptable to the Roman Catholic Church. As the Catholic Church gained confidence and became more politically powerful, encouraged by the political leadership of Daniel O'Connell, the Society came under attack for its refusal to compromise on this principle. It was also accused of supporting schools which were in receipt of grants from other educational societies such as the London Hibernian Society and the Association for Discountenancing Vice, which were missionary societies dedicated to the religious conversion of the Roman Catholic poor.

In 1825 under increasing pressure from the Roman Catholic hierarchy the government agreed to set up an education inquiry into the provision of education for the poor. This commission reported the following year and while acknowledging the work done by the Kildare Place Society in providing schools, printing school books and training teachers, it stated that the society was no longer acceptable to the majority of the poor of the country, and that a neutral national board of education should be established by the government to distribute the state grants for education.[4] In 1825 the society was receiving a grant of £25,000 but with the establishment of the Board of Commissioners of National Education in 1831 the parliamentary grant was withdrawn. Lord Stanley, the chief secretary, who established the new National Board, regarded the scheme as an experiment in its early years, and he presented the rules under which it was to function in a letter addressed to the Duke of Leinster, first president of the Board. This 'Stanley Letter', as it was to be known, became the basis on which the national education system was to operate. The letter acknowledged the failure and unhappy position of the Kildare Place Society:

> Although the Kildare Place Society prospered and extended its operation under the fostering care of Legislature . . . the Roman Catholic Church began to exert themselves with energy and success against a system to which they were on principle opposed, and which they feared might lead to proselytism, even though no such object was contemplated by its promoters. When this opposition arose founded on such grounds, it soon became manifest the system could not become one of National Education.[5]

However, from 1811 to 1831 the achievements of the Kildare Place Society were remarkable, particularly in the field of teacher-training and text book publication, and helped to lay the foundations of a system of popular education in Ireland. The training institution and model schools which the Society established in Kildare Place pioneered a course of formal training for teachers and developed the idea of a qualified profession of teachers of the poor. Although the Society itself achieved little after 1831 owing to lack of funds, and it ceased to play a major role in Irish education, it retained legal ownership of the Kildare Place Institution until 1887 when the society was finally wound up.

In order to provide teacher training the Kildare Place Society decided to establish its own 'model' schools in Dublin to which schoolmasters from the country were to be invited to see the 'new improved methods' in practice. In the early nineteenth century the new improved method of education was the monitorial system, based on those of Joseph Lancaster and the Rev. Andrew Bell. It was the Lancasterian system which was adopted by the Kildare Place model schools. Joseph Lancaster, a young Quaker, had opened his first school in 1797 in London in an outhouse of his father's premises. By 1801 he had had to move with his 350 pupils to a larger room in Borough Road, Southwark. His success in attracting pupils nearly 'overwhelmed him'. He was unable to teach them all himself and he was too poor to pay assistants. Therefore, he evolved the plan of using 'monitors'—of allowing the boys who knew a little to teach the boys who knew less. In 1803 Lancaster published his plan in a book *Improvements in Education*; the book was such a success that the third edition was published in 1805, and 'he had evolved not only a new kind of teacher but also a new kind of teaching and a new kind of school management'.[6]

It is not difficult to understand why the monitorial system had such a popular appeal in the early nineteenth century. In the absence of a state system of elementary education, economy was of great importance to the voluntary education societies dependent on subscriptions from members. The monitorial system of Lancaster and Bell was cheap and efficient for as the number of monitors increased the cost of each pupil decreased. One schoolmaster could teach up to a thousand boys. Moreover, the system encouraged orderliness, discipline and cleanliness, the necessary virtues of the nineteenth century poor. Bell's 'Madras' system differed only in detail from Lancaster and he had published his plan based on his experiences working with children in an orphanage in India in a book *Experiments in Education*. It was due to the Quaker connection between Lancaster and Bewley that the Kildare Place Society decided to adopt the Lancasterian system, and in seeking 'a well ordered system of education of the Poor which shall combine economy of time and money and bestow due attention on cleanliness and discipline',[7] the answer was to be found in the monitorial system. It also provided a useful method of recruiting young boys and girls to become teachers. Able pupils in the elementary schools were selected and served an apprenticeship as monitors under a master, thus learning to become teachers themselves. The majority of teachers in the nineteenth century were trained in this way, and only a select minority was 'called' for training at an institution. Training colleges did not become an essential feature of teacher training until the end of the century.

Joseph Lancaster himself was present at the opening meeting of the Kildare Place Society on December 11th 1811. Although the Society refused to have formal links with the Royal Lancasterian Society in England (soon to become the British and Foreign School Society), a request was sent to London for a suitably qualified trained official to inaugurate the teacher-training scheme. In 1813, John Veevers came to Dublin to take up the appointment. He had been trained by Lancaster himself at the Borough Road Institution and had taken up a post in Birmingham. However, Lancaster had recognised Veevers' particular talents and he persuaded him to come to Dublin. He wrote to Bewley:

> I have at last a young man in view for you, one whom success will attend, who has been tried and proved for ten years and has the root of the matter in the very grain and soul of him.[8]

Veevers was only 23, 'of mild disposition and an accomplished mind'. He was reluctant to stay in Dublin for more than six months, but in fact he was to stay for forty years. He was persuaded to leave his employment in Birmingham and the British and Foreign School Society paid him an allowance of £100 for two years in addition to his salary of £200 from the Kildare Place Society. He proved an able and energetic young man and it was due to him that the Kildare Place Training Institution earned its high reputation.

When Veevers came in 1813, the Society had not yet been able to build its own model schools; therefore, a room in the School Street Schools in west Dublin was rented so that Veevers could begin 'to exhibit his system' and young men could come to be trained. The School Street Schools had been founded in 1786 in the heart of the Liberties in Dublin to provide both daily and Sunday schools for the poor children of the city. Some members of the School Street Society Committee, such as Samuel Bewley and John D. La Touche, were also members of the Kildare Place Society and they saw the new society as a national extension of their original work in the city.[9]

Veevers began his training school in School Street and the Society advertised that instruction would be offered 'free of all expenses' to young men who wished to learn the new methods. Students were expected to provide their own 'diet and lodgings'. In 1814 sixteen men were trained, and in 1815, seventeen. Among the first students were James Maye, aged 26, from a school in Lurgan, Co. Armagh, Daniel Horan, aged 38, from Francis Street School, Dublin, and Joseph Flynn, aged 19, from Co. Down. Both Maye and Horan were experienced teachers but Flynn was a novice. The students were recommended for training by a specific person or a committee; Maye was recommended by a Mrs. Brownlow, Horan by the governors of his school, Flynn by the committee of his school. The non-denominational principle was upheld: Maye and Flynn were Protestants and Horan was a Roman Catholic. The training course lasted only three to four weeks after which the students returned to their schools.[10] Each successful student received a certificate of which Mr. Flynn's is an example:

> This is to certify that Joseph Flynn hath diligently attended the School of the Society for Promoting the Education of the Poor in Ireland in School Street, Dublin, for the last six weeks, by which he hath had an opportunity of being acquainted with the mode of instruction recommended by the Society.
>
> Signed *John Veevers*

Encouraged by the initial success of its training school, the Society pushed ahead with its building plans. In 1815 a parliamentary grant of £6,980 was obtained for the specific purpose of purchasing a site and erecting a model school and seminary for the instruction of masters. The Society was fortunate to purchase a site in Kildare Place which was in a fashionable area of the city, yet where there would be a demand locally for education from the lower classes. Nearby in Kildare Street, Leinster House, the splendid town mansion of the Duke of Leinster, had recently been acquired by the Royal Dublin Society for its headquarters. 4 Kildare Place became the headquarters of the Kildare Place Society. It was a large Georgian house on the south side of the Place, with its side windows on to Kildare Street. The model schools were built on the long piece of ground to the side of No. 4, and were designed by the Dublin architect, William Farrell. There were two large school rooms, one for boys and one for girls. The front design of the schools was plain and classical, topped by a large pediment in keeping with the Georgian architecture of the surrounding houses. These schools were to remain in use until the 1930s and although they were refaced in a Victorian style by the Church of Ireland Training College in the 1890s, the school rooms themselves changed little in the 120 years. The whole site is now occupied by Agriculture House.

Meanwhile, Veevers continued his work at the School Street School. The increased funds of the Society enabled it to begin to give financial assistance

> to such young men as were properly commended and appeared to the committee not to possess the means from any other source, to enable them to undertake the journey to Dublin and to remain here for a length of time sufficient for their instruction.[12]

In the next year 17 young men trained assisted by the grant, and another 12 trained without it.

How beneficial the few weeks training at School Street were to these young teachers was difficult to assess. One way of finding out was to visit some of the Society's schools where the recently trained teachers were working. The Society's system of inspectors was only beginning; therefore, in 1818 Veevers himself set out in a gig to visit schools in chosen counties. On his return he wrote a detailed report for the Society, and being an honest man, he stated that although almost half the schools he visited 'were in the charge of a teacher trained by the Society . . . most of them acted as if they had never been trained at all'. The following year he made another tour of schools in Leinster and Munster and this time he was able to make a more encouraging report and wrote:

> most of the schools conducted by teachers trained in the Model School of the Society, are evidently superior to the neighbouring seminaries where masters have not had this advantage.[11]

Veevers' reports encouraged the Society's committee to consider the long term value and nature of the training course offered. The effectiveness of the training had been limited not only by the shortness of the course but also by the fact that the young men were only day-scholars at School Street. It was suggested that the benefits of the training course would be much increased if the young men resided together for the five or six weeks. Therefore plans were made to provide residential accommodation for the students at Kildare Place, and the importance of an enclosed seminary life for teachers in training was recognised. It was noted that living in the seminary would

> provide greater security for the morale and habits of the young men thus bound to observe regularity in hours and conduct, than if being lodged in one part of the city, and instructed in another, they were exposed to the occasions and temptations of misconduct, incident to a great metropolis.[14]

The model schools and seminary at Kildare Place were officially opened in 1819, and Veevers was appointed superintendent of both. The Society was aware of the increased responsibilities which it was undertaking. All the young men coming up from the country to be trained would be obliged to reside at Kildare Place and the Society would stand *in loco parentis*.

From 1819–1831 the model schools were highly successful. Under the firm guidance of John Veevers, an efficient and well-organized course of training in Lancasterian school management was developed. Although the work of the Society was, during the decade, to be bitterly criticised on many charges, its training methods were widely praised. The 1825 Commission Report acknowledged:

> While the Society have succeeded beyond their own sanguine expectations in some of their objects, they have failed in others . . . and it is observable, that in matters wherein they consider of less importance for instance . . . the training of masters and mistresses . . . they have conferred the most extensive and undoubted benefits on Ireland.[15]

As the prestige of the model schools increased the number of applicants for training likewise increased. By 1825 there were up to 48 students residing in the training institution. Most of the applicants were recommended personally by a patron, often one who had already built a school and appointed a master. The Society sent out a circular addressed to 'Local Committees and Managers of Country Schools', in which they stressed that school masters should be selected with great care. All persons recommended for training should have:

> A competent knowledge of the rudiments of Spelling, Writing, Reading and Arithmetic; that in temper they should be patient; in disposition mild but firm; of diligent habits and unblemished character; and above all they should be fully convinced of the importance of inculcating upon the young mind, a love of decency and cleanliness, of industry, honesty and truth.[16]

The seminary was 'open to admissions of all persons properly recommended and desirous of learning the improved method of teaching without any conditions being imposed as to the reputation of the school in which they may afterwards be engaged'.[17] However, the Society was prepared only to pay the maintenance costs and travelling expenses of those teachers who were being trained specifically for schools conducted on the Society's principles. The cost per master was seventeen pounds, but this expense does not seem to have deterred many applicants because of 52 men who trained in 1820, 24 received instruction only without fee and their maintenance and travelling costs were paid either by themselves or by their patron.

The following is an example of a letter of application received by Mr. J. Devonsher Jackson, secretary to the Society:

> We never had a school in this district until two years past, at which time we built a schoolhouse at our own expense, and employed a young man to teach the children of the neighbourhood, and we are happy to say he answers our most sanguine expectations, by his good conduct, sobriety, and the improvement which the children have had under his care; and as such we beg leave to recommend him to the Committee through your kind mediation, and with very great respect, entreat you will be pleased to admit him to the Model School to learn the new system of education . . . We are sorry to state that this young man's circumstances do not enable him to support himself during the period of instruction at the Model School, but being informed that the Committee are pleased to allow something towards the support of such young men, we are emboldened to solicit them to accept this young man (Patrick Gallagher) on our behalf, in order to prepare him with the necessary qualifications to enable him to diffuse useful and approved learning more extensively amongst us, and our children, which will confer a blessing on this district

at large; and we pray their laudable exertions may meet their just rewards in Heaven.

We have the honour etc.

Signed . . . . . .
28th March 1818[18]

(Mr. Patrick Gallagher, a 21 year old Roman Catholic teacher from Killery, Sligo, was accepted and trained by the Society from 30th September to 11th November 1818, and was awarded his certificate).

The training course at Kildare Place at first was only four to six weeks but in 1822 it was extended from six to eight weeks. At the end of the course the students were examined by Mr. Veevers and were given a certificate. Originally, there were three classes of certificate—'Fully Competent', 'Competent' and 'Having had an opportunity of being made acquainted with it'. Not surprisingly these titles caused some confusion so they were changed to three simple graduations—first, second and third class certificates. Most of the students reached the required standard in the eight weeks but if Veevers was not satisfied with their knowledge they had to remain for another month. If after that the student was still below standard, he was sent away without a certificate.

The Society made no attempt to extend the length of the training course. In the face of the great demand for teachers it was considered more important to maintain a large turnover of masters each year than to train a smaller number for a longer time. The average turnover was about 150 to 200 masters per year. There was also another sound reason for keeping the course short. Mr. Samuel Bewley, a founder member of the Society, when asked by the Commissioners of Irish Education Inquiry in 1825 if he thought it a desirable plan to have a seminary for teachers where they would stay for four or five years, replied:

> I think Masters so trained would not have the same effect and influence upon the population of the country where they go to teach, as those whose habits and manners would be in unison with the habits and manners of the country.
>
> They might be made too great gentlemen and not have the same agreeable influence as those with whom the population were acquainted, they would be looked upon as a different race of beings, as foreigners.[19]

It was feared that a longer course would make the elementary school teacher socially superior to his pupils. This could not be allowed to

happen—the status of the elementary school teacher must remain low and the education given him suitable for obedient lower classes. Elementary teacher training was to uphold this maxim throughout the century, and hence life at a training college was to be spartan and severe. In a profession where the majority of members received no formal training other than a monitorial apprenticeship under a practising master, students who were 'called' to a training institution were, by this fact alone, made superior to their fellow teachers, and the training course itself could not be allowed to encourage further ideas of grandeur. As it was, many of the students who received training at the institute, aspired to higher jobs such as clerks, private tutors and coastguards, to which their further education gave them access.

The two month training course at Kildare Place was an intensive one in school management. The students received little further education, the emphasis being on training. During the first few days of the course they listened to some lectures from John Veevers, but after that the majority of their time was spent in observing and teaching in the model schools. Five days a week, from ten o'clock in the morning to three in the afternoon, the students watched and practised the Lancasterian plan of school management. The Kildare Place schools were regarded as an excellent example of what could be achieved under this system: 'The Order, Disposition, Cleanliness and Accuracy so desirable in conduct of schools, have attained a high degree of Perfection' was the report of the commissioners in 1825.[20]

In a large single room, four hundred boys were divided into 'drafts' for reading and writing. The reading drafts, consisting of ten to fourteen pupils, stood in small semi-circles down the sides of the room, each under the supervision of a monitor. The other pupils, seated at the desks down the centre, practised their writing on slates. At a signal from the master standing at the top of the room, the classes changed places with promptness and precision. The system was dependent on orderliness and an elaborate drill. Under the supervision of Veevers each trainee teacher practised conducting the reading and writing drafts, studied the widely praised Pestalozzian methods of teaching arithmetic, and learnt to organize the monitors and give the correct commands for the changing drill. He also had to master the administration of a Kildare Place Society school—to fill in the 'Daily Report Book', in which the children's attendance was recorded, to keep the 'Register' in which each child's age and place of residence were noted plus his progress in reading, writing and arithmetic, and to make up the 'Class Lists' sharing the divisions for each subject. In addition a student had to learn how to manage a school library as well as schoolbooks, such as the *Dublin Spelling Book* and the *Dublin Reading Book*, for use in the classroom, and these were now readily available to schools. In 1825 the Society published *The Schoolmaster's Manual* which recommended the best methods of organizing a school. The suggestions in the book ranged from details on how to plan and build a school house to model timetables and the correct methods of teaching reading, writing and arithmetic. The influence of Pestalozzi, the eighteenth century Swiss educator, was very marked at Kildare Place. Johann Heinrich Pestalozzi had been born in Zurich in 1746. In his youth he was much influenced by the writings of the French philosopher, Rousseau, and in particular by his educational novel *Emile*. Pestalozzi became a farmer and cared for orphan children. He published two books on education—*Leonard and Gertrude* (1781), a novel of family life, and *How Gertrude Teaches Her Children* (1801) which described his educational methods. In 1805 he established a training college at Yverdon in Switzerland where teachers from many parts of Europe came to study and observe his methods.[21] Pestalozzi believed that the school should recreate the atmosphere of a loving home, and that the basis of learning was a knowledge of the general mental development of the child. The teacher's task was to foster and direct his development with the aid of carefully graded and concrete learning experiences. Reading was taught by the syllabic method, beginning with words of one and two syllables and progressing to those of three and four. Writing was taught first by drawing lines and curves to train the eye and the hand, and then by copying headlines. Arithmetic was taught using tangible and concrete objects, followed by the use of the Pestalozzian charts which developed the concept of number and of addition, subtraction and division. Pestalozzi's theory of the importance of 'number, form and language' in the early education of a child was given a central place at Kildare Place and the rigidity of the monitorial system was tempered by the emphasis which Pestalozzi placed on kindness and encouragement and on learning by activity. The Kildare Place Society was one of the first advocates of Pestalozzi's educational ideas in Ireland. These had been introduced into Ireland by 'Pestalozzi John' Synge of a leading family in Co. Wicklow who had been inspired by Pestalozzi's ideas when travelling in Switzerland. He had returned home and set up a printing press near his father's estates at Roundwood, Co. Wicklow, where he began to publish Pestalozzian reading and arithmetic charts.[22]

It is probable that the training course at Kildare Place closely followed the methods laid down in *The Schoolmaster's Manual*, which the young masters were encouraged to refer to regularly. The book also provided a useful guide to teachers who had not attended the institution. The main attributes of a good teacher were described as order and punctuality, and to have a time and place for everything, and everything in its time and place. A teacher was expected to set his pupils a good example by never deviating from the rules laid down for his own conduct, 'by being patient in temper, and kind in manners; by being cleanly in his person, and correct in his conversation; but above all by strictly adhering to the principles of honesty and truth and showing the utmost respect and obedience to the Sacred word of God'.[23]

The training course remained unchanged throughout the decade though by 1830 more time was given to further education and school subjects. Geography was becoming part of the school curriculum as well as geometry and these were not included in the course:

> In addition to the fullest details of school instruction on the improved system, the male teachers are taught Arithmetic on the Pestalozzian plan, Geometry to a certain extent, Geography and book-keeping; those who have a talent for it are instructed in Drawing, the lay-out of Gardens etc. They receive information on the building and filling up of School-houses, and they are trained in strict habits of cleanliness, order, regularity and propriety of conduct.[24]

The residential aspect of the students' training was regarded as being of central importance. The daily routine was strictly organized and little free time was allowed. The students resided in the house in Kildare Place. From eight to ten o'clock each morning and from six to eight o'clock each evening they were required to write exercises, and study. In the winter months from October to March the men were forbidden to leave the premises after half-past four in the evening, and were always under strict supervision. Occasionally one or two of them rebelled. The usual punishment for 'irregularity of hours' was to be forbidden by Veevers to leave the premises at all for a few days. However, in 1825 Veevers informed the Commissioners of Irish Education Inquiry that in all the years he had only had to expel a few students—two or three for being intoxicated, one for being involved in a 'brawl in the street'.[25]

True to the leading principle of the Society 'to afford the same facilities for Education to all classes of professing Christians', Roman

Catholic and Protestant students lived together in the seminary. The proportion of each depended on the number of applicants, though there were usually more Protestant than Roman Catholic students. By 1825 out of 771 students trained, 461 were Protestants and 310 were Roman Catholics. The life of the seminary was kept strictly non-denominational. Reading of the scriptures was optional except when teaching in the model school, where according to the Society's rule, the Bible was read 'without note or comment'. On Sundays the students were required 'to appear dressed at breakfast, to attend a place of worship', and 'to conduct themselves in a manner becoming the day'. Occasionally in the evening, the students voluntarily met together for bible reading but Veevers forbade any religious discussion or controversy. At first he kept a book which the students had to sign on Monday morning stating where they had attended worship but he soon abolished the regulation because the students complained that he was too strict. The Society was always at pains to emphasise that the students lived together in 'perfect harmony and goodwill', and that the benefits of a 'mixed' education were important for teachers living in a society torn by religious acrimony. Mr. Devonsher Jackson, the secretary of the Society, giving evidence before the Commission of Irish Education Inquiry in 1825 stated that the cohabitation of Protestant and Catholic was

> ... very useful in the Country in resolving prejudices that have gone abroad. Their sojourning with us cannot fail to have a good effect upon the Teachers ... Individuals of different Persuasions live together like the Members of one Family. They have no Differences between them, and have often questioned them upon the Manner in which they were employed out of School Hours, and how they lived together, and I have always been answered by such Individuals expressing great satisfaction and even Surprise that they could live together so happily, differing as they did. I am sure the very best consequences have resulted.[26]

The success of the seminary in training masters encouraged the Kildare Place Society to consider providing similar facilities for female teachers. The Society decided to acquire the two neighbouring houses, 10 and 11 Kildare Street, and to provide accommodation for up to 24 women. It was intended to restrict the number of women accepted as 'propriety was still more apparent with respect to school mistresses than instance of school masters'. The two houses backed on to the model schools and thus had direct access to them.

Miss Jane Edkins was appointed superintendent of the women's residence with salary of £100 per annum, 'furnished apartments plus coal and candles'. Prior to the opening of the new women's department, Miss Edkins who had been a governess, was sent on a tour of women's training establishments in England including the British and Foreign School Society's College at Borough Road, London. She was expected to stay away only a few weeks but she found the experience so useful and informative that she stayed for three months. In May 1824 she wrote to the Society's committee to explain her decision:

Female Lancasterian School, Borough Road.
May 14th, 1824.

Sir,

In obedience to the desire of the committee on Wednesday the 5th and after taking a slight view of the schools of Liverpool, Manchester and Birmingham arrived in London on the evening of the 12th. Having learned that persons wishing to learn the system pursuant at the Borough Road School were sometimes admitted to the house, on paying a very moderate sum weekly, and judging that nothing could so much facilitate my improvement as a residence in the very spot where mistresses are in training, I immediately applied for and received admission. I have attended the school yesterday and today —. I this morning had the pleasure of seeing Mr. Millar, Secretary to the Committee here, who appeared to take a lively interest in the success of your new establishment, pointed out those schools which he judged best deserving of observation and expressed an earnest wish for me to remain longer here.

On my reply, that my instructions rendered it impossible, he kindly proposed writing to you to procure a longer leave of absence for that purpose. I fear, Sir, that such an application may be displeasing and beg to say, that if my return before 1st June be still the desire of the Committee, I feel little doubt that I shall by that time be enabled to fulfil their intentions in the management of the training school.

Yet I fully agree in opinion with Mr. Millar, that longer residence here must have *very great* advantages, much greater than would be sufficient to compensate for the time and money so devoted. I have been so fortunate as to receive kindness and [?] from every person acquainted with the object of my journey and feel particularly indebted to Mr. Benjamin Wood of Liverpool, Mr. Lloyd and his family of Birmingham and Miss Springman, the Superintendent of this establishment.

I remain Sir, with great respect,
Your very obedient servant,
Jane Edkins.[27]

The Committee complied with her request but in June she wrote again to say that she could not yet fix a time for her return—her doing so 'did not indeed arise from negligence but from the advice of those best informed on the subject and most warmly interested in the success of her important undertakings'.[28]

She eventually returned in late July and in the autumn of 1824 the women's department opened. Six girls entered for training, five Protestants and one Roman Catholic. Their ages ranged from 18 to 24. Anne Shiel recommended by Mr. O'Neill, was training for a school at Garryhill, Carlow; Frances Wheatley was recommended by Mrs. Bayly, for a school at Ballyarthur, Co. Wicklow while Eliza Millet was recommended by Mr. R. Pollock for a school in Chancery Lane, Dublin. The other three were all experienced teachers: Eliza Fitzhenry taught at a school in Tanderagee, Co. Armagh, Margaret Christian in a school in Sligo, and Mary Cooke at a school in Doonass, Co. Clare. In January 1825 another twenty-three girls were accepted for training.[29]

The female students' course was similar to the men's in that school management was the major study. However in the women's course there was a strong emphasis placed on the domestic arts and skills. Half the time was spent in household duties in the residence house itself and in learning cookery and laundry-work. The students were divided into two divisions of four drafts each. One division spent the first four weeks engaged in domestic duties, acting as housekeepers, cooks, housemaids and laundresses, while the other division was engaged in academic study and practical teaching duties. At the end of four weeks the two divisions reversed their duties. The Society 'impressed with the importance of improving the domestic habits of the poor in Ireland, . . . thought it right to make it part of the discipline of school mistresses sent up to the Training School, that they shall take part in the domestic management of the Institution'. It was hoped that by doing so they 'would acquire habits of order, neatness and regularity and learn to prepare cheap and wholesome food'.[30] This emphasis on the domestic training of the female students became a feature of training college life in the nineteenth century, and whereas servants had to be employed to cook and clean for the male establishment, the female one was run by using the students' own labour. Miss Edkins presided over the residence house and supervised these domestic duties. Mrs. Julia Campbell was head of the female model school, and she supervised the girls' teaching practice. Each girl was required to keep an 'Observation Book' of her training course in the model school. Two of these books are preserved in the Kildare Place Society archives, one belonging to Martha Donaldson, the other to Elizabeth Crowther. Martha Donaldson's book is headed, 'The following Description and Observations were written in the Model School, Kildare Place, Dublin by Martha Donaldson, Between the 11th day of May and the 15th day of July 1836'. The book, beautifully hand-written, gave an account of the organization of the school, and how the pupils were divided for reading, writing, arithmetic and needlework. In addition 'Hints to a Young Schoolmistress' showed examples of a Daily Report Book, a Register and a model timetable. The lists of daily, weekly, monthly and yearly duties were carefully recorded to show the value of regularity and planning. In her first month Miss Donaldson was given the wise advice 'to be more solicitous to teach well than to teach much. Keep brisk industry awake but do not embarrass yourself or your pupils by commencing too many subjects of instruction'. The Society's lending library scheme was also mastered as was the 'New Ticket' system whereby a pupil earned tickets of increasing value and purchased a useful object such as a story book, an apron or a pair of scissors. The book ended with the sound advice:

What ever you do, do it heartily
As unto the Lord and not unto man.[31]

As the female school became well-established candidates had to be selected. Those chosen were persons most 'likely to prove qualified to impart instruction to the rising generation of Females in proper management of their families and dwellings' and were persons of 'Christian principles, Common sense, good temper, Integrity, Energy, orderly habits and good talents'.[32] Students had to be acquainted with reading, writing, arithmetic and scripture and a high standard of needlework was desirable. By 1831, 482 girls had qualified from Kildare Place, the female establishment was as flourishing as the male one and the students had little difficulty in obtaining posts afterwards.

The degree of success and influence of the Kildare Place Training Institution was limited. It was the first major attempt to provide a formal training for elementary teachers in Ireland. By 1831 2,380 teachers had been trained but the Commissioners of Irish Education Inquiry had estimated that there were about 12,532 teachers in Ireland. The Society itself made every attempt to show how beneficial the training course was. Their own inspectors' confidential reports gave accounts of the improvements of their schools. In 1820, of 320 schools visited the inspectors stated that good teaching, with a few exceptions 'is manifest in those masters who have been trained in the Seminary for that purpose'. The Society also regularly received letters from grateful school managers and patrons informing it of the great benefits which their teachers had obtained from the training course. Some of these letters were published in the appendix of the Society's annual reports, for example:

November 18th 1824

Sir,

I enclose the Master's receipt for £7.10s for which he seems most grateful. I trust that after the next inspection of the School, by your visitor, so much improvement in the school and the children will have occurred as to entitle the Master to an advanced gratuity. I can assure your Committee that since the return of the Master from Kildare Place the improvement of the children is most extraordinary . . .

I remain, Sir,
Your obedient humble servant.[33]

The Society had had a system since 1820 of paying gratuities to deserving teachers and it was obviously hoped that after this letter the teacher would obtain a further one. The Society also received grateful letters from ex-students who, on returning home to teach in a crowded school house, found their new training most beneficial:

23rd December 1820

Sir,

. . . I had conducted Schools in divers parts of Ireland, for 16 years previous to my admission into your Model School in April last, and I candidly confess that I can render more service, and with less trouble to myself, to the 300 children, who are in attendance under me, in three months than I could to 50 in the ordinary manner of teaching, in nine.

I have the honour to be
yours and the Society's most
humble servant.[34]

One of the Training Institution's most distinguished admirers was the Rt. Rev. Dr. James Doyle, Roman Catholic Bishop of Kildare and Leighlin. Although a strong critic of the Society's religious principles, he told the Select Committee of the House of Commons in 1830 that when he set up schools in his own diocese, he appointed masters educated at Kildare Place to take charge of the model schools in the diocese. He said 'The persons conducting these schools have been well educated and conduct them in an excellent manner', and he recommended that other young masters in the diocese should train under them.[35]

The training institution was, therefore, beginning to have some affect and to earn a high reputation when sadly it lost its financial support. In 1831, with the establishment of the Commissioners of National Education by the Government, the parliamentary grant of £30,000 was withdrawn from the Kildare Place Society, and it found itself solely dependent on voluntary subscriptions. The Society attempted valiantly to continue to collect these and sent a travelling secretary on a tour of England to advertise their case, but with little success, and the scale of the Society's work had to be radically curtailed. The Training Institution continued to function for another fifteen years, still offering a thorough training course, but its numbers declined as schools began to enter the national system and teachers began to train at the National Board's new training college at Marlborough Street, Dublin. In 1834 John Veevers resigned after 20 years of service, though he remained in Dublin, became High Sheriff in 1850 and continued to serve on the Society's comittee. In 1840 the Training Institution itself closed down leaving the model schools only which continued to offer training. Thomas E. Irvine became head of the male school on the resignation of Veevers, but he was paid a salary of only £100 whereas Veevers had been receiving £300. Irvine left in 1841 as he had obtained a better appointment in England as master in the Lower School of the Royal Naval Asylum Greenwich and his assistant, William Thomas Wilkinson, was appointed. Wilkinson proved to be a very able young man, and it was largely due to him that the model schools survived and were able to continue to offer some form of training. He began a course in the 'Science of Education' and taught the theory behind the school's daily practice. He was a man of remarkable energy and stamina, and the Society's inspectors had much admiration for the work he was doing despite all the difficulties:

> This teacher appears to be faithfully discharging his very onerous duty. His exertions are constant and unremitting, and nothing but great zeal and singleness of purpose could enable him to overcome the labour which is imposed on him. Labour, the amount of which may be measured by consideration of the great number of advanced boys who attend (260 in the Scripture class alone) and the wide ranging instruction which they claim at his hands; a range of instruction which whatever may be done to enlarge

> or improve it it is quite vain to suppose (if the present high character of the school is to be maintained) will now admit of being, curtailed in quality or extent.[36]

In 1847 W. Cooke Taylor of Trinity College, who published a book *Notes on a visit to the Model Schools (Dublin, 1847)* which supported the system of national education, wrote that although he did not approve of the Kildare Place Society's rule on the compulsory reading of the Scriptures, he had to admit that its model schools were very fine:

> I found the management of the Model Schools excellent; the teacher of the boys' school is as enlightened an educationist as ever I met; he is a thorough Pestalozzian and has completely worked out Pestalozzi's admirable system.[37]

On the women's side, Miss Jane Edkins remained in charge until the 1840s when on the closure of the training institution she was dismissed with a 'flattering testimonial and half a year's salary'. She was unable to find further employment and was forced to run a lodging house instead. Mrs. Julia Campbell, the head of the female model school, resigned in 1833 when she obtained a post at the National Board's Training Institution in Marlborough Street. After 11 years she was reluctant to leave the services of the Kildare Place Society but when she was faced with a reduction in her salary she had little choice. She was a widow and had to provide for her family. She pleaded with the Society but it could not maintain her salary so she tendered her resignation. She wrote to the Committee:

> 7th March, 1833
>
> Gentlemen,
>
> In consequence of the altered and very embarrassing circumstances in which from the reduction of my salary, I found myself placed, and which I intimated to the Committee by my letter of January last,—several friends who felt interested for me strongly urged the necessity of my seeking for a more lucrative situation—and through them I have obtained an appointment under the Board of Education.
>
> I therefore take the earliest opportunity of acquainting you that I respectfully beg leave to resign the charge which I have for so many years held.
>
> In justice to my feelings I cannot omit saying that it has cost me a most painful struggle to relinquish a situation in which all the energies of mind and even my affections have so long been engaged and that nothing but a

sense of paramount duty which as a parent I owe to a dependent family, could have induced me to seek for a change.

I have only to add that I shall feel obliged by being relieved from the charge as early as may suit the convenience of the Committee.

I have the honour to remain Gentlemen,
Most respectfully your obedient Servant,

(signed) *Julia Campbell*[38]

Julia Campbell became head of Talbot House, the female section of the National Board's Training Institution. She brought with her knowledge and experience of the Kildare Place system and she used it to advantage. The course at the National Board's institution was broader and included more lectures and formal classes as well as practical training. The emphasis on the domestic arts remained and all the students at Talbot House were taught needlework, cookery and laundry-work. Thus the influence of Kildare Place was brought directly into the national school system, and the pattern of teacher-training continued.[39]

Although the Kildare Place Institution was short-lived and its contribution small, in the long term its influence and that of the Society were very marked. The monitorial system became the accepted method used in national schools in Ireland, and the National Board's teacher training institution was modelled on that of Kildare Place. It was residential and non-denominational and upheld the belief of the value of 'mixed' education for teachers in training. The Society's schoolbooks were used as models for the National Board's lesson books, and the system of inspection was based on that pioneered by Kildare Place. The traditions of the training institution were retained at Kildare Place itself, and the later colleges continued to honour these.

Faced with a dwindling income and a decreasing number of applicant teachers, the Society was relieved when, in 1846, it was approached by the newly formed Anglican education society, the Church Education Society, for permission to send a group of students each year to train at Kildare Place. The request was granted and nine years later the Church Education Society itself took over responsibility of running the training institution. Thus 'Kildare Place' entered a new phase.

II

The Church Education Society Training College, 1855–1878

When the national school system was set up in 1831 by the Whig government, the majority of Church of Ireland clergy were opposed to it on the principle that under the rules of the new National Board, religious instruction was to be separate from secular and moral and that the reading of the Bible other than the agreed 'Scriptural Extracts' was forbidden except in these separate hours. Archbishop Whately of Dublin, who was one of the first Commissioners of National Education, was the only major leader in the Church of Ireland to support the new system. The established church was affronted because it had been one of the major agencies of education in the early nineteenth century, and it believed that it had a right to use the education system for missionary work among the Roman Catholic poor. The new national system was strictly non-denominational and forbade any interference with pupils' religious beliefs. The rigid separation of religious and secular instruction was to ensure this.

Whereas the other two major churches in Ireland, the Roman Catholic and Presbyterian Churches, went into the National system and worked from within to change its rules and gain recognition for their denominational rights, the Church of Ireland, being the established church and sufficiently wealthy, opted out and maintained a separate voluntary school system of its own.[1]

In 1839 the Church Education Society was founded to support schools and provide Anglican children with a scriptural education, that is, an education where the Bible was given a central role in the curriculum and the teacher could refer to it throughout the school day. Religious instruction, it was argued, could not be separated from secular, and was fundamental to the education of the child. The policy of the Church Education Society was to provide financial support for parochial schools by way of grants for school requisites and gratuities for teachers. In all schools receiving aid, the Society required that the 'Scriptures in the Authorized Version' be read daily, that all anglican children learn the catechism, and that the teachers should be anglicans. All books used in the school had to be approved by the Society.[2] The Society was very prestigious and the presidents were the archbishop of Armagh and eleven other bishops, and the vice-presidents were leading Protestant gentry such as the Earl of Courtown, the Marquis of Downshire, the Earl of Mayo, and Viscount Adare, plus the deans and archdeacons of the Church. The Society had a co-ordinating central committee of both clergy and laity but the basis of its strength lay in the diocesan committees which organized the society at parochial level and collected funds. From the outset the Society was very well supported and had large financial resources, such was the determination of the Church to resist the National school system and never to accept state aid. By 1850 its income was over £5,000 and it was supporting 1,882 schools. The Church was determined 'never to avail of any system in which the Scriptural instruction of every pupil is not recognised as the fundamental principle of a Christian Education'.[3]

Teacher training was regarded as one of the major functions of the Church Education Society and although it was originally proposed to set up a model school in each diocese, teacher training became the responsibility of the central committee in Dublin, and it was agreed that the Society would use part of its income to support teachers while training and to give them gratuities in addition to their parochial salaries. A 'Model School Sub-Committee' was established in 1839 which consisted of Rev. Dr. Singer of TCD, Rev. J. B. Woodward, Rev. A. Irwin, and Mr. T. Stewart, and whose purpose was to organize a model school in Dublin. The committee agreed: 'It is expedient to establish a school in Dublin in connexion with this Society and an enquiry be made respecting the practicality of establishing such a school in one of the following districts—1. Deanery of St. Patrick's and St. Nicholas Within. 2. Parishes of St. Peter's and St. Mark's. 3. Parishes of St. Mary's, and St. Paul's and Grangegorman.'[4]

St. Peter's schools were chosen as the model schools and the Church Education Society provided books, school effects and a clock. The latter was considered an essential item of equipment for a model school because of the emphasis on punctuality, regularity and order. The arrangement with St. Peter's was seen as a temporary measure only, like that of the Kildare Place Society with the School Street

Schools thirty years earlier, and the Society hoped to be able to build its own schools. In 1841 Rev. Thomas Newland was sent to Britain to visit two of the leading training institutions, the Normal School at Norwood, founded by the English educationalist Kay-Shuttleworth, and the Glasgow Normal Seminary, founded by David Stow.[5] In 1846 the 'New Model School Committee' was set up and this seems to have had a more realistic view of what the Society could afford. It visited the Kildare Place model schools and, being pleased with what it saw there, it was agreed to enter into an arrangement with the Kildare Place Society whereby twelve students each year would be sent to the model schools and the Church Education Society would pay 12 shillings per week for their support, and a salary of £30 for an assistant mistress in the school.[6]

This arrangement between the two Societies worked quite amicably for some years. There were, however, fundamental differences between them in that the Kildare Place Society was strictly non-denominational and run by laymen, while the Church Education Society was dedicated to denominational education and was dominated by churchmen. The main area of conflict which emerged at the training institution was over the selection of candidates. The Kildare Place Society had always required applicants to have an appointment at a school before being accepted for training, whereas the Church Education Society insisted that their applicants would be recommended by the clergy and should be trained whether they had an appointment or not. The Church Education Society was quite thorough in its procedures. It printed an official application form which was sent to candidates to be completed in the presence of the clergyman of the parish. The form included some 'examination questions' which the candidate was required to answer as well as giving an example of his handwriting and mathematical ability. The application form of Andrew Roark of Brosna, Abbeyfeale, Co. Limerick is preserved in the Church Education Society archives.[7] He applied to the Society in 1848 and answered the 'Queries' on the form in a locked room to which his rector, Rev. Edward Norman, 'had the key'. He was aged twenty and had been employed as a 'check clerk' on the public works organized during the Famine of 1847. He was asked to state the contents of the Church Catechism, to write a short life of Paul of Tarsus, to give the meaning of the words 'miracle' and 'parable', to describe the situation of Ireland and to parse the sentence 'A fine February spoils the rest of the year'. He was able to perform all these exercises satisfactorily.

By 1853 there were 53 students in training for the Church Education Society at Kildare Place and the Society considered that it was necessary 'to enlarge the sphere of its influence in this department and connect the training of teachers more closely with the system of the Church Education Society'. Therefore, in 1855 a formal agreement was made with the Kildare Place Society to lease all the premises in Kildare Place and Kildare Street, including the model schools and the training college. This was a sad but inevitable decision for the Kildare Place Society. Its support and income had dwindled and it felt that it could no longer fulfil a useful function. The majority of the schools which the Society had supported by now had entered the National system or were being assisted by the Church Education Society while the National Board's Training Institution was qualifying teachers for national schools. The Kildare Place Society remained the legal owners of the Kildare Place premises, but the traditions and prestige of its schools were carried on by its successors, albeit under different religious principles.[8]

For twenty years the Church Education Society college in Kildare Place flourished and served the established church well. A high standard of training was attained, and the course broadened to provide the students with an extensive general education as well as professional training. The religious life of the college was central to its function, and students were expected to acquire a thorough knowledge of the Holy Scriptures, and of Church Formularies. Teaching was a religious vocation, and the teacher was seen as the willing assistant of the clergyman in parochial life. In an address to the students leaving the Training School in 1850 the Archdeacon of Emly (Henry Irwin B.A.) stressed the importance of a teacher's Christian example:

> Yours is a high sacred office, the School is the porch of the Church: out of it the members of the Church, for the most part, must come; and only second in importance to the office of minister is that of a truly qualified teacher . . .
>
> Education is a process to fit children for life, and that life is to fit them for eternity; it is a training up of a mortal for immortality, and no system will be regenerative unless it is decidedly Christian . . . Therefore a teacher should not be the mere main spring of the machine, but the living principle of a living body; it is not enough that he should have knowledge and an aptitude for imparting it, but he should have a character openly exhibiting the fruits of the Christian faith.[9]

When the Church Education Society took over the Kildare Place college in 1855 it was in a position to adapt the training course to suit its own ends. Religious instruction had been deliberately excluded from the training course of the Kildare Place Society except for Bible reading 'without note or comment' in the model schools. The Church Education Society now made religious instruction the central subject in the course, and the students' devotional and religious life became all important.

The college continued to offer training to 'not only those who intend to devote themselves to the education of the poor . . . but as many as possible of those engaged in teaching should have the advantage of such training'. Therefore, the training course was restricted to 24 weeks so that there could be two sessions per year. Around 50 students per session could be accommodated in the college so 100 students per year passed through, though many of the women students stayed for a second session. The men students numbered around 20 and resided in 4 Kildare Place and the women, who numbered around 30—40, lived in 10 Kildare Street, while most of the staff resided also and so a community and collegiate life developed.

The head and key figure in the college was the Reverend Alexander Leeper, D.D. He had been first appointed catechist to the students in 1846 when the Society had entered into the arrangement with the Kildare Place Society, and in 1855 when the Church Education Society took over the college Leeper was appointed chaplain and superintendent of the model schools. He lived on the premises, received a salary of £200 per year 'plus coal and gas', and was responsible for the religious instruction of all the students. Leeper had been born in Dublin in 1805 and entered Trinity College, Dublin in 1834. He graduated with a B.A. in 1840 and M.A. in 1850. He was a scholarly and able man, and he presided over the training institution with a firm and wise hand. He combined his duties at Kildare Place with those of rector of St. Andrew's Parish in the city and general secretaryship of the Church Education Society itself. He continued his own studies and was awarded his B.D. in 1859 and his D.D. in 1865. It was largely due to Leeper's initiative and determination that in 1878 the General Synod of the Church of Ireland was persuaded to take over the training college, and Leeper continued as chaplain there until his death.[10]

The main day-to-day running of the college was undertaken by William Thomas Wilkinson, previously headmaster of the model schools. Wilkinson had been retained by the Church Education Society when it took over the schools, and he served the college with dedication and vigour. He was promoted to 'Training Master' and paid a salary of £180 per year, but he did not live in. He lectured both the men and women students in the 'Science of Education' and he developed a thorough and detailed course in the theory of education, giving the students an understanding of the basis of classroom practice and management. An outline of his lecture course was eventually published under the title *The Training of Teachers—Lectures in Education* (Dublin, n.d.) and he became a well-known figure in the city of Dublin. It was under his influence that the college began to develop a broader course of training for the students both in general subjects such as English, Geography, History and in the theory of education, as well as practical school teaching.

The women's department of the college was run by Miss Henrietta White and her able assistant, Miss Jane Lewis. In 1855 when the college was being re-organized, the Church Education Society had applied to the Home and Colonial Infant School Society in London to send over two of their best teachers to run the training institution. The reply came that the two best teachers were already in Dublin. Miss Henrietta White and Miss Jane Lewis had both trained at the Home and Colonial College, Gray's Inn Road, London and had come in 1854 to teach at the Irish Church Missions' Schools in Luke Street, Dublin. Therefore, they were invited to transfer to Kildare Place, which they did, and the two were to work together for twenty years to develop the college. Miss White eventually retired owing to ill-health in 1873 but Miss Lewis, who was head of the girls' model school, remained as vice-principal when the college was taken over by the Church of Ireland, and she died in office in 1889. The Lewis Memorial prize for the best lessons in Holy Scriptures was founded in her memory, and her portrait hangs today in the boardroom of the Church of Ireland College of Education in Rathmines.[11]

The link with the Home and Colonial Society in London was an important one for Kildare Place and the emphasis on infant education, which became a feature of the college, dated from this time. The Home and Colonial Society had been founded in 1836 to promote infant education. The chief influence in its work was Dr. Charles Mayo and his sister who had written a book based on the ideas of Pestalozzi entitled *Lessons on Objects* which became widely used. The book consisted of a series of lessons designed to teach children through observation and 'first hand examination' of natural objects such as animals, flowers, fruit and substances like glass, slate, stone etc. The 'object lesson' became a feature of infant education, and immensely popular. The Home and Colonial Society published a series of text-books such as Miss Mayo's *Practical Remarks on Infant Education* and these were to be used at Kildare Place. The Church Education Society itself opened a book depository in Kildare Street and began to sell useful books for education including the manuals of the Home and Colonial Society. In 1856 a visit was paid by some of the staff of the Gray's Inn Training Institution to Kildare Place and the college were very pleased to be assured by their visitors that they 'had been more successful in the application of Pestalozzian principles than any other educational establishment they had seen in Ireland'.[12]

The college maintained a staff of up to fifteen people including a singing and a drawing master as well as a needlework mistress. The head of the boys' model school was Mr. Edward Taylor who, with his wife Anna in her capacity as matron, supervised the male department. He acted as assistant to Mr. Wilkinson and received a good salary of £125 plus residence.

Vocal music was taught by Mr. James Hill, who had joined the staff in 1847, and drawing by Mr. William H. Murray. These two taught both the pupils in the model schools and the student teachers.

The students who came to the college were drawn mostly from the Society's own schools and many of them were already employed as school-teachers. The college accepted Church of Ireland students only and all students were required to participate in the religious training. Teachers were often expected to act as parish clerks as well as to undertake a variety of parochial duties, such as leading the choir or playing the harmonium in return for a free residence. A married teacher or a brother and sister were particularly welcome as they could offer a variety of services. Salaries varied from £30-£60 a year but extra fees could be earned by offering tuition to able pupils seeking entrance to the university. The following is an example of an application sent to the college:

> Rev. John Powell of St. Anne's, Newtown Forbes, in the diocese of Ardagh wants a schoolmaster with a wife or sister to teach needlework. The master is to act as Parish Clerk, and therefore sing well. Both must be active, diligent, neat and cleanly in their habits and pious. The school is 2 miles from the church. The emolument is £50, a house and about an English acre of land value £5. A gratuity is given for children promoted at inspection and £3 for school fuel.[13]

Students entered the college twice a year. Entry to the women's department was competitive but there were often insufficient numbers for the men's. Emigration and the better prospects elsewhere drew away many men and the scarcity of good male teachers much concerned the Society particularly in the 1850s after the famine. It was noted that the shortage of male teachers was 'partly arising from the circumstances that many of the best masters have been drawn off to the more lucrative employments elsewhere and still more from the multitudes which have been borne across the Atlantic to the distant land'.[14]

A formal qualifying entrance exam was held to see if the candidates possessed the 'prescribed amount of information'. This examination was based on the four proficiency scales laid down for a Church Education Society school. These proficiency scales clearly showed the influence of the Home and Colonial Society, and began with syllabic reading and 'counting with objects' and a knowledge of natural objects. The 4th class programme included a knowledge of the Holy Scriptures, reading, writing 'including dictation', English grammar, history, mental arithmetic, geometry and geography. Not all the students, particularly the men, reached the required standard but they were allowed entry. The college looked for qualities other than academic, placing equal importance on 'Religious and Moral Principles' and on 'Natural Disposition and Abilities'. It was considered 'that the primary object of early education is to cultivate in children religious principles and moral sentiments, to awaken in their tender minds a sense of their evil dispositions and habitual feelings before they become callous by daily intercourse with vice'.[15]

On applying to the college a student was required to give full personal details, including whether he was a communicant member of the Church, the occupation of his parents, where he had been to school, and whether he was free of debt and was presently employed. He was asked to give his reasons for wishing to become a teacher and whether he had taught in Sunday Schools, and to state that if he was trained he would 'devote himself in the future to the education of the poor'. The fee at the college was £6 per session which covered tuition, board and lodging. All were required to stay at least one session, but to encourage a student to stay longer the fee for the second session was £4 only. A reference from 'one or more respectable parties' as well as a parochial clergyman were required and referees were asked for their opinion of the candidate's moral character and whether he had 'a disposition amiable, cheerful and contented and that his domestic habits were steady, sober and regular'.[16]

Thus the college looked for students who had both the necessary personal and academic qualifications, who would set a good example and have sober habits fit for a parochial assistant. These qualities were seen to have as much importance as intellectual knowledge. All the students' names were entered formally in a register which noted their date of birth, post-town, name of referee, and classification on leaving. An attempt was made in the early years to follow up the students after they left and this information also was entered in the register. In the first class of 17 men in 1855 all but one qualified successfully. James Duff (of Edenderry) recommended by Rev. T. C. Murray obtained a first class certificate but died shortly afterwards. George Crawford of Hacketstown, recommended by the Archdeacon of Leighlin, and James Hunter of Westport, recommended by Miss Aldridge, also obtained first classes. Among the second class candidates were Thomas McDonough of Dublin, recommended by Rev. A. Leeper himself, Thomas Hull of Oldcastle, James Dougherty of Clones and Joseph Howe of Mountrath. Thomas Thorpe of Ferns was the only one not to complete the course. In the female department there were up to fifty girls in each session and most of them found employment. Among the first class entrants in 1855 were Mary Jane Aughlin of Dunmanway, recommended by Rev. R. D. Sloane, who went to a school near Nenagh and then to England where she married; Mary Crossley, recommended by Rev. C. Donovan, who went to America after teaching for six years near Clonmel; and Margaret Carroll who taught in a school in Co. Wexford and then became the matron of St. Anne's Parochial Boarding School in Dublin. The majority of the girls married after teaching for some years—Emily Browne of Dublin married and went to live in Liverpool; Charlotte Manseragh of Miltown Malbay 'married a sergeant in the army', while Elizabeth Jane Grey of Portadown became mistress of the Kilkenny Infant School and married there.[17]

Each student attended the college for a minimum of one half-year session but most of them stayed for two. Some of the female students remained for a third because the demand for female teachers was less than for male. At a time when training was not compulsory there was little incentive to remain at the training institution longer than was necessary, particularly if a suitable post became available. In the 1860s it was estimated that 31% of male students failed to complete their training while for female the percentage the much lower figure of 23%.[18] It was essential therefore that the course in each session contain both academic and practical training. The timetable was an intensive one and it was estimated that the men students spent up to 63 hours per week in organized activity of which 32 hours were in lectures, 8 in school practice and 23 in study. For the women the total was 49 hours per week of which 8 were spent in school practice. An attempt was made to cover all aspects of education in a short course, and therefore there was little time for individual thought or recreation. The reduction in the amount of time spent in school practice and the increase in lectures in general subjects and educational theory were a marked change from the 1820s and 1830s.

The course for the male students was organized by Mr. Wilkinson and covered the basic school subjects—English grammar (3 hours per week), geography (4 hours per week), history (1 hour per week), mathematics (5 hours per week). The theology course (8 hours per week) was given by Canon Leeper and this already lengthy course was followed up each evening by a session of 'Scripture Preparation' supervised by Mr. Taylor in the residence house. Wilkinson attempted to broaden the students' general knowledge and he included some lectures on 'Social Science' and 'Natural Philosophy'. The study of social science was in its infancy in the mid-nineteenth century and in this he was very advanced. His course covered aspects of political economy such as the theory of labour, the use of money, and the role of capital. In 'Natural Philosophy' he attempted to deal with simple mechanics and the theories of motion and gravitation, and he taught by giving practical examples from everyday life—e.g. 'Why will a rider or passenger be thrown forwards when a horse or vehicle is suddenly stopped?' or 'Why is it dangerous to stand against a wall in a thunderstorm?' In 'Natural History' he taught the classification of species, flora and fauna, as well as aspects of physical geography. Again, everyday illustrations were used—'Why do April showers bring forth May flowers?' or 'Why is it dangerous to sleep in a damp bed?'.[19]

Wilkinson gave similar though less extensive courses to female students and thus he hoped to deepen their knowledge and understanding of the world around them.

It was however in his 'Science of Education' course that he was ahead of his time and showed himself to be an able educationalist. There was no similar course taught at the National Board's Training Institution, Marlborough Street, and it was not until the 1890s that 'science of education' courses were introduced widely into the training colleges. Wilkinson's course covered the philosophical and psychological principles of education, raising such issues as 'What is education?' 'What is the true purpose of a school' and 'the real work of teacher?' as well as 'The Mental and Moral Constitution of Man' and the 'General Truths respecting the Mind'. The course was divided into four sections entitled—(*i*) 'The Science and Art of Education', (*ii*) 'The Principles and Practice of Teaching', (*iii*) 'School Economy' and (*iv*) 'The Teacher'. It examined the aims of education, with some historical background on the educational ideas of Lancaster and Bell, Pestalozzi and Froebel. The organization and management of the school as well as the desirable personal qualities of the teacher and his relationship with his pupils, his parish clergyman, and the community at large were discussed. Thus the student teacher was given insight into his role in society as well as a broad perspective of education and its function.[20]

In addition to all these courses, drawing, music, elocution and book-keeping were offered together with domestic economy and needlework for the female students. The musical training was first based on the 'Hullah method' which had been used in elementary schools since the 1840s. Invented by John Hullah of London, it used the tonic solfa to teach singing and enabled large numbers of children to enjoy choral music. However it was based on a 'fixed doh' aural scale which presented many difficulties, and by the 1860s it was being replaced by the Tonic Solfa Method of John Curwen which used a 'moveable doh' system. Curwen (1816–1880) founded the Tonic Solfa College in London and many teachers trained under him. The method was so successful that teachers often did not attempt to teach their pupils the staff notation afterwards. Choral singing was regarded as a moral and uplifting activity for poor children and the discipline and control were an extra benefit.[21]

The students' practical training took place concurrently in each session with the theoretical work. As had been the case in the days of the Kildare Place Society, the model schools played a central role in this training. The boys', girls' and infant model schools were situated in the big schoolrooms at the back of Kildare Place and the students attended daily, learning to organize and manage a school. They observed the staff at work and 'criticism' lessons were held where the staff and students taught in front of each other. Much importance was placed on infant education with the female students, due to the influence of the Home and Colonial Society, and the infant model school was divided into a 'senior infant' and a 'baby' school and the children were taught formal lessons in 'a gallery'—a raised stepped platform at one end of the schoolroom. The college also established special 'practising schools' which was a farsighted move. One of the disadvantages of the large city model schools for training was that they were untypical as the majority of students would be working in small one- or two-teacher rural schools, with all age classes. Therefore the training staff at Kildare Place organized a 'model one-teacher school' using a group of pupils from the big model schools, and each senior student was placed in charge for two weeks, in which time he learnt to organize and manage the school and to teach children of all ages. This idea of a 'model one-teacher school' was to reappear seventy years later when Principal Hodges of the Church of Ireland Training College organized a similar experiment in the 1930s.

Student life at the college was highly organized and very busy. As was the pattern of a nineteenth century training college there was little time for individual choice or relaxation. The students rose at seven o'clock and began the day with study and scriptural preparation. Lectures were held from nine to eleven o'clock, and the period from eleven to two o'clock was spent in the model schools in class teaching. Dinner was eaten at three o'clock and a period of recreation was allowed. Study began again at seven o'clock and continued until nine. Saturday was a half day and the students had some free time. On Sundays they went as a group to St. Andrew's Church where Canon Leeper was the rector, and some went to the chapel of the Magdalen Asylum in Leeson Street. And though a mixed college, the male and female departments were kept quite separate, and the students were always under strict supervision. The college built up a well-stocked library of books which the students were expected to study. The publications of the Home and Colonial Society including their *Hints for Infant Teachers* and *Elementary Instruction* were required reading, as were John Gill's books on *School Management* and Sheldon's *Manual of Elementary Instruction.* Cornwell's *School Geography* (1847) and Keith's *Use of Globes* (1850) were set texts, as were Bonnycastle's *Algebra*, Thomson's *Arithmetic* and Lardner's *Euclid.* The Church Education Society stocked these books in its shop in 10 Kildare Street, and the students were expected to purchase copies for themselves. This would have added considerably to the basic cost of £6 for the training course. Formal written examinations in all subjects were held at the end of the course and certificates were awarded in three classes. In the 1860s it was estimated that 25% of the male students gained first class certificates but only 17% of the women. The men were often older and more experienced and despite staying for one session only, reached a high standard in that time. [22]

Thus the Church Education Society ran a well-organized and professional training college of which it was justly proud. The key figure was undoubtedly Wilkinson who dominated the college, and provided intellectual and enthusiastic leadership both to the female and male departments. He developed thorough and rigorous courses, offering his students a wide range of knowledge. He could be criticised for attempting too much and for relying too heavily on formal instruction and his own lecture programme was very heavy:

Tuesdays:

9–10	Educational Science (male students)
10–11	Arithmetic (female students, juniors)
11–12	Mathematics (male students)
12– 1	Map Drawing (female students, juniors)
1– 2	Grammar etc. (male students)
2– 3	English Literature (male students)

But he was a man of energy, stamina and vision.

On the female side, Miss Henrietta White and Miss Jane Lewis provided a stable and dedicated partnership and, despite Miss White's ill health in the later years, they offered a thorough and well-structured course. The two women set a high standard of piety and personal devotion to the teaching profession and trained their students for a life of service. The female department was always the larger one, with a number of its students remaining not just for two but for three training sessions, and by 1867 there were sixty-six girls in residence.[23]

By the mid 1860s the college was at its height, with 115 students in residence. However, serious problems were beginning to appear and grave doubts grew as to whether it could continue. Some of these problems stemmed from the decline of the Church Education Society itself, others from developments in Irish education. The fortunes of the Church Education Society began to decline in the late 1860s, when, after the Church Disestablishment Act of 1869, the resources of the church were seriously curtailed. The annual income of the Society had been nearly £7,000 in 1855 but by 1860 it had dropped to £5,000 and by 1866 to £4,500. The Society found itself unable to give sufficient financial support to parochial schools and these began to feel the loss. In 1860 Archbishop Beresford of Armagh, himself a president of the Society, sent a circular to clergy who were patrons of the Society's schools in the diocese of Clogher in which he advised that if a parish was unable any longer to support a school on its own it should apply to become a national school and receive state aid from the National

Board. This circular was regarded as heresy by many churchmen and seen as a great betrayal, so much so that Beresford was called 'Judas Iscariot'. The Society which had staunchly supported the cause of scriptural education launched a campaign to defend its policy and to uphold the rights of church schools to teach the scriptures throughout the day. A bitter pamphlet war ensued between the supporters of the Church Education Society and those of the National Board, and parishes argued furiously about the merits and demerits of placing a church school under the National Board. The truth was that the Church of Ireland could no longer afford to run its own separate voluntary school system and unless it was prepared to accept some state aid, the education of Church of Ireland children would suffer. The national system had *de facto* if not *de jure* become a denominational one by the 1860s, and the rights of a denominational manager were fully recognised. In a 'non-vested' national school (one where the building itself was built without aid from the National Board), the manager had the right to exclude religious instruction except that of his own denomination, though the pupils retained the right to withdraw. No clergy of any other denomination had right of entry and, therefore, in a Church of Ireland 'non-vested' national school, Anglican instruction only could be given, albeit at a specific hour each day. By 1868 the majority of national schools were 'non-vested' and the denominational managerial system became firmly entrenched. In 1860 a further incentive had been offered to small Church of Ireland schools when the National Board introduced a new rule whereby a school of fifteen pupils or under would qualify for aid, and those of fifteen to twenty pupils for assistance towards a teacher's salary. In 1860 the number of Church of Ireland children in the national system was 30,868, that was 5.63% of the total; by 1870 this figure had risen to 74,237, which was 7.44% of the total enrolment. Meanwhile by 1868 the number of pupils on the rolls in the Church Education Society schools had dropped to 63,549 of which 50% only were Anglican. There was little doubt that both Church of Ireland and Roman Catholic children were being drawn off into national schools—the number of Church of Ireland children attending the Society's schools had dropped from 47,090 in 1863 to 44,378 by 1868, and the number of Roman Catholics from 9,662 to 6,871.[24]

In view of the serious financial decline of the Church Education Society, the heavy burden of running a training college came to be questioned. The annual cost of the college was about £2,000 per annum which by 1866 was nearly half the Society's income. The college was the responsibility of the central committee but there were those who argued that the money would be better spent assisting small parochial schools throughout the country rather than maintaining an expensive training institution which only a limited number of teachers could attend. By 1868 the college had trained over 700 students but the majority of teachers in the Society's schools had received no training at all. In 1861 the Society had set up an endowment fund for the college of £1058 13s. 0d. which had been vested in government stock, and this income plus the students' six pound fees had helped to cover some of the costs, but these were steadily increasing and the staff salaries had to be maintained.

In addition it was found that with limited financial resources the local clergy could no longer afford to pay a teacher who had been trained at college. Trained teachers were in a position to demand a higher salary than those that had not been trained and the clergy now preferred to appoint an untrained teacher at a lower salary, rather than to have to pay a trained one at a higher rate. The highest salary which a teacher in a Church Education Society school could expect was around £50 per annum, and while this had compared favourably with the highest basic salary paid in a national school, the situation changed in 1872 when the National Board introduced the system of payment-by-results. Under this scheme a national teacher was paid a bonus in addition to his basic salary, according to his pupils' performance in the annual examination. Thus it became possible under the new regulations for a national teacher to earn up to 3s. 6d. for each pupil who passed successfully in first class, up to 14s. 6d. per pupil passing in sixth class. Extra subjects such as French, Latin and drawing were eligible for further 'result fees' and therefore the position of the teacher in a Church Education Society school began to look less and less favourable in comparison with his counterpart in a national school. Regarded by the clergy as expensive luxuries yet unable to qualify for a government salary, the Kildare Place teachers found themselves in an unenviable position.

It was not surprising, therefore, that the numbers attending the college declined in the 1870s and more began to train as national teachers instead. The course at the Marlborough Street college was free and the same length as the Kildare Place one. Church of Ireland students had always attended the state college in small numbers since its foundation in 1839, and in 1873 there were 51 in residence. At the end of this training course the teacher could qualify for the higher salary offered by the National Board.[25]

In 1868 the Royal Commission on Primary Education in Ireland was set up to examine the system of National Education, and other agencies providing education for the poor. The commission was chaired by Lord Powis and seven of its members were members of the Church of Ireland including Samuel Butcher, bishop of Meath and Master William Brooke Q.C. who was a vice-president of the Church Education Society. Brooke was Master of the Chancery Court and a staunch evangelical. He played a leading role in the new General Synod of the Church of Ireland set up in 1870 after disestablishment to govern the Church.

The Church Education Society was anxious to defend its policy and explain why it found it impossible to accept aid from the National Board. It submitted substantial evidence to the commission to show the extent of its work and its contribution to the education of the poor. It once again explained why it could not accept the separation of religious from secular instruction as required by the rules of the National Board:

> The Church Education Society holds that Scriptures being the divine rule of faith and practice ought to be made an essential part of education, and that not only should they be read at certain stated hours but also that the teachers should be at liberty on every suitable occasion to refer to them, whether in administering reproof or enforcing a duty, or illustrating a lesson, and it declines to undertake the education of children on any other terms.[26]

Leeper as general secretary of the Church Education Society, and Wilkinson as training master at the college, were both invited to give evidence to the commission. Both were questioned closely about the necessity of being able to refer to the Scriptures throughout the school day. When asked whether such would not be an 'interruption' in a geography class, Leeper replied, 'We would not regard it as an interruption. We feel ourselves not only free but bound to teach what is higher and better than geography while at the same time teaching geography, or whatever school lesson it might be'. Both men gave an account of their work at the training college and described the organization there. Wilkinson was forced to admit that a ten and a half hour day of literary instruction was too much for a trainee teacher but when asked whether he thought that a smaller number of subjects and a fewer number of hours would be more conducive to real instruction, he replied, 'I do, but the session being five months, and a cessation then for a month, they are relieved of much; and after the training of two sessions they are free; but however I have not found the health of anyone of the teachers break down. I am willing to admit that the work is severe'.[27]

Nonetheless the training college received a favourable report when visited by the commissioners and the overall recommendations of the Powis Report favoured denominational rights in education. However, the fundamental rules of the National Board were unchanged, and the Church Education Society found itself still unable to accept aid. The National Board's own training college at Marlborough Street had received a critical report from two of Her Majesty's Inspectors from England who were on the Powis Commission, Scott Nasmyth Stokes and Reverend Benjamin Cowie, and who recommended that radical reform was needed if the state college was to survive. The college had stagnated since the 1850s when, because of its non-denominational status, the Roman Catholic hierarchy had refused to allow Catholic students to attend. Since the Synod of Thurles in 1850 Archbishop Cullen and the other Roman Catholic bishops had conducted a vigorous campaign demanding denominational education for Catholic children, and the recognition of denominational colleges for teacher training. In 1862 a ban had been placed on the Marlborough Street college and Catholic children were forbidden to attend the model schools of the National Board. Therefore, the number of untrained teachers was growing each year and one of the recommendations of the Powis Commission was that the National Board should give aid 'to training schools under the management of committees, voluntary societies or religious bodies on certain conditions, or to allow denominational boarding houses to be attached to Marlborough Street'.[27] This policy however was not to be implemented for another ten years and meanwhile the Kildare Place training college had to struggle on.[28]

Throughout the 1870s the fortunes of the Church Education Society declined. Its position was further reduced by the administrative re-organization of the Church of Ireland which took place after disestablishment. In addition to the setting up of a General Synod Board of Education, diocesan boards of education were established to assist church schools and to ensure that adequate religious instruction was provided in both national and church schools. These diocesan boards began to replace the old Church Education Society committees and local support for the Society dwindled. By 1872 the total annual income of the Society had dropped to £3,000 and so the cost of running the training institution was prohibitive. The Society began to consider whether it could transfer the college to the General Synod and persuade the Church to take over the responsibility of the training of teachers. At a meeting of the General Synod in 1873 a resolution was adopted whereby a fund should be established

> to provide the means whereby masters and mistresses of our primary schools may be adequately prepared as teachers of secular knowledge and still more they should be well instructed in the Holy Scriptures and in the formularies of our church and apt to teach others.[29]

It was agreed that some of the fund should be used to support the Kildare Place Training Schools but that part of it should pay clergy to give daily religious instruction to the Church teachers training under the National Board, and to supervise a residential boarding house.

This resolution illustrated the dilemma which the Church faced and showed that it had not yet decided whether its future education policy lay with trying to maintain a separate denominational system or whether, in the long run, it should accept the rules of the National Board and encourage its schools to apply for aid. This dilemma was very marked in the training college question. One of the recommendations of the Powis Report had been that denominational boarding houses should be established in connection with the Marlborough Street College. This arrangement would provide the necessary religious safeguards for the students in training to satisfy the Churches' demand, while still preserving the non-denominational status of the state college. Such a plan, however, was not acceptable to the Roman Catholic Church which was seeking state support for full denominational colleges.

In 1874 the Chief Secretary, Sir Michael Hicks-Beach wrote to the National Board urging that a solution be found to the teacher training issue. He referred to the proposals made by his predecessor, Chief Secretary Fortescue, who in 1866 had suggested that a system of grants be paid to private training schools, and to the recommendations of the Powis Commission.

The National Board debated the request but were unable to come to agreement. Professor J. H. Jellett of Trinity College (later Provost 1881–1888), one of the Church of Ireland commissioners on the National Board, eventually proposed a motion to support a boarding house scheme for Marlborough Street:

> The Commissioners are of opinion that the system at present in force at Marlborough Street Training School might advantageously be modified by permitting those who are admitted to the Training School to reside in private boarding-houses to be approved by the Commissioners and to

> receive a grant sufficient to defray the cost of living of the pupils so resident.[30]

Jellett's motion was carried but an amendment was proposed that the Board should consider a scheme put forward at the previous meeting by Sir Patrick Keenan, the resident commissioner. This memorandum which became known as 'the Resident Commissioner's scheme' was the plan on which the denominational colleges scheme was eventually to be based. It proposed that the state should support denominational colleges for the training of national school teachers provided there was a model national school on the premises. The state was to pay up to 75% of the college's expenditure including a capitation grant for each student in training who completed two years' service in teaching after leaving the college. The training colleges were to be treated under the same rules as 'non-vested' national schools in that ownership and management of the college would be retained by the church but the curriculum, standards and staff qualifications were to be controlled by the National Board. The members of the National Board, particularly the Protestant ones, were reluctant to surrender the fundamental principle of the national system—namely that of 'mixed' education but they were outvoted and the memorandum was adopted. Details were sent to Hicks-Beach but nothing further developed. It would appear that the disagreement on the National Board and the formal protest made later by the Education Committee of the General Assembly of the Presbyterian Church convinced the government that it would be unwise to move on the issue. However, the two schemes, Jellett's 'boarding house' proposal and Keenan's denominational colleges, now were both 'on the books' from 1874.[31]

The Church Education Society continued to press the General Synod of the Church of Ireland to take over the Kildare Place college. In 1875 the college was £500 in debt and the number in residence, particularly men, was declining. By 1876 the Society had finally decided that it could no longer justify using its dwindling resources to support the college, since the Society itself 'no longer received the *hearty* support of an overwhelming number of the clergy and laity of the Church of Ireland' and that the opinion was 'spreading even among members of our own church that religious and secular education may be lawfully separate and that where one or the other must be given up secular should be retained'.[32]

Therefore, in June 1878 the Church Education Society presented the General Synod with an ultimatum. Canon Leeper as Hon.

Secretary of the Society wrote to the standing committee of the General Synod to say that the Society had decided that unless aid was forthcoming from the Church it would have to close the male department of the college. It could no longer afford to pay the high salary of Mr. Wilkinson, and the small number of male applicants did not justify keeping the department open. Thus the future of the Kildare Place college hung in the balance, and the outcome depended on the decision of the standing committee of the General Synod and even more on the Church's choice of its future policy towards state aided primary education. For over twenty years the Church Education Society had carried the burden of providing trained teachers for Anglican church schools and had run a first class denominational college. If the Church of Ireland wished to retain a denominational college, then the Kildare Place college was the foundation on which to build; if on the other hand it wanted to move towards closer co-operation with the National Board, a boarding house attached to the state college would be a better proposition. The outcome depended as much on the development of events in the whole national teacher training issue as on the particular decision of the Church of Ireland itself.

III

The foundation of the Church of Ireland Training College, 1878–1890

Part I: The decision of the General Synod, 1878–84

When the standing committee of the General Synod of the Church of Ireland received the letter from the Church Education Society in June 1878, it was fortunately in a position to take an immediate decision regarding the Kildare Place college. At the meeting of the General Synod in May that year it was decided that the Board of Religious Education of the General Synod should 'be authorized to undertake the management of any institution for the training of teachers in connection with the Church of Ireland, any arrangement to be laid before the Synod at its next session for approval'.[1] This resolution left the way open for the Church either to run its own voluntary church college, or to seek state aid by establishing a boarding house at the Marlborough Street college.

Therefore, in June 1878 it was agreed to set up a temporary management committee to run the Kildare Place college for a further six months provided £1000 was forthcoming in subscriptions. The committee consisted of six able members of the Board of Religious Education, four laymen and two clerics. William Brooke, Master of the Chancery Court was chairman. He was a member of the Church Education Society and was determined to keep a voluntary church college in operation. He was ably assisted by Henry Fitzgeorge Colley, J.P. of Mount Temple, Clontarf who had also been an active member of the Church Education Society. The other two laymen were Tankerville Chamberlain, a barrister, and John H. Nunn, a solicitor and law agent for Trinity College. Nunn was a member of the Kildare Place Society and provided a useful link with it. The two clerical members were Dr. C. K. Irwin (later archdeacon of Armagh) and Canon H. J. Tombe of Co. Wicklow.

This management committee worked to raise the necessary funds to keep the college open while a second sub-committee was set up to examine the possibility of establishing a boarding house in connection with Marlborough Street. The latter wrote to the Commissioners of National Education in February 1879 to seek information on whether Professor Jellett's 'boarding house' proposal of 1874 could be implemented. The National Board replied sending a copy of the relevant minutes and resolutions which had been printed in the parliamentary papers in 1875, and stating that they had written to the Chief Secretary Hicks-Beach, but still awaited a reply.

Therefore, when the General Synod met in April 1879 two alternative proposals were presented. William Brooke's training college committee recommended that the Church should try to go it alone and maintain an independent college, while the other sub-committee recommended that the Church should apply for a boarding house scheme attached to the state college, and obtain a maintenance grant for Church of Ireland students. This second proposal meant the official recognition by the Church of the national school system, and the conservative forces in the Synod still prevailed. The less radical proposal, that of continuing to run an independent college, was accepted, and the boarding house scheme was dropped.[2]

Therefore for three more years the Kildare Place college struggled on. But lack of financial resources and of male applicants made the task impossible. The desire to train at a church college was growing less and less as the opportunities for and salaries of national teachers improved. In 1881 William Brooke died; he had been the main force behind the church college. By 1882 the management committee could no longer continue to pay the staff (for both Leeper and Wilkinson had been retained at high salaries) and college was faced again with the closure of the male department.

It was at this stage that William Conyngham, Lord Plunket, bishop of Meath emerged as the leader and prime negotiator. He had been chairman of the college management committee since 1879 and was determined to see it survive. Plunket was a member of the Co. Meath landed family and his uncle, Thomas, the second Lord Plunket, had been bishop of Tuam. As a young man he had suffered ill-health but after ordination in 1857 he had worked closely with his uncle in supporting the evangelical campaign of the Irish Church Missions in West Connaught and had written about its work. He became treasurer of St. Patrick's cathedral, Dublin, and in 1876 bishop of Meath. An able, energetic leader, he foresaw that the future of the Church of

Ireland primary education lay within the state school system and that the Church must face the reality of its post-disestablishment position and accept state aid. The eventual success of the Church of Ireland Training College and the gradual acceptance of the national school system by the Church was due more to Plunket's influence than to any other.[3]

In this work he was much helped by three able laymen. William Graham Brooke, nephew of William Brooke, was a barrister and an active participant in education affairs. A bachelor, quiet and tactful, he was a strong advocate of women's education, and he served on the Council of Alexandra College, Dublin, for twenty-seven years. In 1895 he was a member of the deputation to the Board of Trinity College, which requested the entry of women into the university. His wisdom and negotiating skills were to prove invaluable to the training college.[4] Rt. Hon. Sir Frederick R. Falkiner, Q.C., the recorder of Dublin, was another active supporter. His prestige and powers of persuasion were to have much influence in the debates in the General Synod. He served for twenty years as chairman of The King's Hospital and in 1906 published a history of the school. Finally Lord Justice Gerald Fitzgibbon played a leading role in the legal and political negotiations in the coming years. As a young man he had been law adviser at Dublin Castle where he had become a close friend of Lord Randolph Churchill whose father, the Duke of Marlborough, had been lord lieutenant (1876–80). In 1878 he had been appointed a lord justice of appeal and in the 1880s he served as one of the judicial commissioners on the Educational Endowments Commission. He also became a commissioner of National Education from 1884–96. Fitzgibbon's legal expertise and political influence were to be of immense benefit to the Church of Ireland as a whole.[5]

When the General Synod met in 1882 a definite decision had to be made regarding the future of the Kildare Place college so the 'boarding house' proposal was revived. Such a scheme would give the Church increased clerical supervision over its teachers who were attending the state college at Marlborough Street, without the burden of full financial responsibility. Since disestablishment an increasing number of Church of Ireland schools was entering the national system. In 1870 7.4% of national pupils were Anglicans; by 1880 this figure had risen to 10%. In 1873 there were 332 exclusively Protestant schools in the system; by 1883 this had risen to 620, and the number of Church of Ireland schools entering each year about 40. In addition many Church of Ireland children were attending the model schools of the national system (in 1873 34% of model school pupils were anglicans). Therefore, it was clear that a growing number of Church of Ireland children were receiving their primary education within the national system, and that the Church would have to acknowledge this. About 50 Church of Ireland students per year were in training at Marlborough Street, and the Church had kept a chaplain there.[6] A resolution was put forward at the Synod by the Right Rev. Bishop R. S. Gregg, now bishop of Cork:

> that the Board of Religious Education be instructed to enter into communication with Government on the basis of the resolution of the Commissioners of National Education of Ireland ... and also with Commissioners to ascertain whether and how far they will agree to such a modification of the Timetable as shall allow for religious education to teachers in the evening hours.[7]

Opposition to this resolution was so strong in the Synod that a division of the house and a vote by orders was called for. The outcome was a vote in favour, the clergy by 97 to 22 votes, the laity by 64 to22. However, the situation was so serious that radical action was required, and it was decided to set up a special negotiating subcommittee of the General Synod itself rather than to leave the matter in the hands of the Board of Religious Education. On a proposal of F. R. Falkiner, Q.C., the recorder of Dublin, a special twelve-man committee consisting of six members of the Board of Religious Education and six appointed by the Synod was given powers to negotiate with the government about the boarding house scheme. Four days of protracted debate ensued at the Synod as the fears and prejudices against the state system of education were voiced, but eventually, due to the influence of Plunket, Falkiner and Brooke, the resolution was passed. The Recorder's committee, as it came to be known, began negotiations immediately, first with the training college management committee and second with the Commissioners of National Education. This committee included Lord Plunket, W. G. Brooke, Sir Andrew Hart, the Vice-Provost of TCD, Dr. C. K. Irwin of Armagh, Canon J. F. Peacocke (later archbishop of Dublin, 1897–1911) and Canon J. G. Scott (later archdeacon of Dublin, 1883–1907). The training college committee was reluctant even at this stage to surrender part of its premises for a boarding house but the influence of Plunket, who served on both committees prevailed, and by December 1882 the Recorder's committee were in a position to write formally to the CNEI requesting a grant for a boarding house for Church of Ireland students in Marlborough Street in accordance with the resolution of 1874. The letter was signed by Brooke and Falkiner.[8]

It appears that this bold move by the Church of Ireland re-opened the whole question of the future of denominational teacher training colleges, and encouraged the government to act. Throughout the 1870s the Roman Catholic Church had maintained its demand for state grants for denominational colleges on the pattern of the English system. The Church had been hopeful when the Conservative government came to power that some action would be taken, but the chief secretary, Hicks-Beach, failed to follow up his original initiative of 1874 because of Protestant opposition, particularly from the Presbyterian Church, which strongly supported the non-denominational state training college at Marlborough Street. However, by 1883 the situation had changed, the Church of Ireland having shifted its position towards accepting state aid. Gladstone's Liberal government was anxious to seek conciliatory measures following the 'Kilmainham Treaty' of 1882 and the Phoenix Park murders. Earl Spencer and George Otto Trevelyan had been appointed lord lieutenant and chief secretary respectively in May 1882 and they were much influenced by Sir Patrick Keenan, the resident commissioner of the National Board, in seeking to find a solution to the teacher training issue which would placate the Roman Catholic hierarchy. Therefore, in January 1883 when the Commissioners of National Education wrote to the Chief Secretary regarding the request from the Church of Ireland for a Church of Ireland boarding house attached to Marlborough Street, the government was prepared to act. On March 6th 1883 the Chief Secretary wrote to the Commissioners to say that not only was the government willing to grant a boarding house to the Church of Ireland, but that it was now prepared to sanction a full grant to non-vested training colleges for the training of national teachers. On March 9th this news was announced in the House of Commons and the Commissioners were invited to submit a plan (which would be probably Keenan's plan of 1874) for approval. Thus the Church of Ireland was overtaken by events. Details of the denominational colleges scheme were not yet available when the Synod met in early April. The scheme was sanctioned on the 12th and the correspondence published by order of the House on 26th April 1883. Therefore, the Church of Ireland decided wisely to accept the boarding house scheme and await further developments.[9]

In September 1883 eighteen men came into residence at Kildare Place, lodging at the expense of the CNEI and attending courses at Marlborough Street. This scheme served as a useful stepping-stone for the Church of Ireland by creating a favourable contact with the National Board, and breaking down distrust. So much so that by January 1884 the standing committee had decided to request the government to extend the scheme to a female boarding house. The Church was still reluctant to commit itself to accepting a full denominational college although by September 1883 the two Roman Catholic colleges, Our Lady of Mercy, Baggot Street, and St. Patrick's, Drumcondra, founded by the Vincentian Fathers, had both entered the scheme. Throughout the spring of 1884 the standing committee awaited a reply from the government. In March a deputation went to see the under-secretary, Sir Robert Hamilton, at Dublin Castle to press the Church's case, but when the Synod met in April no reply had been received. On the sixth day of the Synod, W. G. Brooke finally received a letter from Hamilton refusing the Church's request for an extension of the boarding house scheme but stating that it was open to the Church to apply for support for a full denominational college under the 1883 scheme.

The Church, therefore, was faced with continuing the Kildare Place college half as a residence for men and half as a college for women, an arrangement which would prove most expensive. Bishop Plunket and Brooke urged the Synod to accept the full denominational scheme, stressing that it would give the Church increased control over the college and would enable them to run a full two year course of training. Finally the Synod agreed and the Church of Ireland Training College for national teachers came into existence.[10]

This decision by the Church of Ireland to accept the 1883 scheme was a crucial one both for the Church and for the national school system. Although the two Roman Catholic training colleges had already accepted the 1883 scheme, the entry of the Church of Ireland ensured its success. If the Church of Ireland had maintained its support for Marlborough Street, the development of teacher training might have become less rigidly denominational. Although a small number of anglican students continued to train at Marlborough Street, it became largely a Presbyterian college.

The establishment of the Church of Ireland Training College (CITC) marked the official acceptance by the Church of the national system and had considerable influence on both the Church and the national system. The denominational aspect of the system was strengthened by the guarantee of the continued existence of separate Church of Ireland schools with their own trained teachers. Church of

Ireland clerical managers upheld along with their Roman Catholic counterparts the Church's rights in education and the first principal of CITC, Canon H. Kingsmill Moore, was a strong advocate of the rights and privileges of the denominational colleges. Protestant children were increasingly to receive their education within the national system and share a common curriculum with the rest of the community. The Church's schools were to be well maintained and equipped, and national school teaching became an honourable profession for Protestant boys and girls.

However, the decision of 1883 was seen by many churchmen as a bitter surrender of the rights of 'scriptural education' which had been fought for since the foundation of the national system in 1831, and the very existence of CITC was for some years in jeopardy. But the wise compromise of including within the college a 'non-government department' for the training of teachers for the church which remained independent of state aid, helped to allay the fears of the church party, and the continued emphasis on the devotional and spiritual life of the students convinced clergy that the new national teachers would be suitable persons to run their schools. The success of the new college depended on what support it could gain from the Church as a whole and on the energies and enterprise of its governors and staff in fulfilling the requirements of the state so that its students would qualify to serve in the national system.

The months following the decision of the Synod in April 1884 to apply for a licence to become a denominational training college for national teachers were to be very busy. Immediate action was needed if the Kildare Place college was to be reorganized and ready to open in September 1884. The church college had to be wound up, and the premises re-leased from the Kildare Place Society. The model schools had to be transferred to the National Board, and a new principal and staff appointed. Under the terms of the 1883 scheme the Commissioners of National Education had to be satisfied with the management, premises and staff of the new college.

Therefore, in May 1884 the standing committee appointed a subcommittee to act as an organizing committee for the new college. Bishop Plunket acted as chairman, W. G. Brooke as secretary, and F. R. Falkiner, the recorder, advised on legal matters. The other members were Archdeacon Scott of Dublin, Archdeacon Stuart of Dromore, Dr. Hart, Vice-Provost of TCD and Dr. Anthony Traill FTCD (later Provost, 1904–14). This committee held a series of meetings in Dublin, Cork and Belfast to raise support for the college and collect donations. The new college would need about £2,000 a year from voluntary subscriptions to cover costs not borne by the state. It was essential that if the venture was to succeed solid support from all dioceses be forthcoming. Plunket who was himself to become archbishop of Dublin later that year, invited Archbishop Trench to be the Visitor and a management committee consisting of both clergy and laity was appointed to represent a wide range of Church interests. Most members of the management committee of the former church college were incorporated into it. The members were:

Archbishop Plunket of Dublin (chairman)
Bishop R. S. Gregg of Cork
Bishop W. Pakenham Walsh of Ossory
Bishop W. R. Chester of Killaloe
Dean A. H. Leech of Cashel
Dean H. H. Dickinson of the Chapel Royal
Dean J. Lefroy of Dromore
Archdeacon J. G. Scott of Dublin
Archdeacon G. Nugent of Meath
Hon. Justice Harrison
Dr. A. S. Hart, vice-provost of T.C.D.
F. R. Falkiner, recorder of Dublin (Hon. Sec.)
Rev. J. S. Bell, LL.D.
W. G. Brooke, Esq. (Hon. Sec.)
T. T. Chapman, Esq.
Rev. F. C. Hayes M.A.
E. H. Kinahan, Esq.
Henry F. Colley, Esq.
Rev. Canon T. B. Warren, M.A.
Rev. J. J. Robinson, M.A.
Rev. Wm. Sherrard, M.A.
A. Traill, Esq., F.T.C.D.
James Wilson, Esq.
Rev. Canon F. R. Wynne, M.A.

Of these, eighteen members had served on the church college committee, including the bishop of Ossory and the bishop of Killaloe. Only one member of the previous managment committee, J. H. Nunn, resigned. He objected to the placing of the Kildare Place model schools under the National Board which to him, as an old member of the Kildare Place Society, was the final betrayal.[11]

The decision of the organizing committee to continue a 'non-government' training department within the college was a prudent one. This department which would receive no state aid was to have its own separate executive committee and was to have no connection with the National Board other than that the students attended the same classes as the national teachers in training. This compromise move enabled the college to maintain a viable number of students in its early years, helped to allay the fears of the Church party, and increased support for the college from the Church of Ireland as a whole. The non-government department continued to exist until 1903 when it was finally closed owing to lack of demand. By that time national teachers and national schools had become fully accepted by all churchmen.

The transfer of the premises in Kildare Place to the Church of Ireland involved difficult and lengthy negotiations with the legal owners, the Kildare Place Society. The organizing committee were anxious for the legalities to be settled as soon as possible so that the necessary maintenance and repairs could be carried out before September. 10 Kildare Street was already in use as the boarding house for men, but No. 11 was occupied by tenants of the Kildare Place society. Eventually when the time came for the college to open the top floor only of No. 11 was available. The final legal negotiations were not to be concluded until 1887 when, under a scheme of the Educational Endowments Commission the total property was transferred to the Church of Ireland and the Kildare Place Society, after seventy years of honourable existence, was wound up.[12]

The next most important task was the appointment of a principal of the college. In this the organizing committee was to be most successful. The Reverend Henry Kingsmill Moore was appointed principal in 1884; he was to serve the college for over forty years in that office. He was to be responsible, more than any other, for the establishment of CITC as a respected and flourishing training college. T. F. Kelly in an essay on education in *Irish Anglicanism 1869–1969* described Kingsmill Moore as 'perhaps the greatest single influence on Church of Ireland education for the entire generation'.[13]

Kingsmill Moore was born in 1853 in Liverpool but moved to Ireland at the age of ten when his father, Dr. Moore, was appointed headmaster of Midleton College, Co. Cork. Kingsmill Moore was educated first at Midleton and then at King Edward VI Grammar School, Bromsgrove where a number of Irish boys were sent. He went up to Balliol College, Oxford, in 1873 and was ordained for the diocese of Cork in 1877. He first served as a curate in Queenstown, Co. Cork where he married Constance Turpin of Cork in 1880. He later moved to Fermoy where he became involved in the educational work of the church. In 1881 he was appointed by Bishop R. S. Gregg of Cork as diocesan inspector of schools. His job was to inspect all the primary schools both church and national in the diocese. The conflict between church and national schools was still very strong in Cork but Bishop Gregg was determined that the church should recognise its responsibility to children attending national schools, and eventually gained agreement for the expenses of a diocesan inspector to be shared between the two types of schools. Kingsmill Moore travelled the length and breadth of the diocese, visiting schools in remote parts of west Cork and examining the pupils for results fees. In national schools he examined in religious knowledge only but in church schools in all subjects. It was arduous and responsible work and he gained valuable experience of primary education.

As a result of this work Kingsmill Moore wrote a pamphlet entitled *What We are Doing for Our Children* which made him well known in church circles. When in May 1884 Bishop Gregg asked him to organize a meeting in Cork in connection with the new training college, Kingsmill Moore first met F. R. Falkiner, the recorder, who had come down to address the meeting. Kingsmill Moore recalled that it was Falkiner who first broached with him the subject of applying for the principalship of the new college, and Bishop Gregg strongly encouraged him. He was interviewed with four other candidates, all clergymen, and was appointed on the 18th July 1884. He came up immediately to Dublin and throughout the summer resided in Maples Hotel in Kildare Street, opposite the college. A close relationship was established with Archbishop Plunket whom Kingsmill Moore liked and admired, and the two men worked together tirelessly for the development of the college. Kingsmill Moore was a confident, able and energetic man of thirty. He had experience of primary education at the basic level from his work in Co. Cork, and he understood the attitudes of churchmen to the national system. His bold, sometimes arrogant, actions were tempered by the wisdom and tact of the archbishop and Kingsmill Moore was prepared to accept the archbishop's advice on most matters.[14]

Kingsmill Moore's first task was the appointment of his new staff. This posed a somewhat difficult problem as the staff of the old college had to be retained, yet new and younger personnel were required.

Canon Leeper, who had been head of the college since 1855, gracefully retired but served as chaplain until his death in 1891. W. T. Wilkinson, the master of training, now an ageing man, also retired but continued to serve as a diocesan inspector for the Church Education Society which recognised with gratitude his long service. This left the way open for younger men. The college was very fortunate in finding four who, like the principal, were to serve the institution for forty years. Jeremiah Henly was appointed headmaster of the boys' model schools, and training master. He was a gifted and experienced national schoolteacher. Trained at Marlborough Street, he had obtained a first class certificate and as headmaster of the Christ Church, Leeson Park schools in 1883 he had been awarded the Carlisle and Blake prize, one of the National Board's coveted awards, conferred annually on the eighteen best teachers in the country. Henly was also a founder member of the Irish National Teachers' Organization. While a young teacher in Calary, Co. Wicklow, he had founded a local teachers' association and helped to organize the national association in 1868. Along with a group of young national teachers he had approached Vere Foster, the philanthropic and social reformer for his advice and assistance on how teachers' grievances could be made public. Henly had already begun to write articles for Chamneys, the Dublin publishers of journals, and it was through them that the contact with Vere Foster was made. Eventually it was agreed that Chamney would edit and publish a new monthly journal *The Irish Teachers' Journal* for which Henly would be the chief leader writer. Thus from 1868 Henly wrote regularly for the journal, commenting and criticising government policy in education and providing a tutorial section to assist teachers to pass their promotion examinations. The journal became the official organ of the Irish National Teachers' Organization and provided an important political platform for national teachers. Henly was to continue to contribute under a nom-de-plume for many years, when the journal became *The Irish School Weekly.*

CITC were fortunate to recruit Henly, and were sensible enough to accept his writings and political activities on behalf of the teachers' union. A shy, stern person, he was a strict disciplinarian, and he was to advise and assist Kingsmill Moore on all matters relating to the practicalities of teaching and the professional role of the teacher. He provided a valuable link between the college and the profession, and national recognition for his services was given, when as an elderly man, he was invited by the government to serve on the Dill Committee on the national school inspectorate in 1913.[15]

The other three men who joined the staff in 1884 were university graduates who reflected the increasing academic status of training college work. The men were given the title of 'professor'. James C. Rea, who was appointed Professor of Mathematics and Natural Philosophy, was a graduate of the Royal University of Ireland, having attended Queen's College Belfast. (His name is one of those carved on a desk top recently preserved at Queen's University. The desk top which had been used as part of a bench at Cherryvale Playing Fields, Belfast, was presented to the university for safe-keeping in 1982.) Rea was born in Castlewellan, Co Down in 1857, and was a first class trained national teacher. He built up the scientific and mathematical side of the college's work but owing to ill-health he retired early in 1912.[16] John Cooke who was appointed Professor of Geography, Physiography and General History, had a first class degree from Trinity College, Dublin. He developed drawing and craft subjects at the college, and was honoured by being invited in 1898 as an expert witness to the Belmore Commission on Manual and Practical Instruction in primary schools. Born in Ulster in 1850, he was a retiring, quiet man, devoted to cycling and fishing. He wrote a popular textbook *Elementary Geography*, and edited two useful guide books, *Murray's Handbook of Ireland* (1896) and *Wakeman's Handbook of Irish Antiquities* (1903). He was a member of the Royal Society of Antiquaries of Ireland and of the Royal Irish Academy, and when in 1922 the college formed official links with TCD he was appointed lecturer in geography by the university. John Cooke remained on the staff until he was eighty, and he died in 1931.[17]

Laurence Edward Steele, who was appointed Professor of English, was also a first class graduate of Trinity College. Born in 1855, he was the son of W. E. Steele, the director of the Science and Art Museum. A gifted public speaker, he became well known for his popular lectures. He edited several books for English teaching, *Essays from the Tatler* (1896) and *Sir Richard Steele, Essays* (1902) and was a vice-president of the Royal Dublin Society and vice-chairman of the National Library. His chief interest at CITC in addition to his English lectures was the maintenance of links with past students and he kept meticulous records of their subsequent careers. Always a gentleman, 'Larry' Steele was a much beloved figure at CITC; 'a slice of Lamb' was his favourite phrase in class. He retired in 1930 at the age of seventy-five and died in 1944.[44]

CITC was very fortunate in obtaining the services of such loyal and able men who devoted their life work to the college. On the women's side two senior staff members, Miss Jane Lewis and Miss Mary Jane Smith were retained. Miss Lewis became vice-principal of the female department until her death in 1889. Mary Smith was much younger—born in Gowna, Co. Cavan in 1853, she had been a student at the Church Education Society college in 1869 and had stayed on as a member of staff. A gifted musician, she was to develop a very high standard of singing and choral music in the college, and she studied at the Tonic Solfa College in London, obtaining specialist qualifications there. A devout and dedicated teacher, she was to give a life of service to the college until her sudden death in 1914.[19]

The other important section of the college staff was the teachers in the three model schools. These schools which had always been a feature of Kildare Place, were now formally recognised as national schools and as practising schools for the teachers in training. There was considerable opposition to the transfer of the schools of the National Board, but W. G. Brooke tactfully handled the matter himself and became first manager of the national schools. Mr. Henly was assisted in the boys' model school by Mr. Hamilton who had just qualified from the college, being one of the eighteen boarders who had resided at Kildare Place while training at Marlborough Street. Miss Agnes Brown became head of the girls' model school, a position she was to hold for thirty-four years. Miss Brown a first class trained teacher, had been head of the national school in Carrickfergus, and was a capable leader. Miss H. C. Heron, who had been an assistant in the school, was reappointed and she taught needlework both to the girls and the students. Miss Bessie Robinson, who had been head of Inchicore National School, was appointed head of the infant model school. Her assistant, Sarah Boyd, had been a student at the church college and was already working in the school. Thus the model school staff played a vital role in the college, and, being resident, assisted with the supervision of the students.

The re-opening of the new national model schools, freshly painted and refurbished, took place in August, 1884. Bishop Plunket used the occasion to make a speech reminding parents and the clergy that the religious teaching of the children would be central to the schools' work and that under the National Board's regulations adequate provision for religious instruction was provided, albeit at a separate and definite hour. The enrolment of children from the city at the schools was to be indicative of the confidence which they gained. In 1884 numbers attending the schools were 96 boys, 97 girls, and 73 infants; by 1888 these numbers had risen to 189, 237 and 119 respectively.[20]

With the re-organization of the college well under way negotiations with the National Board proved a pleasant task. The organizing committee applied for a licence as a denominational college in June 1884, and within a month W. R. Molloy, the chief of inspection, and H. Fitzpatrick, head inspector, inspected the college premises. Kingsmill Moore appreciated the courtesy and encouragement which he received from the officials of the National Education Office. The resident commissioner, Sir Patrick Keenan, personally gave advice where needed. He was pleased that the Church of Ireland had agreed to accept the 1883 scheme, which had been mainly his own plan. W. R. Molloy, 'the Chief', gave constant guidance to the college in its initial months and Kingsmill Moore was to seek his advice on all National Board regulations for years to come.

Under the 1883 scheme the college was entitled to receive a grant of up to 75% of its annual expenditure. This grant was paid out of a credit fund which accrued to the college from the grants earned by each qualified student who successfully completed two years teaching after leaving the college (the grants amounted to £100 per male student and £70 per female). In the first five years, however, this rule did not apply, and the grant was paid out of a central fund. The officials of the National Education Office advised Kingsmill Moore to spend as much money as possible in the initial years, and after that to save to build up the credit fund. This policy enabled the college to equip and launch itself in style. CITC differed from the other two denominational colleges in that it was co-educational, and therefore the grants scheme worked out somewhat differently. Under the 1883 regulations a maintenance grant of £50 per male student, and £35 per female student was paid and, therefore, it was very important for CITC to maintain high numbers in the male department.[21]

The college was formally re-opened on 9th September, 1884 by Archbishop Trench, the Visitor. It was an occasion for rejoicing, and Bishop Plunket made a fine speech on the importance of reconciling the Church's interests with those of the national system. There were 87 students in residence, 62 in the government department, training to be national teachers, and 25 in the non-government department, training for church schools. In the government department there were two types of students—the 'Annuals' who were already certificated teachers on leave of absence from their national schools, and the 'Biennials' who were younger students, taking the new full-time two year training course. The number of male students was small, 14 only in the government department, two in the non-government. The first year for the new denominational college was of vital importance for it had to show that its students could reach the required standard of the National Board examinations, and win the confidence of the Church so that the clergy would appoint students to their schools. The future financial stability of the college depended on its students obtaining posts in national schools and at a time when it was still possible for an untrained teacher to be appointed to a national school, it was imperative to show that the new two year college trained teacher was superior in every way. Therefore, Kingsmill Moore was very pleased when at the end of the first session the CITC students headed the result list in the National Board examinations, and the college was well up to the standard of the other two training colleges, St. Patrick's, Drumcondra, and Our Lady of Mercy, Baggot Street. In his report at the end of the year he wrote that they were very thankful and must give 'recognition of His Hand by Whose special help preventing us, our efforts have been brought to good effect'.[22]

Part II:
The early years, 1885–1890

Once the first year was accomplished, CITC began to expand and flourish. The self-confidence of the college increased as it gained the support of the Church of Ireland community and as it became recognised in the broader educational world. In the next five years Kingsmill Moore laid the solid foundations on which the college was to build. He was full of energy, drive and enterprise and was ably backed by Archbishop Plunket, the Recorder, and W. G. Brooke.

The first important task was to develop the Kildare Place site and improve the buildings for the students and staff. Early in 1885 Kingsmill Moore went on a tour of English denominational training colleges, including Battersea and Chester, and returned home inspired by the facilities which these colleges could offer. Legal ownership of the Kildare Place site, however, still lay with the Kildare Place Society, which, although a dying organization, was reluctant to part with the historic site. The Educational Endowments Act of 1885 which had set up a body of commissioners to reorganize educational trusts and endowments, helped to provide a solution. Early in 1887, the Kildare Place Society and the CITC management committee submitted a joint scheme to the Educational Endowments Commission which was accepted and came into effect in 1888. The scheme allowed for the transfer of all the property and endowments of the Kildare Place Society to CITC for use as a training institution and the constitution of the governing body of the new college was laid down. Lord Justice Gerald Fitzgibbon as one of the judicial commissioners of the Educational Endowments Commission was responsible for drawing up the scheme.[23]

The site at Kildare Place was confined and the old buildings run down. The houses, 10 and 11 Kildare Street, were plain classical houses as was 4 Kildare Street which adjoined them. The model schools built behind in the 1820s consisted of a large classical fronted two storied hall. To Kingsmill Moore and other men of the late nineteenth century these buildings seemed dull and ugly, and Kingsmill Moore's visit to England had given him ideas of what a Victorian training college should look like. The most pressing need was for a dining-hall for the female students, so this project was undertaken immediately and completed in 1886. The new hall, a spacious building with a beamed roof and windows on both sides, was designed by an eminent architect, Thomas N. Deane, who had designed the Museum Building in Trinity College and had recently completed the new National Museum and National Library in Kildare Street. Archbishop Plunket had wished for a plainer style hall which would have fitted in with the existing eighteenth century buildings but the influence of Kingsmill Moore and the Recorder won the day, and from then on the rest of the college had to be redesigned to match the new Deane dining-hall.

To raise money to pay for the new hall a 'Great Bazaar' was organized in 1886. This occasion provided a meeting point for all those interested in the welfare of the college. The bazaar lasted six days in General Synod week in May. Each diocese undertook to run a stall and Thomas Deane and his son designed a huge 'educational cloister' for the stall, each with a painted shield of the arms of the diocese placed above. (These shields afterwards hung in the dining-hall itself, and are preserved in the CITC research area). The 'Great Bazaar' was successful in raising nearly £1,000 which was needed to clear the debt on the hall. Among the attractions which drew the crowds was the formal opening by the lord lieutenant, Lord Aberdeen, a 'Wizard's Den' designed by Professor George Fitzgerald of TCD which showed scientific experiments, a concert given by the choirs of St. Patrick's and Christ Church cathedrals, and the sale of the new badge of the training college, designed by Archbishop Plunket's sister. This badge consisting of an open Bible on a celtic cross became the crest of the college, and the inscription 'Pro Christo discere ac docere' ('For Christ to learn, for Christ to teach') became its motto.[24]

However, the raising of capital by a sale was not a feasible proposition for long-term regular income. The government grant covered only three-quarters of the college's expenditure and, therefore, between £1,500 to £2,000 had to be raised annually from voluntary sources. In 1887, Archbishop Plunket, the Recorder, and Kingsmill Moore toured the country speaking at meetings held in the main dioceses. Local collectors were appointed and lists of subscribers were published annually in the college reports. Subscriptions were invited for four separate accounts—the 'Immediate Needs Fund', the 'Government Department Fund', the 'Non-Government Department Fund', and the 'General Fund' thus enabling subscribers to choose which section of the college they wished to support. In 1884—85 an initial £6,000 had been raised, and after that about £1,500 per year was forthcoming. When, by the 1890s, the voluntary subscriptions began to decline, the college had been firmly established on a sound financial basis. The non-government department despite receiving no state aid managed to pay its way with help from the 'General Fund', while the 'Immediate Needs Fund' was changed into a 'Reserve Fund' which accumulated capital for building purposes. Undoubtedly the college owed a great debt to the public relations efforts of its first management committee for establishing itself so well in the church community and in making the college financially secure.[25]

Meanwhile the educational work of the college forged ahead. A new two year training course had been introduced by the National Board in 1883, and the college staff worked with enthusiasm to fulfil its demands. This course was a radical innovation in teacher training and its success depended much on the work of the new denominational training colleges. Prior to this the training courses had been only six months in length, and had been, as at the Church Education Society college, intensive ones in professional studies for experienced teachers. Now students were to be recruited directly from primary schools and were to be offered a full course in general education as well as professional training. While many of the students would have been already employed as monitors in their national schools while studying for the training college entrance examination, called the Queen's Scholarship, the function of the training college was to provide them with initial training prior to a full-time appointment as a teacher in a school. Thus the function of the college was to show that it could combine the general further education of the students with the mastering of the skills of teaching and school management, and to prove that this form of training was superior to the old apprenticeship system of monitor and master teacher.

For the next twenty years CITC continued to run two types of teaching course concurrently: a one year course for the 'Annuals', the already certificated national teachers who were granted leave of absence from their national schools and sought to improve their classification under the National Board, and a two year course for monitors and other candidates recruited from national schools who were known as the 'Biennials'. The two groups of students attended the same classes but the 'Annuals' tended to be older and had much to offer the college in the way of practical teaching experience. The 'Annuals' averaged about ten in number each year, almost equal numbers of men and women. This course continued up to 1910 when the National Board decided that it had fulfilled its function, because the majority of national teachers had by then been fully trained at a college.

The biennial students were officially called 'Queen's Scholars' after the competitive entrance examination held each year in July by the National Board. The standard of the examination was that of the third grade classification examination for teachers. A basic knowledge of English grammar, arithmetic, algebra, geometry, geography, agriculture and book-keeping, was required as well as a good standard of reading and penmanship. Algebra and geometry were optional subjects for girls but plain sewing and knitting were compulsory instead. All students had to show a knowledge of school organization and to have read P. W. Joyce's *Handbook of School Management* (1863). Joyce, who was master of method at Marlborough Street College, was later to become well known for his work on Irish place names. His book on school management remained for fifty years the standard text book for all national teachers in training.

Candidates who sat for the Queen's Scholarship examination had to be in good health and be eighteen by the first day of January subsequent to taking the examination. Younger candidates were also eligible if they had completed their training as monitors in a national school. CITC selected from the successful candidates those whom it wished to attend the college. An examination in religious knowledge and vocal and instrumental music was held at the college in September and all applicants were expected to be communicant members of the Church of Ireland. In the early years the number of applicants, particularly male, who were successful in the July examination was small, and the college had little choice of candidates, but as time went on the entry became competitive, particularly among the women.[26]

The students came up to the college each September. No fees were charged other than an admission fee of eight guineas for men and nine for women. However, all students had to sign a written undertaking that they would 'take advantage of the public funds solely in order to qualify themselves for becoming Teachers in Elementary Schools, entitled to Government Aid'. This rule was to ensure that the college was not used just as a cheap means of further education. It did not deter some from using their college training as a basis for a university degree or other qualifications, but it did mean that the students had to give service first in national schools. This was essential if the college was to earn its credit grants under the conditions of the 1883 scheme.

The majority of the students at CITC came from the north of Ireland. In the first five years out of 392 students trained at the college, 223 came from the northern dioceses whereas 80 and 73 only came from the eastern and southern dioceses. Only 16 had come from the west. The largest financial support for the college came from the east, particularly from the diocese of Dublin, Glendalough and Kildare, and the college governors were constantly urging the northern dioceses to contribute more. The college register recorded each student's age, home address, diocese, school attended prior to entry, qualification on entry (i.e. grade obtained in the entrance examination or certification under the National Board), final classification on leaving, and the school where the first post was obtained. Subsequent postings and promotions were added, and two small photographs (one taken in each college year) completed the profile. Among the first male 'Annuals' of 1884–85 were William Douglas aged 21 from Banbridge, Robert Allen aged 21 from Dromahair, Co. Leitrim and Robert McKelvey aged 24 from Plumbridge, Co. Tyrone. Douglas went on to teach in Bantry, Co. Cork, while Allen and McKelvey returned to their home towns. Among the women were Dorinda Armstrong aged 19 from Drumcliffe, Co. Sligo, Alice Fox aged 20 from Ballymahon, Co. Longford, and May Gordon from Newtownbreda, Belfast. These girls were all certificated teachers who returned to their own schools. Margaret Kennedy from Garvagh, Co. Derry, went to teach in Killarney and after returned in 1892 to be head of the infant model school at Kildare Place.

The 'Biennials' were younger and had often been serving as monitors in their national schools. Among the 1884–86 male class were David Horgan from Bandon who had been in the Cork Model School, Robert Jackson of Portadown who had been at Derrylard School, David Kilpatrick from Newtownstewart, John George Kingston from Clonmel and George Twiss from Killarney. All later obtained posts in national schools. David Horgan was appointed to the Kildare Place model schools and subsequently obtained a M.A. degree and a LL.D. from TCD; and married Miss Patience Lynch, one of the teachers in the infant school. In 1911 at the college centenary celebrations, Horgan, who was then principal of Castleknock National School, chaired the meeting of past students which presented Kingsmill Moore with his portrait.

Many of the women 'Biennials' came from the northern counties—Sarah Benson from Belfast went to teach in Moira, Co. Down; Jane Carson from Florencecourt, Co. Fermanagh, went back to teach in Maghera; Margaret Dinesmore came from Castleblayney, Co. Monaghan, and Harriet Forsyth from Skea, near Bailieborough. The latter emigrated to Australia as a missionary but returned to the college during the centenary celebrations in 1911. Elizabeth Smye who came from the coastguard station at Annalong, Co. Down, obtained a post at the Kildare Place model school. From the south there were girls from Cork, Kerry, Clare and Waterford—Sarah Chambers from Dunmanway, Elizabeth Farmer from Mallow, Mary Haigh from Waterford and Rebekah Mustard from Enniskerry, Co. Wicklow.[27]

The two year course which these students took was an arduous but varied one. The students were expected by the end of the two years to have reached the standard of the second class classification examination for teachers. The subjects covered were English grammar and composition, geography, arithmetic, geometry, algebra, elementary mechanics, book-keeping, agriculture and methods of teaching and school organization. The higher branches of mathematics were optional for female teachers but courses in hygiene and domestic economy were offered instead. It was hoped that if the teachers were 'to exercise a civilising influence among the people they ought to have knowledge of the principles which accrue to healthy bodies, and some insight into the method and system which are calculated to ensure healthy homes'. Under the system of 'payment by results' operating in national schools since 1872 it was possible for a teacher to earn extra money by offering 'extra subjects' for which he could claim additional result fees. Therefore, both Latin and French were taught at the college as optional subjects by Kingsmill Moore and L. E. Steele, and students could obtain the National Board's proficiency certificates in them. These subjects though 'not essential in themselves for primary education' were considered to be of the 'utmost value for private tuitions—no small matter in the light of reduced incomes and the difficulties of sending children to a distant school'. Classes in drawing and handicraft were offered by John Cooke, and with the demand for scientific subjects increasing the college also began to participate in the examinations of the Science and Art Department, South Kensington. This department offered results fees also, so on the strength of these the college was soon able to employ another member of the staff, Professor Charles Smith, who prepared the students for the South Kensington examinations in theoretical mathematics, sound, light, heat, magnetism and electricity. Agriculture was a compulsory subject for men, and the students enjoyed the eight mile walk each week out and back to the National Board model farm at Glasnevin. It was believed that teachers in rural schools should have a basic knowledge of farming and so improve their pupils' understanding of agricultural methods.[28]

Some of the women students specialised in infant education and took the certificate in the kindergarten method of Froebel. Miss Bessie Robinson, head of the infant school, was an expert in this method and wrote a standard textbook, *The Kindergarten Practice* (Belfast, 1887) on the subject. Froebel's ideas of play and creative activity for young children were becoming increasingly popular in the 1880s and CITC was in the forefront of the movement. Miss Robinson in the foreword to her book wrote:

> To students at the several Training Colleges and to young and inexperienced teachers, I would say a word of encouragement. Be self-reliant and energetic: cultivate a bright sympathetic manner: make your pupils understand that you are interested in their studies and their games, and they will quickly though perhaps unconsciously, imitate you; they will catch up at once your animation, and adopt your tone of speaking and manner of acting.[29]

Music also played an important part in the curriculum. Mary Jane Smith was an expert in the Tonic Solfa method of John Curwen, and she conducted the college choir and encouraged the students to take the certificates of the Tonic Solfa College. This method enabled a young teacher to learn to teach singing without formal music training. Instrumental playing, particularly of the piano and of the harmonium, was also encouraged, and Mr. Charles O. Grandison, the organist at

Booterstown Church gave classes assisted by his daughter. Extra fees (25 shillings for men and 15 shillings for women) were charged for these lessons. A college organ was sorely needed and a special fund was opened to which past students were urged to contribute. Mr. Grandison served on the staff until his death in 1911 and contributed much to the musical life of the college. He composed the college song 'God's Work is Ours' the words of which were written by Kingsmill Moore, and which was sung on many occasions by the college choir:

We saw the Mighty River in its course
Blessing the many lands thro' which it sped.
We knew the distant springs where it arose
The hundred streams whereby its strength was fed.

Come springs and streams, come in exultant throng.
Helpless alone, together ye are strong.
Come bringing blessing, as we rush along.
God's work is Ours.[30]

Teaching practice remained, however, the most important part of the students' training. It was imperative for the training college to do this practical work very well to show that a fuller general education enhanced rather than hindered a young teacher's ability to handle the realities of classroom management. At CITC the organization closely followed that seen by Kingsmill Moore during his visit to the English training colleges. School practice was based, as previously, on the model schools, and the students taught regularly in them, concurrently with their own academic studies. Lesson notes were carefully scrutinised and 'model lessons' were introduced by Kingsmill Moore who considered it 'the most valuable and certainly the most searching of all methods'. In the presence of the principal, staff and fellow students, each student was required to teach a group of children from the model school, and the lesson was afterwards publicly discussed. 'All in turn are exposed to criticism which though kindly never fails to be impartial and outspoken', and 'the hope of succeeding and the fear of failure at a criticism lesson exercises a healthy stimulus over the whole of the students' course'. The ordeal of these criticism lessons and the nervous strain induced was very hard on many young students, and the method came to be condemned in later years. (Students remember how helpful the pupils from the model schools used to be in these lessons, being more experienced in these matters than the students themselves!) The model schools remained the focal point however of the practical training and this was why the staff of these schools was so important. The girls' model school in particular became a source of recruits for the training college, and a special class was organized there for girls to prepare for the Queen's Scholarship entrance examinations. Miss Agnes Brown presided over the students' training in the model schools and gave valuable advice to all. Miss Margaret Kennedy who had been one of the first annual students at the college, replaced Miss Robinson as head of the infant model school in 1892; and she held this post until 1899 and trained many infant teachers. She had been the first ex-CITC student to win, in 1889, a Carlisle and Blake premium, the coveted prize awarded annually by the National Board to the three best teachers in each school district.

Student life at the college was active and arduous. In common with other nineteenth century training colleges, the main emphasis was on the moral and religious life. Discipline was strict and the male and female departments functioned quite separately. 'Simplicity of dress and modesty of demeanour' was required by all. The students rose at 7 a.m. and attended a daily service with an address by the principal before commencing classes until noon. The women students were expected in addition to carry out their orderly duties and weekly marks were given for neatness and proficiency, and all were encouraged to take a pride in keeping their rooms well. The men and women students ate separately, and a number of domestic servants had to be employed to cook and serve the meals in the men's department. To that extent the men were encouraged to consider themselves as 'gentlemen' though of a humble nature. Little free time was allowed though the students were allowed out for regular walks. The men were given more freedom and responsibility and under a prefect system ran their own residence. All were expected, though not obliged, to become members of the Church of Ireland Temperance Society and to take a pledge of total abstinence.

Kingsmill Moore encouraged the men to enjoy a collegiate life and it was with this in view that he founded the Literary and Debating Society which held fortnightly meetings on Saturday evenings in the dining-hall. The Society was founded in October 1885, and was at first named 'The Church of Ireland Training College Students' Association and Mutual Improvement Society' but this clumsy title was changed in 1886. The CITC debating society was modelled on an university debating society such as the College Historical Society at TCD, and reflected the efforts of the principal to raise the intellectual and cultural standard of the college. The aim was 'the advancement of the interests of the National Teachers, and the mutual improvement of its members by means of General Debatings, Readings and Recitations'. Kingsmill Moore was the first president, and David Horgan (1884–86) was first secretary and J. G. Kingston (1884–86), vice-president. T. W. Pettipice, an annual student (1885–86) from Co. Sligo was the first treasurer and other committee members were George Twiss from Killarney, Robert Jackson from Portadown, John Greet from Co. Sligo, John Elliott of Banbridge, and J. M. Moore of Brookeboro, Co. Fermanagh.

Papers were read, and debates and musical entertainments held throughout the term. Members of staff were invited to attend and took turns to preside. In the first year (1885–6) papers were read on 'Teachers' Independence' by J. M. Moore, 'The Scripture Examination, 1886,' by R. Jackson, 'Teachers' Salaries' by J. G. Kingston, 'The National School Teachers' Programme' by W. Canning and 'The Education and Social Status of the Church of Ireland Primary School' by W. E. Ellis, a member of staff. All the topics were closely linked with the students' work. Some debates did cover a wider area with topics such as 'Is Sunday Closing beneficial to Ireland?' (carried), 'That the Abolition of Capital Punishment is desirable' (lost), 'That the Warrior is of greater benefit to the community than the Poet' (carried).

One function of the society was the running of a 'news room' where the daily and weekly papers were displayed. Disagreement took place regarding which papers should be purchased, and the political views of the students were evident. In December 1885 T. W. Pettipice proposed that *Freeman's Journal*, the nationalist newspaper, should be dropped and the *Belfast Newsletter*, a unionist paper, substituted. In the second session 1886–7 *The Irish Times*, *The Belfast Weekly News*, *Harper's Magazine*, *The Irish Teachers' Journal* and *The Church of Ireland Parish Magazine* were agreed on, and a number of other journals such as the eminent *The Nineteenth Century* and the strident *The Church of Ireland Temperance Advocate* were rejected. The Literary and Debating Society undoubtedly provided a focal

---

ILLUSTRATIONS:

1 *Kildare Place with the Model Schools in the 1820s.*

2 *Kildare Place in the early 1900s with the statue of Archbishop Plunket in the foreground.*

1

2

3

4

meeting point for the male staff and students and an annual dinner was held. Kingsmill Moore presented a prize for oratory and the Saturday evenings were to be 'long remembered with gratitude not merely for the healthy amusement which they afforded, but for the valuable qualities which they developed and called into existence'.[31]

On the female side the ladies' committee provided a valuable social service for the girls. This committee provided a valuable social service for the girls. This committee, formed in 1884, organized outings and musical entertainments. Miss Brooke, sister of W. G. Brooke, Miss F. Leeper, sister of Canon Alexander Leeper, the Hon. Miss Plunket sister of the archbishop, and Mrs. Kingsmill Moore were active members. For instance, in 1885 they hired a tram to take the girls to the Phoenix Park to see the Prince and Princess of Wales, and in 1888 Miss Brooke arranged through Sir Andrew Hart, the Vice-Provost of TCD, for the girls to use the university Botanic Gardens in Ballsbridge for recreation in the afternoons. The ladies' committee worked closely with the Church of Ireland Girls' Friendly Society to which many of the students belonged, and in the absence of any women members on the governing body of the college, this committee provided an important service. While the attitude of the ladies to the young country girls may have been patronising, they did provide a link with the 'outside' life of Dublin and they opened their houses to the students. The annual excursion and picnic to Bray and Killiney where both the ladies and students gathered were happy occasions.[32]

The most important day in the college year was Commemoration Day, held every July to mark the end of the college year. The annual prize-giving took place in the big school room, presided over by Archbishop Plunket and attended by past pupils, friends and relations of the students. The principal read his annual report using the occasion to publicise the achievements and aspirations of the college and the day ended with a musical entertainment led by Miss Smith's choir.

A special feature of Commemoration Day was the return of past students who were welcomed warmly back to the college. Many of them stayed the night having travelled up from the country. Every

---

ILLUSTRATIONS:

3 *Front entrance to the College from the Plunket Quadrangle.*

4 *The men's department and the 'Nuns' Walk' with the clock tower, designed by T. N. Deane and Son.*

effort was made to forge lasting links with these past students, the college knowing that they were its best ambassadors, and the mentors of new recruits. *The Church of Ireland Training College Magazine* was begun in the 1880s to provide a regular contact with college events. The magazine consisted of two pages of college news which were placed at the front and back of *The Church of Ireland Parish Magazine* and later of *The Church Monthly*, and was published three times a year, in April, July and October. An attractive black and white ink cover showed the college crest surrounded by the arms of the dioceses, and Professor L. E. Steele himself edited the account of college events and the news of past students' achievements. He instituted the system of 'red forms' in the 1880s whereby students were encouraged to send in each year a statement of their present position and this information was entered into the college register.[33]

To encourage academic and practical achievement a series of prizes was instituted. By 1889 there were ten of these, the most important being the Lewis Memorial medals for the teaching of the Holy Scriptures instituted in memory of Miss Jane Lewis, the first vice-principal; the Smyth Memorial Prize for Ancient and Modern History, donated by Mrs. O'Brien in 1888 in memory of her brother; and the Trench Memorial Prize for Needlework presented in 1886 by Hon. Mrs. Chenevix Trench in memory of Archbishop Trench. Later on the Mackay Wilson medals for the teaching of the Holy Scriptures by male students were donated by Mr. and Mrs. R. H. Wilson in 1894, and in 1905 they also presented the Wilson Suffern medals for the best women teachers of the year. Mr. Grandison and his daughter presented two prizes for instrumental music; the Helen Smyth Memorial prize for senior year needlework was presented in 1893, and J. T. Wood Latimer, M.P., founded a prize for the best essay written in the vacation.

These prizes became coveted awards and were treasured by the recipients for many years to come.[34]

Thus by the close of the 1880s CITC had established itself as a stable and well-organized institution. It had gained the confidence and support of the Church of Ireland clergy and community and was sending well-qualified teachers out to the Church's national schools throughout the country. All the students were classed under the National Board's regulations on the results of their final examinations. Some of the 'Annuals' achieved first class grades, the 'Biennials' were placed in the second class grade. By 1889 three students only had failed. This record pleased the college very much as it compared favourably with the other colleges, particularly with that of Marlborough Street which was considered a rival. After the establishment of CITC about 50 Church of Ireland students per year continued to attend the state college, attracted by the non-denominational atmosphere there. CITC students regarded themselves as superior to Marlborough Street ones and this tradition continued up to the 1920s. However, Marlborough Street never presented a serious rival to CITC and it became predominantly a Presbyterian college.[35]

The non-government department at CITC also proved a success, though the members were small and decreased gradually (in 1884 to 25; in 1889 to 11). The students trained for posts in church schools, where the salary was often lower than a national school but a residence was provided. Some of the girls entered private employment as governesses. However, the college ensured that these students, if they wished, could become national teachers later. At the end of their year's training course they sat the same examination as the first year 'Biennials', and if successful were given a third class grade classification under the National Board, so that they would be eligible for a post in a national school. No fees other than admission fees were charged in the non-government department, and so the students had to give a written pledge 'to teach for at least two years after leaving the college (if required to do so by the Committee) in non-government schools'. The department was a heavy drain on the college's voluntary income, about £500 per year, but in the long run it served a most useful purpose for it allowed for the gradual change from the support of church schools towards acceptance of national schools, and it made it possible for the clergy to support the college, regardless of their views. It also gave time to show that state support and the national system could serve the church's needs without any loss of faith.

However, CITC faced serious problems which would have to be tackled in the next decade. The first of these was ensuring that all the students obtained posts on leaving the college. At first the college had difficulty in persuading Church of Ireland school managers to apply to the college when they had a vacancy. In 1887 at Commemoration Day, Kingsmill Moore had urged managers not to appoint untrained teachers, saying that such appointments 'injure those appointed, for the higher salaries are now rigorously denied to untrained teachers; consequently all who wish to teach, might, for their own sakes, be compelled to go to training'.[36] Two moves helped to ease the problems. The first was the new rule introduced by the National Board in 1888 whereby trained teachers only could be appointed to posts in national schools, trained teachers being those who had trained at a college, or were classified by examination.[37] This was the first time the Board had been able to enforce such a rule and it marked the beginning of a qualified teaching profession. The second development was the increasing number of Church of Ireland schools entering the national system thereby increasing the number of teaching posts available. In 1883 there had been 620 exclusively Protestant national schools, but by 1890 this had risen to 979. Since part of the college's income from the state was earned retrospectively by the service of its students in the national system for two years after leaving, it was essential that as many as possible obtained immediate employment.

As soon as the 1888 rule was introduced the college found that it could not meet the demand for qualified male teachers. The number of male students had remained small throughout the 1880s:

Annual Figures for Biennial Students at CITC, 1884–1890[38]

	STUDENTS		
Year	*Male*	*Female*	*Total*
1884–5	7	35	42
1885–6	16	54	70
1886–7	28	60	88
1887–8	28	67	95
1888–9	21	66	87
1889–90	31	68	99

Many of the male applicants did not reach the required standard of the King's Scholarship examination. Primary teaching was slowly becoming in the 1880s a female dominated profession, partly because of the alternative occupations opening for men in the civil service, banking, and the constabulary, and partly because of the growth of the idea that younger children needed a woman teacher. Froebel's concept of 'mother care' in the infant school was now a strong influence and in an all-age one-teacher school a woman would seem to provide this role better than a man. By 1886 CITC had filled its male department to capacity, and if more men were to be recruited a more spacious male department would have to be built. Also, since under the government scheme the grants for male teachers were higher, the college financial stability would be strengthened by the growth of such a department.

However, like the other training colleges, CITC faced the problem of finding capital funds for improvements. The 1883 government scheme provided the colleges with maintenance and running costs but the system of retrospective payment made it difficult for the colleges to build up sufficient credit to expand. For instance, CITC would have to develop its larger male department in the 1890s on the grant-earnings of a smaller group of male students who had been trained in the 1880s. Therefore, the college along with the other training colleges began to demand capital grants from the government in order to develop and expand its facilities. A library and a gymnasium were needed as well as a new male residence, and the principal still lived out in his own residence in Palmerston Park, Rathmines, because there was no suitable accommodation for him and his family in the college. Therefore it was with high hopes that the college entered the new decade. Firmly established it was ready for the challenges ahead. The 1889 report concluded:

> The certainty of increasing expenses without the certainty of increasing income is the prospect of its immediate future. In itself the prospect is not encouraging, but when taken along with the memory of innumerable difficulties which by God's help have been surmounted in the past few years, it does not afford ground for alarm . . . Ours it is to labour on fearlessly in the name of the Lord Jesus believing that whatsoever the work requires our Father will provide.[39]

IV

The 1890s: A decade of expansion

The 1890s mark in the history of CITC the most important years of development. As a result of the Balfour 'Free Home' scheme of 1892 the college became financially secure and was able to expand and rebuild its premises. The male and female departments were filled to capacity and the status of the college rose rapidly. The principal, Kingsmill Moore, was at the height of his powers, negotiating with the government and becoming the leading spokesman on Church of Ireland educational policy. The academic and cultural life of the college flourished as the staff gained in experience and so by 1900 the college had reached its zenith where it was to remain until the outbreak of the First World War.

The first major development was the building of the new men's department at the rear of Kildare Place, alongside the model schools. In 1889 the college obtained a loan of £2000 from the Board of Works and Thomas N. Deane was again asked to be architect. He designed a tall five storied red brick building with ornate decoration in the popular 'Queen Anne' revival style of the period, which contained accommodation for 40 students with dormitories, a class room, dining room and infirmary. The dining room was to be fitted out with shelves so that it could be used as a library. This room was later to become the pride of the college. It had an 'inglenook' fireplace, and beautiful oak shelving from Italy presented by the past students.[1]

On the strength of this new building the college proposed to increase its male students to 40 per year in an attempt to meet the demand for male teachers. A special appeal was launched to encourage both clergy and teachers to send young men to the college to be trained. In 1889 the college had warned that 'if the supply of masters should fail, the Church must lose control over the education of the most important part of the rising generation i.e. boys who showed most promise'. Kingsmill Moore himself wrote a special letter of appeal which was sent to 29 newspapers throughout the country, and Professor Steele contacted past students and sent circulars to the national schools. As a result of these efforts the college in 1890 received 54 applications from male candidates of whom 24 passed the qualifying examinations, and therefore for the first time the department was full. However, the lack of good male candidates caused much concern, and although the college considered that 'it ought to be easy to induce young men to enter a profession which not only ensures a high class education but which promises employment—certain, honourable and remunerative', it was not the case. At the official opening of the new men's department by the lord lieutenant, the Earl of Zetland, in February 1890, Archbishop Plunket proposed in his speech that the college should consider providing a preparatory class for male candidates within its own walls. He argued 'just as the most promising boys in our primary schools are obliged to leave school there remains an interval of some two years before they can come here to be trained, and naturally rather than remain idle, they embark on some other calling'. It was with the idea of providing accommodation for such younger candidates that the archbishop announced that the college now wished to extend the men's department by building a new façade across the front of the old model schools. The splendid Victorian front of Deane's new building contrasted like 'Beauty and the Beast' with the plain old school house, and Deane had been asked to submit a design for the extension.[2]

The capital required for such a project, and for a gymnasium, was nearly impossible for CITC to find. However its difficulties, along with those of the other training colleges, were to be largely solved by the new 'Free Home' scheme introduced by the Conservative Chief secretary, A. J. Balfour, in 1892, which gave the colleges a series of thirty-five annual payments based on the valuation of their buildings.

From the outset the denominational colleges had protested against the terms of the 1883 scheme which provided them with only 75% of their annual expenditure. The Marlborough Street state college received 100% expenditure but as Sir Patrick Keenan had been at pains to point out at the time if such a rate had been granted to the denominational colleges they would have had to renounce their voluntary status.[3] However, Archbishop William Walsh, the Roman Catholic archbishop of Dublin, began a vigorous campaign to persuade the government to increase its grants to the training colleges. In September 1885 on a visit to St. Patrick's, Drumcondra, Dr. Walsh denounced the injustice of the 1883 scheme which provided no capital funding for the colleges. He argued that whereas the voluntary colleges had had to provide their own sites and erect their own buildings, Marlborough Street College had been built entirely with state funds. In 1889 he wrote a memorandum which covered all the Catholic Church's grievances regarding public education in Ireland, including the training college issue, and this memorandum was published in 1890 under the title *A Statement of the Chief Grievances of Irish Catholics in the Matter of Education*. It received wide publicity, and the matter was debated in Parliament.[4]

Meanwhile the Church of Ireland had raised its voice in support. As early as 1885 the matter of the inequality with the state college had been raised at the Dublin Synod, and in 1889 at the General Synod the Recorder, F. R. Falkiner, had proposed a motion instructing the governors of CITC to press a claim on the government in view of the necessity of extending the male department, and W. G. Brooke had proposed 'that the Synod regards the claim of the Church of Ireland Training College to be put on a footing of equality with Marlborough Street Training College in regard to the expenses of Queen's Scholars as one which cannot with justice be refused'. A deputation consisting of Archbishop Plunket and the Recorder had gone to London to see the attorney-general but with little success. However, in August 1890 A. J. Balfour, the chief secretary, announced that he was proposing to bring in a new scheme of capital funding for the denominational colleges, the details of which were announced in November. All the colleges were to be placed on an equal footing regarding fixed capitation grants for students plus a diploma bonus of £10 for males and £7 for females for each year of training, for each student who successfully taught for two years afterwards in a national school. In addition the buildings of the denominational colleges were to be valued by the Board of Works and the colleges to be granted a loan equal to that sum, the interest on which was to be paid by the CNEI for a period thirty-five years. This scheme of Balfour's came to be known as the 'Free Home' scheme because it reimbursed the voluntary colleges for their existing buildings which had been provided from private sources.[5]

However, the scheme required an act of parliament to allow it to be implemented, and so early in 1891 a bill was introduced 'To Provide for the Reimbursement of the Training Colleges in Ireland on their Sites, Buildings, Appurtenances, Premises and Fixtures'.[6] Opposition to this bill arose because it was seen that state grants were to be paid to support denominational institutions, and it seemed as if the whole scheme would founder. CITC in anticipation of the bill had launched on its building plan to extend the front of the men's department and by April 1891 had signed a contract with T. N. Deane and Son. By July the bill was still held up, and CITC became very concerned. Kingsmill Moore recalled how one day in mid-July he received an urgent message from the resident commissioner, Sir Patrick Keenan, to warn him that the bill was likely to fail, and even if it did pass CITC might not receive a loan because its buildings had been erected by the Kildare Place Society with a state grant. Archbishop Plunket and Kingsmill Moore decided to cross to London immediately to see the chief secretary in person. A momentous meeting took place at the House of Commons between the two men and Balfour and Mr. Jackson, financial secretary to the Treasury. Balfour indicated that the ambiguous situation of CITC and Kingsmill Moore protested that the college buildings had been completely renovated by them and that two new large buildings had been erected since 1884. He recalled the discussion:

> 'Surely, Mr. Moore,' said the Minister, 'you don't expect the government to pay twice for the same thing?' 'Certainly not,' I replied, 'but it is for a different thing we ask payment. Nearly eighty years have passed since that old grant was made, and if you calculate the large sums spent since then on repairs, alterations, renovations, and additions, it will not be easy to find traces of the old grant.'[7]

The outcome of this meeting was that Balfour was persuaded that CITC should be eligible for the new loan scheme; and Archbishop Plunket remained in London to try to add his influence but eventually the bill had to be dropped. Balfour then devised a clever alternative plan whereby the colleges were paid annual capital grants over a period of thirty-five years which would be based on the valuation of their existing property and which would be paid out of the annual educational expenditure and so did not require an act of parliament. All the training colleges were delighted with the scheme and plans for expansion could now get under way. St. Patrick's, Drumcondra, was able to build a new wing and repay much of the loan which Cardinal McCabe had given it from church funds. Our Lady of Mercy College was to move out to splendid new premises at Carysfort House, Blackrock in 1901, while CITC was able to reface all the old buildings and build the gymnasium.[8] The attentive concern which the

Education Office gave to the training colleges is illustrated by this personal letter received by Kingsmill Moore from Sir Patrick Keenan in August 1891:

Private.

Delville
Glasnevin
Aug. 23rd 1891

Dear Dr. Moore,

The Treasury have instructed Sir John Bull-Greene to undertake the valuation of the Denominational Colleges. I write this line lest you might be thinking of leaving town and also to suggest to you to have all the documentary evidence of expenditure ready at hand.

Ever Yours faithfully,

(Signed) *P. J. Keenan*[9]

As a result of the valuation, CITC was awarded an annual capital grant of £1031 7s. 6d. for the next thirty-five years. This grant was credited to the reserve fund and enabled the college to complete its new buildings and reface the rest. In 1893 a new front was built across the old model schools, and a connecting cloister and underground passage linked the front and the back of the college. This cloister became known as 'the Nuns' walk' because the women students were not allowed to walk across the open quadrangle but had always to use the covered way. A clock tower was built at the corner of the quadrangle, which chimed every quarter and 'regulated' the life of the college.

The new gymnasium was built in 1893 on the south side of the quadrangle. Mr. George Spencer of London, one of the leading authorities on the subject, advised on its design and equipment. A separate cookery and drawing room was built over the top which contained specially-designed desks and stools and modern gas cookers. A model classroom was constructed in the men's department for use for the 'Crit. lessons'. It had 'German style single desks in which to command and be commanded by the lecturer'. There were an adjustable blackboard, cases for maps, and a compass painted on the ceiling, and examples of the metric and imperial measures marked on the walls. 'The scheme of decoration, artistic in effect, hygienic in colour and introducing a variety of educational devices in such a way as to add not only to the beauty but to the utility of the room,' was to be the most modern and advanced that the college could provide. A college organ was installed in 1892 in the dining-hall. The funds for this had been collected by past students, and a concert and social gathering was held on St. Patrick's night to mark its opening. It was built by T. W. Magahy of Cork and had 16 stops and two manuals. The keys falls were of Irish maple and the keys of the ivory. It was placed on a gallery at one end of the hall and was to be used regularly by both men and women students for practice. In 1893 the college were honoured by a visit from Mr. and Mrs. Curwen of the Tonic Solfa College in London, and by Sir Robert Stewart, Professor of Music at TCD, and the musical life of the college continued to flourish.[10]

By 1895 the female department along Kildare Street was the only part of the college left which had not been modernised. Thomas Manly Deane, son of T. N. Deane, presented plans for the reconstruction of these houses. The cost was heavy and the college hesitated. However after the death of Archbishop Plunket in 1897 it was decided to undertake the work in his memory. The rebuilding of the Kildare Place front and of the Kildare Street houses began in 1899 and was completed by 1907. Under Deane's plan the old entrance doors in 4 Kildare Place and 10 Kildare Place were closed off and the girls in future entered through the doorway of No. 11. A connecting passage was built along the back of the two houses so that it was no longer necessary to go through from room to room as before. This led to various flights of stairs going up and down, and to an old CITC cry, 'You have to go up, to come down'. A new main entrance hall and board room were built at the back of No. 10, and dormitories were placed above them. The lady superintendent's quarters were situated on the first floor, and the old sash windows along the street front were made into bow windows enlarging all the rooms. One tragic loss in the reconstruction was the original Kildare Place Society tablet which had been attached to the Kildare Street front. Deane planned to place the tablet on a new gateway entrance which was never built and the tablet was lost.[11]

Thus, due to the Balfour 'Free Home' scheme, CITC became a fully equipped college housed in spacious buildings on a well-kept site and the architecture of T. N. Deane and Son made it a landmark in Dublin.

The second major public issue which CITC became involved in during the 1890s was the survival of the small rural school. By 1900 there were over 8,000 national schools of which a large proportion was either one- or two-teacher schools. Although the overall population of Ireland was declining, the number of schools was increasing. In

1891 the population of Ireland was 4,704,750; by 1901 it had dropped to 4,458,775. In 1890 there had been 8,298 schools in operation with 828,520 children on roll. By 1900 there were 8,684 schools but only 770,622 on roll. The entry of the Church of Ireland schools had increased the problem as these schools were often small, since each parish wished to retain its own parochial school. In 1903 an English H.M. Inspector, F. H. Dale, was asked by the government to report on the Irish public elementary school system and compare it with the English one. Dale commented critically on the multiplicity of small schools and showed how the denominational divide within the national system had increased this trend. The rules of the National Board which allowed a 'non-vested' school to enter the system and receive capitation and salary grants had enabled a large number of Protestant schools to join. If the National Board had insisted on investigating these claims for aid more closely, it might have been able to apply the rules as for 'vested' schools where, if there was already a school within three miles, no new schoolhouse could be built. Dale commented:

> The increase in the Protestant schools has not been confined to one denomination. During the last ten years there have been added among non-vested schools alone, no less than 214 under the management of the Church of Ireland, 56 under Presbyterian, 30 under management of Methodist and other denominations.[12]

CITC's interest in the small school was two-fold. It wished to uphold the rights of Church of Ireland children to attend a school under the Church's management, and it wanted as many teaching posts as possible to be available for Protestant students. Under the National Board rules the smallest school which could be recognised for a capitation grant was 15 pupils. The Church of Ireland was anxious to lower this figure to 10. Requests were made to the Education Office but were of no avail owing to Treasury objections. Therefore, in January 1890 a deputation including Kingsmill Moore went to the Castle to see the chief secretary, A. J. Balfour. Kingsmill Moore recalled that this was the first time he had acted as an 'educational politician', and the first time he met Balfour and his secretary George Wyndham (who was later to become chief secretary in 1902). The meeting with Balfour was cordial but unproductive. Later that year the government introduced the Local Taxation (Customs and Excise Bill) under which a portion of the customs dues (commonly known as the 'whisky money') was to be allocated to Irish education.[13] The Church of Ireland again pressed its case and

Kingsmill Moore on the advice of Archbishop Plunket and W. G. Brooke, went to London to lobby for amendments to the bill. He argued the case for the small school and had two meetings with the chief secretary, but to no avail.

However, later that year in November 1890, the archbishops received a public letter announcing that in view of the strong case presented to him in favour of the small school, Balfour had advised the National Board that the Treasury had withdrawn its objections and that capitation grants would be given for schools with an average attendance of ten. The Church of Ireland were jubilant and the two archbishops sent a joint letter to their clergy and laity urging them to avail of the advantages now offered:

> We consider it to be of the utmost importance that the children committed to the spiritual care of our church should be early and earnestly taught in schools whose managers and teachers belong to one communion.[14]

Local clergy were advised to establish a school where even a possible attendance of ten children could be found, and to raise local subscriptions to supplement the teacher's salary.

The cause of the small school received further impetus the following year. In May 1891 an Irish Education Bill was introduced whereby primary education was to become free and compulsory.[15] Fees were to be abolished in national schools and were to be replaced by a capitation grant. The Conservative government had introduced free education in England earlier in 1891 and the same provision was now to be extended to Ireland. While the Church of Ireland supported the principle of free compulsory education, it was strongly critical of the proposed scheme of replacing school fees by an average payment of 7s 6d per child. Fees in many Catholic national schools were lower than this, whereas in Protestant ones they were often higher. Kingsmill Moore in a forceful pamphlet published in 1892 entitled *£200,000 a year for Irish Education, How may it best be spent?* argued that the fairest and most productive way of distributing the money was not to replace fees per head, but rather to give an overall increase in the class salaries of teachers and to improve the position of the assistant teacher and the single teacher in a small school. The Standing Committee of the Church of Ireland General Synod established a special subcommittee to watch over the progress of the Education Bill and to present the Church's viewpoint. The committee, consisting of Archbishop Plunket, the Earl of Belmore, the Recorder, W. G. Brooke,

Lord Justice Fitzgibbon, Dr. Kingsmill Moore, Mr. R. Bagwell, the Dean of St. Patrick's and Mr. J. J. Murphy, called a public meeting in November 1891 to which they invited representatives of the other Protestant denominations. A joint Free Education sub-committee was formed to fight the cause of the small school.

The main concern of the Protestant churches was over the small one-teacher school where, if the average attendance was below 30, the National Board paid the teacher a capitation salary rather than the fixed class salary, a system which discouraged young teachers, particularly males, from taking up such appointments. Kingsmill Moore had showed in his pamphlet *£200,000 a year*, that if such teachers could be paid a fixed salary which would be in proportion to their class salary, the incentive to work in small schools would be much improved. It was also argued that all assistant teachers who under the present rules were allowed only a third class salary regardless of their own classification under the National Board, should be eligible for a higher class salary. A large public meeting was held in December 1891 at the Antient Concert Rooms, Dublin at which various Protestant interest groups were represented, and the views of the Church of Ireland were supported. A deputation went to the Castle to present their case and as a result of these efforts when the bill was reintroduced in February 1892 sections of it had been changed to include provision for increases in all teacher class salaries and for improvements in the position of teachers in small schools.[16]

Thus the position of the small national school was secured and a large number of small denominational schools were to survive. By 1909 there were 1,371 national schools under Church of Ireland management and the percentage of children attending exclusively Protestant or Catholic schools had risen from 52.5% in 1889 to 70.7% by 1909. Thus the denominational divide was strengthened, and the Church of Ireland had become a strong supporter of the national system. This newly acquired support was indicated by the Church of Ireland's opposition to the other issue raised by the 1892 Education Bill, namely that of modifying the rules of the National Board to allow the Christian Brothers schools to enter the system. The Church of Ireland had become a staunch upholder of the non-denominational principles of the National Board and did not agree with the changes which these Catholic schools required.[17]

The life of CITC continued to develop and flourish in the 1890s. The overall number of students continued to grow and the college reached over a hundred.

Annual Figures for CITC 1890–99[18]

STUDENTS

	Government Department		Non-government Department		
Year	Males	Females	Males	Females	Total
1890–1	38	64	—	6	108
1891–2	38	67	—	4	109
1892–3	29	70	—	2	101
1893–4	36	69	—	2	107
1894–5	42	70	—	3	115
1895–6	33	69	—	3	105
1896–7	43	71	—	2	116
1897–8	40	73	—	2	115
1898–9	43	71	—	2	116

While there was no difficulty in recruiting good female candidates, the number of male candidates remained disappointing. In 1894 the men's department rose to 42 and the college was encouraged to apply for an extension of its licence up to 50, but the following year the numbers could not be maintained. Out of 33 male candidates who applied, 12 only passed the qualifying examination; the college was again stressing the need for a good preparatory class for boys. The idea of establishing such a class within the college itself had not materialised. Whereas the Collegiate School, Celbridge was fast becoming the main source of supply of well educated female candidates, no such school emerged for boys. The Celbridge School was run by the Incorporated Society for Promoting Protestant Schools, founded in the eighteenth century to board and educate the children of the Irish poor in the habits of industry and in the tenets of the established Church. The Society's schools, commonly known as 'Charter Schools', had earned an ignoble reputation for proselytism and neglect, but in the nineteenth century the Society was reformed and its schools reorganized under the Educational Endowments Commission. Celbridge Collegiate developed in the 1890s into an excellent intermediate school for girls and established close links with the training college, preparing girls for the Queen's Scholarship examination. Kingsmill Moore became a governor and took a special interest in the school.[19]

The growth and development of the female department at CITC was to be one of the outstanding features of the 1890s, and it became the dominant section of the college. It was fortunate in obtaining the services of two very able young vice-principals who both developed the work of the women's training and built up the reputation of the department. The first of these was Miss F. C. A. Williams who was vice-principal from 1889—97 and the second Miss Annie Lloyd Evans who was vice-principal from 1897—1908.

The first vice-principal Miss Jane Lewis had died in office in 1889. She had served the college for 30 years since the Church Education Society had taken over in 1855, and 'she had been conspicuous throughout her long career for the vigour and enthusiasm which she threw into all her duties'. Her death opened the way for a new appointment. Miss F. C. A. Williams came from one of the leading colleges in England, Bishop Otter College, Chichester, which had been founded in 1873 by Miss Louisa Hubbard 'for women of culture and a good general education' who wished to become teachers. At Chichester Miss Williams had been much influenced by Miss Charlotte Mason, then vice-principal of the college and a well-known educationalist. In 1887 Miss Mason had founded the Parents' Education Union which became in 1892 the Parents' National Education Union. PNEU was a movement concerned with the education of children at home and with the training of parents and governesses who undertook this task. In 1891 Charlotte Mason founded her own college at Ambleside, which became a well-known centre for 'home education' and young women and parents came to study there, and to enjoy the lovely scenery of the lake district.[20]

Miss F. C. A. Williams brought to CITC fresh ideas and renewed vigour. Under her leadership the academic work of the female department flourished. She was interested particularly in geography and nature study and enjoyed long energetic walks. The students much appreciated her work, and in 1897 when she resigned to go to teach at the 'House of Education', Ambleside, the senior students presented her with a special scroll, beautifully decorated and personally signed. It read:

ILLUSTRATIONS:

5 *Staff and students in the 1890s. The principal, Rev. H. Kingsmill Moore is seated with the lady superintendent, Miss Annie Lloyd Evans, and Miss Mary J. Smith.*

6 *The model classroom in 1914 with tiered desks, maps and 'motto' board.*

5

6

7

8

To Miss Williams Lady Superintendent of the Church of Ireland Training College from the Students on the occasion of her leaving Ireland.

Dear Miss Williams,

We the students of the Church of Ireland Training College hearing with deep regret of your intended departure from amongst us, beg your acceptance of this address as a small token of our esteem and affection. We have always found you not only a wise and faithful teacher but also a true and considerate friend.

When in trouble we were always sure of your ready sympathy and advice, and your aim was ever to influence our lives for good, and to raise our thoughts and motives to a higher level.

Wishing you all happiness and success in the future.

We remain, Dear Miss Williams,
on behalf of the students,
Yours faithfully,

Annie E. Tombs, Annie Bell,
Jessie Ellis, Annie Pratt,
Jane Blennerhassett,
Sara Thompson.[21]

These students were second year biennials and represented all parts of the country.

Miss Williams became vice-principal of Charlotte Mason's 'House of Education' where she ably assisted Miss Mason whose health was not strong, and she served there until 1921. Miss E. Cholmondeley, author of a book on the life and work of Charlotte Mason, was herself a pupil of Ambleside and she remembered Miss Williams with much affection:

I took the training at the House of Education Ambleside in 1918–19. Miss Williams was Vice-Principal very much loved and revered. She did

---

ILLUSTRATIONS:

7 *The dining-hall built by T. N. Deane and Son in 1885, with the portraits of Rev. H. Kingsmill Moore, and Miss Jane Lewis, the first lady vice-principal.*

8 *The kindergarten classroom in 1914 with floral display and picture charts.*

not lecture but she took us in small groups or singly for walks called 'geography' walks. She must have been in her seventies but she walked at a great pace and shared her deep interest in outdoor things and her great knowledge of the countryside. On wet dull walks she used to recite to us children's poems and stories. She seemed to us students a very great person.[22]

The work of developing the female department begun by Miss Williams was continued by her successor, Miss Annie Lloyd Evans. Miss Lloyd Evans came from Warwick of Welsh parentage and had been educated at King's High School for Girls, Warwick and at St. Andrew's University. She had taught for a short while at Llandiloes Intermediate School in Wales and then at Blackburn High School for Girls. Only twenty-two when appointed to CITC, she gave excellent leadership and contributed much to the college, introducing the study of educational psychology and encouraging a broader approach to education. She had studied education at St. Andrew's University under Professor Meiklejohn and in 1897 had been awarded her M.A. degree.

The first woman graduate to head the female department, Annie Lloyd Evans raised the standard of the academic and cultural life of the college. She was interested particularly in drama and organized plays and 'Tableaux vivants' with the students. On leaving CITC in 1908 she was appointed the first principal of the new Fulham Day Training College in London and in 1915 became principal of Furzedown College, Streatham, a post which she held until her death in 1938. She had a most distinguished career and was one of the leaders of teacher training in London. Furzedown College along with Avery Hill Training College (founded 1906) were two of the most important teacher training establishments of the London County Council, and in 1925 Miss Lloyd Evans became President of the Training College Association, and served on the Central Advisory Committee of the Board of Education for the Certification of Teachers, and on the Training Colleges Delegacy to the University of London. Like Miss Williams, Miss Lloyd Evans was remembered by her students with much affection and admiration. One of the staff at Furzedown wrote of her:

Principal—I can see her now, in one of the light blue dresses which she nearly always wore, moving about the building or sitting in our tiny, stuffy staff-room up the little stairway, her clear bright penetrating eyes reaching to the heart of whatever was going on. She dearly loved a party of any sort, and instituted the yearly play—always Shakespeare then—or a

> Gilbert and Sullivan Opera and various out-of-door entertainments. Her humanity was her strongest trait, "I like people", she used to say, and her interest in the family as well as college life of her students never failed. There must be many who remember her warm human sympathy with gratitude.[23]

CITC was fortunate to recruit two such able women at the outset of their careers. Miss Lloyd Evans kept in touch with her Dublin colleagues and later on Miss J. Kennedy and Miss A. Heaney, two heads of the Kildare Place Infant School, were invited by her to visit Furzedown and infant schools in London.

In the male department Professors Cooke, Rea and Steele continued to extend the training course. One of the most interesting developments of the 1890s was the formation of the Educational Research Club. This club, under the presidency of Kingsmill Moore, was a meeting of staff who were all eligible to join provided they agreed 'to contribute either one literary paper or three sets of Observations'. These 'Observations' were short papers commenting on issues directly related to classroom practice such as discipline, the role of parents, school organization, and character formation. The 'literary' papers were full-length studies presented at one of three termly meetings of the society. Papers were delivered on the history of education, theory of education and educational biography. The club met throughout the 1890s and produced a great variety of papers. These reflected the current issues and problems of the day as well as the interest of the staff. In 1891 Kingsmill Moore read a paper on his visit to English training colleges, Miss F. C. A. Williams one on 'Natural Science in the Elementary School' and Miss M. J. Smith on 'State Education in Her Majesty's Colony of Victoria, Australia'. The model school staff also contributed and 'observation' papers were read by Miss A. M. Brown on 'Religious Instruction—Calendar Lessons', and Miss Heron on 'Interest taken in Religious Education by Pupils'. By 1898 interests had broadened and were concerned with the extension of the curriculum. Kingsmill Moore was working on a history of the Kildare Place Society and he read a paper on the model schools. Miss Lloyd Evans read two papers, one on 'Welsh Intermediate Schools' and another on 'The Kindergarten System'. Professor Cooke offered a paper on 'White Slaves in England' which examined child employment, and Professor Henly spoke on the new mathematics programme for teachers introduced in 1897. The club provided an important meeting point for the staff, and encouraged a study and discussion of educational ideas.[24]

Another feature of the 1890s was the expansion of the college bookshop, the 'Educational Depository' in Kildare Street. Under the endowment scheme of 1887 the governors had undertaken to continue this service and from 1895 were allowed to use the profits of the bookshop for general college funds. The shop was housed at the corner of 10 Kildare Street, and stocked a range of literary and educational books as well as school furniture and fittings. The manager, Mr. J. M. Quinn, encouraged clergy and teachers of Church of Ireland schools to order all their school requisites from the shop and it offered an excellent service by post. Large stationery parcels and 'school prizes' parcels which could be relied on to contain books of 'a healthy tone and by good writers at a low price' were available. Bookbinding, painting and die sinking were offered, and children's books and magazines such as *Little Folks*, *Girls' Own Paper* and *Sunday at Home* could be ordered. The shop obtained the agency for the major school publishers, Longmans, Bells and Macmillans and in 1898 got the sole sale rights on a new set of school readers published by Blackie known as 'The Century Readers' which were used widely in national schools. Thus the shop was a most useful financial source to the college and brought many visitors to Kildare Street.[25]

Throughout the decade the reputation and confidence of the principal, Kingsmill Moore, increased. Having successfully established the college, he turned his interest and energy to an active public life and writing. He was appointed secretary to an educational committee of the Standing Committee of the General Synod, and he became a governor of the Erasmus Smith Schools and of the Celbridge Collegiate School. He continued to take a keen interest in the teaching of religion and in 1898 he became secretary of the Sunday School Society, an office he was to hold until 1930. The headquarters of the society moved to Kildare Place and the close links with the college were to be maintained for many years.[26]

In 1891 Kingsmill Moore founded the Church of Ireland Educational Association which was concerned with the teaching of religion in schools. An annual conference of both clergy and laity was held at the college, and one of the founder members was Rev. J. T. Tristram, a close friend of Kingsmill Moore and a diocesan inspector of schools. He had been a candidate for the principalship of the college in 1884. The two men drew up a programme of religious education for Church of Ireland Schools which was eventually published by the Association for Promoting Christian Knowledge. The Educational Association had many distinguished members including Bishop Gregg of Cork, Rev. J.

H. Bernard (later archbishop of Dublin), Rev. Maurice Day (later bishop of Clogher), Dr. A. Traill, provost of TCD from 1904–1914, and Mr. Alfred Purser, later chief inspector of the National Board.[27]

Kingsmill Moore also became president of the Dublin branch of the Teachers' Guild of Great Britain and Ireland which had been founded to campaign for university degrees for teachers and for professional recognition. In 1891 he gave evidence on behalf of the Irish teachers to a Select Committee of the House of Commons on the Teachers' Registration and Organization Bill, and in 1898 he was called before the Palles Commission on Intermediate Education in Ireland. His experience in primary teacher training made him favour strongly the need for registration and minimum qualifications for secondary teachers.[28]

Kingsmill Moore had also begun to publish a number of books on teaching methods. *Class Room Teaching* (1888) gave practical advice on classroom management and *The Fundamental Principles of Education* (1889) discussed the aims and purposes of education. Kingsmill Moore advocated 'the leading thought' method, where each lesson was built around a theme, and he later published his ideas in *The Way to Teach the Bible* (1915) which proved very popular. He also pursued his own academic studies and became very interested in the history of the Kildare Place Society. He discovered in the basements of the Kildare Place buildings all the papers relating to the society which had been left there, and so he began to sort and list them. He eventually published a full history of the educational work of the society entitled *An Unwritten Chapter in the History of Education, being the history of the Society for Promoting the Education of the Poor in Ireland, known as the Kildare Place Society, 1811–1831* (London, 1904) which was very well received, and further enhanced the reputation of the college and its principal. The book, though partisan, remains to date the standard work on the subject.

Kingsmill Moore's advice was sought on all matters relating to educational policy in the Church of Ireland and he came to occupy a very important position. He also became increasingly autocratic and domineering, and 'Ball' (as he was commonly known because of his constant use of the letters 'Ball. Coll. Oxon.' after his name), although widely respected, was not always liked by his fellow churchmen, colleagues and students. In 1893 he was offered the principalship of the Home and Colonial Training College in London which had maintained links with Dublin, but on the advice of Archbishop Plunket he turned it down. His abilities and interests were extensive, and it may be that in later years when CITC was faced with decline and isolation, he regretted not having accepted such a prestigious post. However, he continued to offer to CITC his full energies and enterprise, though his dominance may have prevented the emergence of more forceful men to lead the men's department, so that it never gained the stature of the women's.[29]

In 1897 Kingsmill Moore lost the guiding hand of Archbishop Plunket who died unexpectedly and was sorely missed by the Church of Ireland. The college was plunged into mourning and a memorial fund was opened to commemorate all his work for teacher training. It had been largely due to Plunket's influence that the rival factions between the Church Education Society and the supporters of the National Board had been reconciled, and that CITC had prospered as a united college. He had also served as a commissioner of National Education and had helped to heal the breach between the Church of Ireland and the national school system. His name was perpetuated at the college first by the college hymn which he had composed, and second by the new frontage of the Kildare Place buildings. The college hymn 'For Christ to learn, for Christ to teach' (No. 599 in *Irish Church Hymnal*) was sung at all formal college gatherings and became a very popular hymn of the Church:

> 'For Christ to learn, for Christ to teach',
> O Lord, may this our watchword be!
> What nobler destiny for each,
> Than thus to live and work for Thee![30]

The tune was composed by Kingsmill Moore. The new frontage was erected with the help of the proceeds of a fund collected by past-students. A carved tablet was placed in 1904 in the newly restored redbrick face of Kildare Place:

> The front of this Building was erected by Members of the Church of Ireland as a Memorial of the Most Rev. William Conyngham, Baron Plunket, D.D. Archbishop of Dublin, to commemorate an Episcopate, distinguished by a lofty standard of duty, by a broad Christian sympathy and by inspiring devotion to the interests of the Church which he loved and served.
>
> Nearly one third of the cost was provided by former students of this College, which in great measure owes its establishment and success to his wise and foresight and able management.[31]

In addition to the college's own memorial there was a desire to erect a public monument to the archbishop who had been a much beloved and respected public figure. Permission was obtained from the Dublin Corporation to erect a statue of Archbishop Plunket in Kildare Place itself and a public fund was opened. The statue was designed by Hamo Thornycroft and was unveiled in April 1901 by the Earl Cadogan, lord lieutenant, in the presence of the lord mayor, the corporation of Dublin and a large crowd. There were plans afoot at that time to extend the National Museum's buildings across Kildare Place, and thus create a square which would 'form one of the most striking sites in this or perhaps any city in Europe; a fitting one in which future ages may be familiar with the form and countenance of him whom we would honour'.[32] Alas, no such plans materialized, and today in the 1980s the lonely pensive figure of the archbishop, hand lifted to his face, is the only visible sign in Kildare Place that it was once the historic site of a respected and honoured teacher training institution.

V

The centenary decade, 1900–1914

In 1911 the college held centenary celebrations to mark the foundation of the Kildare Place Society and its training institution in 1811. These celebrations were largely the idea of Kingsmill Moore who, because of his keen interest in the history of the Kildare Place Society, wished to emphasise the heritage of CITC and its historic role in the development of teacher training in Ireland. In 1911 the confidence of the college was at its height. There were 135 students in residence and its academic work and staff were held in high esteem. All seemed set fair for the years to come, but many problems and difficulties lay ahead and the future of the college was to be very different from that envisaged at the centenary celebrations.

Since 1900 there had been major changes in the programme of teacher training. In 1900 the new Resident Commissioner of the National Board, Dr. W. J. M. Starkie, had introduced a revised programme of curriculum for national schools. This programme attempted to widen the school curriculum to include more manual and practical subjects. The system of payment-by-results was abolished and emphasis on basic literacy and memorization was replaced by a more humanistic approach and child-centred activity. The ideas of Froebel and of the kindergarten methods played an important role in the education of the young children, and the 'Sloyd' method of educational woodwork which had originated in Sweden was used for manual instruction and 'hand and eye' training. Drawing, elementary science, singing, manual instruction and physical drill all became compulsory core subjects.[1]

The Revised Programme for National Schools was based on the recommendations of the Belmore Commission of 1898. This commission on manual and practical instruction in primary schools had consisted of 11 members of the National Board including Archbishop

Walsh and Archbishop Plunket (who died while it was in progress), and four outside experts including T. B. Shaw, an inspector with the Science and Art Department in London. It had taken evidence from many witnesses from England and Scotland as well as Scandinavia, and both Kingsmill Moore and John Cooke of CITC were called to give evidence.[2] The National Board had already introduced a new teacher training programme prior to the changes in the school curriculum and it was on this training programme that both Kingsmill Moore and Cooke were questioned. CITC had not found the change to this new programme easy. The college had been efficiently organized to meet the demands of the old payment-by-results curriculum and this new one placed increased demands on both staff and students. The colleges had been consulted prior to the introduction of the new programme and, while recognising its merits, foresaw the difficulties which the broader and more open course would bring.

The course was now extended to fourteen compulsory subjects—reading, penmanship, spelling and punctuation, English grammar and composition, English literature, geography, arithmetic, algebra, geometry, agriculture, bookkeeping, drawing and theory of education. While geometry, algebra, bookkeeping and agriculture were optional for females, needlework remained a compulsory subject for them. An extensive course in English literature superseded the old one based on the lesson books of the National Board, while the theory of education course demanded a knowledge of the psychology of learning and principles of teaching as well as the practice of school organization. In addition a range of optional subjects were offered, one of which was compulsory for men and two for women. These subjects were vocal music, Latin, French, Irish, history, trigonometry, manual training, domestic economy, practical cookery and science.[3]

In the first year of the new programme CITC had more examination failures than previously. It was the practical subjects such as science and drawing which presented difficulties because they required equipment and special facilities. CITC had been accustomed to offering the science courses for the Science and Art Department examinations, but it found that the new science examinations of the National Board were of a higher standard. CITC now had to encourage the weaker students to take trigonometry rather than science as an optional subject because it was easier.

Kingsmill Moore and Cooke both raised these difficulties before the Belmore Commission. Kingsmill Moore stressed the need for proper equipment to teach science and drawing both of which were now to become compulsory subjects in national schools. Cooke was concerned that drawing had become a compulsory subject at the training college because he considered that many of the students would be unable to reach the required standard. He felt that 'Free hand' drawing was preferable to either 'Object Drawing' or 'Mechanical Drawing' because it was more useful to students for black-board work.

While the attitude of the training colleges towards the new training programme was at the outset positive, it became less so as the difficulties increased and the essential equipment was not provided. The success of the new revised programme of instruction in the national schools depended on the training colleges providing qualified and enthusiastic teachers to teach it. However, sadly, this was not to be the case. T. J. O'Connell, general secretary of the INTO, in his book *A Hundred Years of Progress*, wrote sarcastically of the useless hours spent in his training course at St. Patrick's College on 'handicraft' which consisted of 'paper folding', 'wire-bending' and cutting out models. He recorded that he never taught 'hand-and-eye' training when he became a teacher because the needs of the children for basic literacy and numeracy were paramount.[4] Although the National Board was aware of the need to give the training colleges every support to implement the new training programme, financial shortages, the scepticism of the inspectorate, and the unpopularity of the resident commissioner himself, resulted in such support being very limited.

At CITC many efforts were made in the early years to develop the new practical subjects. The National Board had recruited special organizers from England to help train teachers and A. W. Bevis of the Birmingham School Board ran courses in manual instruction, and W. M. Heller of the London School Board in elementary science. In 1900 W. Mayhowe Heller who was one of the leading exponents of the new heuristic approach to science teaching having studied in London under Professor H. E. Armstrong, the pioneer of modern science teaching, visited the college. He recommended that a specialist teacher of science be appointed and that a laboratory be built for practical work which was an essential feature of the new approach. Mr. Jerry Henly of CITC resigned his position as resident superintendent of the men's department and head of the boys' model schools, and became a full professor of mathematics and elementary science while retaining his position as 'master of method'. Henly, whose health had not been good, was glad of the change, and he went on several training courses to learn the new methods. A new laboratory was built at CITC at a cost of £1,000 and the necessary equipment purchased to enable the students to carry out experimental work. Henly's motto was 'Find out for yourself' which he passed on to generations of students, working in his science classes.

However Henly remained a realistic and astute classroom teacher and as the years went on he became increasingly doubtful about the advantages of the new training programme. As early as 1898 he had read a paper to the CITC Educational Research Club expressing the view that the new mathematics programme was much too difficult for the average student. In 1903 at a general meeting of the County Dublin committee of the INTO, Henly was reported in the press as having publicly expressed his criticism of the 'new system of education' which he said 'deprecated the position of the teacher and emasculated the programme so far as the pupils were concerned'. The paper *The National Teacher* reported Henly as having 'cut the New Programme into shreds and very ably showed up its defects and shortcomings'.[5]

As a result of these press reports, the Commissioners of National Education wrote to Archbishop Peacocke of Dublin, as manager of CITC, to demand an explanation, and expressing the opinion that since 'the duties of Mr. Henly involve the training of King's Scholars in a knowledge of the details of the Revised Programme of Instruction, and also the inculcation of obedience on the part of National Teachers to the Board's rules and regulations, it was most improper of him to use the language, or to express the views in regard to the Revised Programme attributed to him'. The Archbishop immediately asked Henly to submit a full account of the meeting and to state whether he had been reported correctly in the press. Henly drew up a trenchant reply denying the allegations and claiming that he had been misquoted in the press: 'I am not aware that I employed any words in what purports to be a summary of my speech. The statement extracted from the leading article of *The National Teacher* that I cut up the Programme into shreds is absolutely false'. Henly went on to explain that he had attended the meeting as a visitor only and had been invited to speak from the floor. He said that contrary to what the CNEI were suggesting, he had made an effort to encourage the new programme and had undertaken the new teaching in elementary science and manual instruction. However, he defended his right to speak out on educational issues. His letter concluded:

> I trust Your Grace will not consider it inconsistent with the efficient discharge of my duties in the College that I should be allowed to exercise and

> to express an independent judgement on educational questions, outside the College, and to be free to engage in discussions of these questions in temperate and moderate language.[6]

The governors of CITC were satisfied with Henly's reply and wrote to the CNEI to this effect. The matter was let drop but was not forgotten. Henly realised that he would have in future to be more discreet in his comments on the Revised Programme, and the relevant correspondence was placed on file in the minute book of CITC so that there would be no doubt about the importance and outcome of the incident. In 1913 when Henly was invited to serve on the Dill Committee on the national school inspectorate, the CNEI wrote a strong letter to the chief secretary, Birrell, criticising Henly's appointment and enclosing copies of the 1903 correspondence. The letter stated that 'Mr Henly was unfit to be a member of that commission' because he had identified himself with determined opposition to the 1900 programme and he had written a series of critical articles under the pseudonym 'Beta' in the teachers' journal *The Irish School Weekly*. Dr. Starkie, the resident commissioner, was particularly angry about Henly's appointment because neither he nor any member of the National Board had been invited to serve on the Committee. Birrell, however, took no notice and Henly remained a member. Although an elderly man, his vigorous questioning and deep knowledge of the workings of the national school system made him a most useful and influential member of the Dill Committee which recommended many reforms in the inspectorate system.[7]

CITC along with the other training colleges had every hope in the early years that it would receive extra financial support to enable it to implement the new teacher training programme. However, this was not to be. The National Board did not have the support of the government or the Treasury for its new reforms and, after 1902 when the Balfour Education Act was passed in England, the Conservative government adopted a policy of 'starving' Irish education in order to encourage a move towards local rating and local education authorities as had taken place in England.

The annual education grant from central government was increased following the 1902 Act, and in accordance with established precedent, Ireland was entitled to receive an increased proportionate 'equivalent' grant. However, much of this 'equivalent' grant was to be diverted from Irish education to the land reform which was achieved by the chief secretary, Wyndham, under his Land Act of 1903.[8]

Therefore, when in 1901 the heads of the three male training colleges applied to the National Board for grants for building new laboratories and purchasing equipment for manual instruction and woodwork, the request was refused. The National Board wrote to the Treasury but achieved nothing. The heads of the training colleges then asked for the correspondence between the Board and the Treasury to be made public but this also was refused. The colleges were particularly frustrated at the refusal because not only were they denied support for their work on the new programme but also under the new regulations their practising model schools had lost their special grants. In their letter to the CNEI in 1903 the three principals expressed their anger at the whole situation:

> Nothing has been put forward from any quarters which could defend or excuse the withdrawal of grants from the practising schools. The New Programme has put a severe strain upon the Training Colleges in many ways. Your Report recognises the loyal way in which the colleges have co-operated with you in the introduction of the new subjects. Is it equitable to mark your sense of our co-operation by a reduction of our grants when added expense is imposed upon us? Have we not a right to expect, not alone the maintenance of the grants formerly enjoyed but in addition the willing gift of any additional sums which may have become necessary?[9]

The anger of the denominational colleges was further increased in the following year when Marlborough Street Training College was granted a large sum of money to build a new residence house for students later to be known as Marlborough House. While this residence was much needed by the state college, many of whose students still lived in a house in North Great George's Street, the other colleges were very jealous of its position. In March 1904 Kingsmill Moore and Fr. Peter Byrne of St. Patrick's College wrote an open letter to the CNEI which was published in the press. The two principals claimed that under the Balfour scheme of 1890 the principle of equality of treatment for all the training colleges had been established and therefore the denominational colleges had a right to expect a grant similar to that given to Marlborough Street. Funds were much needed by the colleges 'to fit up halls and provide apparatus for the teaching of Elementary Science as required by the Revised Programme' and if the Training College in Marlborough Street was to be 'now started by the Treasury free of debt and fully equipped, our own colleges ought to be placed in a similar position'. The *Irish Independent* and the *Irish Times* both wrote leading articles in support of the colleges but the case was not conceded by the government.[10] In 1904 the National Board was forced to curtail the programmes in elementary science and manual instruction and the college felt that much expenditure had been wasted.

Meanwhile support for the new revised programme of curriculum had decreased outside the training colleges. In 1900 the old system of payment-by-results had been abolished and a new system of graded salaries for teachers introduced. Under this scheme all qualified teachers commenced in the third class grade and progressed by triennial increments for good service to the second and first class grades. However, the number of teachers eligible for each grade was fixed by a 'standard number' and promotion depended on there being a vacancy in the grade. Promotion depended on an annual satisfactory report from an inspector and these had to be consecutive over a period of three years. The scheme while giving teachers a standard salary scale created much anger and resentment because some teachers suffered a reduction in salary and the system of 'standard numbers' prevented well-deserved promotion. The relationship between the teachers and the inspectorate became very strained, particularly because promotion now depended on an individual inspector's report rather than a formal examination system.[11]

The Church of Ireland was concerned about the salary changes for two reasons. First, it was feared that since flat rate salaries were to be paid to all teachers regardless of the size of the school, the National Board would demand an increase in the minimum attendance required for recognition of a school; and second because since 1897 it had been agreed that the principal of a small school of 25 pupils should be eligible for promotion to first class, it was feared that this privilege would now be withdrawn and the status of the small school reduced.

The fears of the Church proved correct. In March 1900 when the new rules of the National Board came into operation, the manager of a small Church of Ireland school in Redcross, Co. Wicklow, received a letter from the Education Office informing him that henceforth the minimum number on roll for recognition was to be 25 pupils. The Redcross school had an average attendance of 19 and, therefore, would be no longer eligible to receive a grant. The manager, Rev. J. Wright, rector of Redcross and Dunganstown, wrote immediately to Kingsmill Moore asking for his advice and help.[12]

Kingsmill Moore gathered his forces to put pressure on the National Board to rescind the decision. Since 1892 it had been the agreed policy that the minimum attendance required for recognition was 10, and the church had a right to expect that such a fundamental change in the rules would have been publicly discussed and the schools forewarned. With the able assistance of Lord Justice Fitzgibbon and W. G. Brooke, Kingsmill Moore drew up a resolution on behalf of the Standing Committee which was carried at the General Synod in April. It read:

> To call the attention of the Synod to the recent decision of the Commissioners of National Education declining to take a school into connection with the Board, with an average attendance of less than twenty-five and announcing that capitation payments will no longer be made. And to move that the Standing Committee be requested, forthwith, to take the necessary proceedings, on behalf of the Church of Ireland, to prevent this violation of the Act of Parliament of 1892, and reversal of previous policy and practice of the Board from taking effect, involving as it does the exclusion from state aid numbers of small schools to which alone the children of the Church of Ireland have to look for education through a large part of the rural districts of the country.[13]

At the Synod Dr. J. H. Bernard, lecturer in Divinity at TCD who was one of the Church of Ireland Commissioners of National Education, defended the policy of the Board, saying that in the long run the small school would benefit from the new regulations and in any case he considered the letter to the Redcross school as unofficial. Despite Bernard's spirited defence the resolution was carried. Kingsmill Moore and Bernard continued the argument in letters to the press. W. G. Brooke, meanwhile, had entered into correspondence with the Education Office which he also subsequently published in the press. The letter which he received from the CNEI stated that while the Board would continue to support small schools where the attendance was under 25, reference would have to be made to the Treasury for special approval. Brooke protested in the strongest terms against 'this increased and unlawful power of the Treasury', and declared that under 'the arrangement made in 1892 by them, and the now First Lord of the Treasury, Rt. Hon. A. J. Balfour, schools of an average of 10 or over were entitled to aid without exception'. The case was then taken up by J. H. M. Campbell (later Lord Glenavy), the Irish M.P., in London on behalf of the Church of Ireland. On May 23rd he telegraphed Kingsmill Moore to send him more details of the case, and a copy of the Standing Committee's resolution. A copy was also sent to the Chief Secretary in the Irish Office in London. On May 26th Kingsmill Moore received a personal letter from the prime minister, A. J. Balfour, stating that he had spoken on the matter to the Chief

Secretary, and that it was now under consideration. By the end of May the Redcross school was accepted by the National Board and the case was won. The Church party was much relieved and jubilant. Kingsmill Moore later recalled that he met a member of the National Board at a private function who informed him that indeed a bargain had been struck between the National Board and the Treasury regarding the reduction in the number of small schools, and the Church of Ireland Synod's resolution had 'blown the whole thing up'.[14]

The survival of the small school was once again secured, but the future position of the teacher in such schools remained in doubt. Under the new 1900 regulations of the National Board, all teachers were to have a starting third grade salary of £44 for women and £56 for men. To be promoted to the second class grade a teacher had to be working in a school with an average attendance of 30–50 pupils, and for promotion to first class grade with an average of over 70 pupils. All assistant teachers were eligible only for third class grade salaries. These regulations meant that for many Church of Ireland teachers promotion beyond third class grade was not possible. Whereas prior to 1900 a teacher could be appointed to the first class grade provided his school had an average attendance of 35, the new regulations put an end to that. In 1903 the Standing Committee published a report of statistics showing the number of Church of Ireland schools in the South of Ireland. Similar reports had been written in 1893 and in 1897 and Kingsmill Moore was largely responsible for the work. The 1903 report showed the crucial importance of the small school to the Church and gave a firm basis on which to argue its case. Out of a total of 497 schools in the Province of Dublin, consisting of the Dioceses of Dublin, Glendalough and Kildare; Ossory, Ferns and Leighlin; Cashel and Emly; Waterford and Lismore; Cork, Cloyne and Ross; Killaloe, Kilfenora, Clonfert and Kilmacduagh; and Limerick, Ardfert and Aghadoe, 357 were government aided national schools and 140 remained 'non-government' church schools. Of the national schools 96 had an average attendance of between 10–20, 75 between 20–50, and 105 between 30–50 pupils. Only 43 schools had an attendance of above 70 and most of these were in the Dublin diocese. There were 8 schools with an average of below 10. Therefore fifty per cent of the church national schools in the south of Ireland had an average attendance of not more than 30. The majority of the 'non-government' schools were in the Dublin diocese where there was still sufficient money to maintain parochial schools without state aid, while the Church Education Society, the Erasmus Smith

Trust and the Irish Church Missions continued to give aid to some very small rural schools.[15]

The Church, however, was not able to persuade the National Board to change the salary structure and, therefore, the prospects for teachers in the small schools declined. Male teachers in particular became increasingly reluctant to work in a one-teacher school, and its status was reduced. The Church was determined, however, to maintain the life of the small rural school despite the drawbacks both educational and financial. For isolated rural parishes the Church school was an essential feature and it was considered imperative that Church of Ireland children attend a school under a Protestant teacher. The training college was also very anxious to prolong the life of the small school as it meant employment and early principalships for the students.

In 1908 the Treasury once again tried to reduce the uneconomic proliferation of small schools in Ireland, and the National Board announced that an average attendance of 30 would be necessary for recognition. This would mean the loss of half the Church of Ireland national system into the mid twentieth century. The denominational successful campaign and with the assistance of J. H. M. Campbell, M.P., in London, and Provost A. Traill of TCD, one of the commissioners of national education, he organised a deputation to London to see the chief secretary, Augustine Birrell. Archbishop Peacocke of Dublin who was in London for the Lambeth Conference, added his support, and together they persuaded the Chief Secretary that the small school was of vital importance to the Church of Ireland, and the new rule was once again dropped.

Kingsmill Moore himself regarded his work for the survival of the small school as one of the most important achievements of his career. The Church of Ireland lobby undoubtedly prolonged the existence of small rural schools in Ireland, and despite the financial cost, and the drawbacks for the teachers, these schools survived as a feature of the national system into the mid-twentieth century. The denominational divide within the national system was also ensured by the continued existence of separate Church of Ireland schools throughout the country.[16]

At the same time as the struggle for the rights of small schools the Church of Ireland became involved in the managerial issue. In 1902 the resident commissioner, Dr. W. J. M. Starkie, made a speech at a meeting in Belfast of the British Association for the Advancement of Science which was subsequently published under the title *Recent*

Reforms in Irish Education (London, 1902). In this speech Starkie analysed the problems of Irish education, one of which he stated was the system of clerical management of national schools. The Church of Ireland along with the Roman Catholic Church immediately sprang to the defence of the managerial system and launched a campaign against Dr. Starkie. A meeting of Church of Ireland managers had been held in 1900 when the crisis over the new rules had arisen. Two years later another conference was called to discuss Dr. Starkie's criticism of the management system. Prime movers in the conference were the Dublin School Managers' Association (Church of Ireland), who in February 1903 wrote to the Standing Committee demanding that the Church should defend its school managers, and refute Dr. Starkie's statement that clerical managers were inefficient and showed little or no interest in their schools. In April 1903 a national conference of over 200 Church of Ireland school managers was held in Dublin, the purpose of which was to form a national school managers' association to act as an official spokesman. The conference drew up a series of resolutions regarding the role and duties of school managers and their relationship with teachers. The resolutions also raised the matter of new teachers' salary structure, of the problems of the revised programme of curriculum, and of the failure of the government to increase the grants to Irish education. The effect of Starkie's attack on clerical school management was to cause the churches to move to its defence and to ensure that as a system of school administration, it was efficient. In 1903 the Catholic Clerical Managers' Association was formed, and the system was strengthened and successfully defended again in 1904 when the Dale Report recommended the setting up of local education authorities to control primary schools. The Church of Ireland's stance on the issue gave extra support to the Roman Catholic Church's case, and assisted the long term survival of clerical school management.[17]

Life in the college itself in this decade went from strength to strength. Once it had come to terms with the demands of the new training programme the college took advantage of the wider scope of the work, and expanded the social and cultural activities. The women's department grew in size each year and by 1914 had reached a maximum size of 110. The newly completed re-building of the Kildare Street front provided spacious and comfortable apartments to live and work in. The men's department on the other hand remained small, never reaching above 47 which it had been at the beginning of the century, and dropping to 25 by 1914. In 1903 the college finally closed the non-government department which had had only one or two female students per year in the last few years. This department had served the very useful purpose of winning the college support from all Church members, but henceforward all students would be training to be national school teachers, and the college would be saved the heavy drain on its voluntary resources.

In 1898 the King's Scholarship entrance examination was moved from July to Easter. This allowed students to obtain their results in good time before being called to Kildare Place for the examination in religious knowledge and vocal and instrumental music. The programme for the King's Scholarship was 'column I' of the revised training programme and required a thorough knowledge of English language and literature, geography, mathematics, book-keeping (for males only), agriculture (for males only), theory of method, and needlework (for females), plus one or two optional subjects, one of which for females had to be vocal music or domestic economy and hygiene, and for men one from Latin, Irish, French, history, trigonometry or elementary science.[18] The main source of female candidates continued to be the Celbridge Collegiate School and the Kildare Place Model School. The male candidates tended still to come direct from national schools where they had been serving as monitors, or from other occupations which they had taken up since leaving school. Many of the men had received no formal secondary education but were self-taught or tutored for the King's scholarship examination, and therefore the standard of their performance in the entry examination tended to be lower than that of the women. The majority of candidates both male and female continued to come from the northern dioceses. In 'Hints to Students Seeking Admission' the college advised that all should 'earnestly meditate as to the disposition and tone of mind necessary for those who hope to become useful and successful Teachers'. They were recommended to cultivate a 'humble teachable disposition and come to their work as *learners*; to keep their thoughts fixed on the *one* object in view, to be cheerful, sober and decorous and to live as brethren in Christian unity'.[19]

Life in the college was full of activity and enjoyment. The two departments continued to operate separately sharing only the facilities and the staff. However, the presence of the other sex on site undoubtedly added to the pleasure of the college life and unofficially many friendships and romances were established. The men's department became known as 'the Sioux' and the women's as 'the Squaws', nicknames which endured for generations of students. The men entered the college by the main gate and had their quarters in the rear of the college, while the women entered through the Kildare Street door. The women were not allowed to cross the 'Plunket Quadrangle' when going to class or to the model schools but had to use 'the Nuns' Walk' or plunge down below to the underground passage which ran under the gymnasium. The girls' dormitories were on each floor of the Kildare Street houses and were known as '1st, 2nd and 3rd dorm', and there was the 'cockloft' in the attic. Each girl had a cubicle with basin and jug and there were bathrooms on each floor—one of which was known as 'the Dive' because it was entered down a set of steps. The women had a large recreation room with a central arch and warm coal fire and comfortable chairs. Meals were served in the dining-hall and the women took it in turns to assist with the orderly duties. The food was plain and wholesome but was supplemented by regular food parcels from home and the Dublin students used illegally to slip off home for fresh supplies. 'Midnight Spreads' were often held in the dormitories after lights out and much laughter and fun enjoyed. On Sundays the women went to St. Ann's Church, Dawson Street in the morning and to St. Matthias', Hatch Street in the evening, the men the reverse. The men had all their meals in their own department and slept in three large dormitories, one above the other, known as 'Junior', 'Cuba' and 'Sion'. It was said the house was haunted and that a ghost walked at night. There was a strict social division between the junior and senior year students both in the women's and men's department, and the 'Seniors' regarded themselves as being much superior. The most able students learnt to play the organ in addition to the harmonium, and this activity provided a useful link between the men and women. Each student was allowed time to practise on the organ in the dining-hall and letters used to be left behind the music to be collected by the next male or female student for delivery to the addressee. Gradually bicycles were allowed for both men and women, and the students used to get out and about for rides. For many of them the two years at the college while being hard work, were a most enriching and enjoyable experience, where friendships were made for life, and the memories treasured for years to come.

The staff continued as before with few changes. Miss Annie Lloyd Evans was succeeded as lady superintendent by her sister Miss Mary Lloyd Evans, also a graduate of St. Andrew's. The two sisters were alike in appearance, tall, handsome women. Miss Annie was more stern while Miss Mary had a soft, gentle manner. One ex-pupil of the

Kildare Place model schools remembers the two Misses Lloyd Evans. 'One was tall and academic with a pince-nez, the other more feminine and approachable'. Miss Mary Lloyd Evans left in 1912 to be married and Miss Elsie Tuckey, a graduate of Trinity College, was appointed. Miss Tuckey was the first Irish woman to hold the post of lady superintendent and this showed a growing confidence in Irish women graduates.[20]

Drama and music both developed at the college. Miss Mary Jane Smith continued her excellent work with the Tonic Solfa method and the college choir became a special feature. Miss Annie Lloyd Evans had introduced the art of 'Tableaux Vivants' and in 1904 the students presented a series of scenes from 'The Odyssey' and 'the Fate of the Sons of Uisneach' at a public concert at the Rotunda rooms in Dublin. These received very favourable comments in the press including an English magazine called *Today* whose columnist Drusilla wrote:

> Her zeal for things Hibernian moved Drusilla to an awful crossing to Dublin, to see some remarkable tableaux. They were given at the Rotunda by the girl students of the Church of Ireland Training College.[21]

Since drawing had become a compulsory subject for all students. Professor Cooke acquired an assistant, Miss Healy, who was remembered by all as an excellent teacher. Professor Henly organized the nature study and science classes in the new laboratory and continued to give his practical and thorough lectures in school management and the routines of keeping the school register and roll-books for which many students were most grateful when faced with the task in their first appointment. His advice was 'If you can get discipline by love, get it. If you can't, get it'. Physical drill was also now a compulsory school subject and Mr. George Hart, director of exercises at the City of Dublin Gymnasium, came to give classes regularly in the college gymnasium. Miss J. T. Sullivan, 'Sully', taught cookery which was much enjoyed by the women students. She presided over the cookery room with a firm hand.

As before the model schools remained a focal point in the training programme. They were renamed 'the practising schools' to emphasise that the students learnt to study and try out school management for themselves rather than seeing the schools as a 'model' to be copied. The schools attracted able and loyal staff who served the college with energy and enterprise and often gained promotion to higher positions. In 1900 Professor Henly resigned as head of the boys' model school; he was succeeded by Mr. Walter Bryson. In 1909 Bryson went to take up a post at Ridley Hall Theological College, Cambridge, and was succeeded by Mr. Hugh Magill. Magill himself moved to Belfast the following year, and Mr. William Caldwell Bradley, an ex-CITC student became head, a position he held for only four years owing to his untimely death. The college much regretted the loss as his work had been characterised by a sincere devotion to duty and the school had prospered particularly well under his headship. Mr. John Perry who had been Bradley's assistant and also an ex-CITC student, was appointed. Perry, a native of Co. Antrim, was a shrewd and confident young man who presided over the men's department with skill and ease until 1918, when he was promoted to the national school inspectorate. His assistant Mr. Walter Bradley, a nephew of Mr. W. Caldwell Bradley, was also promoted to the inspectorate in 1922; he died tragically in a road accident in 1943.

In the girls' model school, Miss Agnes Brown continued to be a most competent head. She was assisted by Miss Heron, Miss Hilda McWhirter and Miss Molly Maguire, all of whom gave their working lives to the college. Miss McWhirter became head of the school in 1918 and Miss Maguire in 1925. Miss J. Kennedy, niece of Miss Margaret Kennedy, had succeeded her aunt as head of the infant school in 1897 and she extended the kindergarten training work of the students. Both she and her successor, Miss Alice Heaney, visited infant schools in London at the invitation of Annie Lloyd Evans, and Miss Heaney became an expert in the newly acclaimed Montessori method and gave a series of public lectures in 1919 on Maria Montessori and her educational ideas.[22]

The college had hoped that the practising schools could be promoted to become a 'Higher Grade School' such as had been developed by some of the school boards in England. These 'Higher Grade Schools' offered an extended curriculum to pupils in the seventh and eighth standard beyond normal primary schooling. The Kildare Place Schools already offered a wide range of extra subjects such as French, Latin, book-keeping, typewriting, shorthand, cookery and domestic economy. They also began to prepare pupils for the Civil Service entrance examination and for commercial posts, and the girls' school had a special preparatory class for pupils working for the King's Scholarship entrance examination. However, the National Board which was itself anxious to develop the idea of higher grade schools was unable to persuade the government to provide the necessary finance, and so the Kildare Place Schools, although one of the leading schools in the south city, remained officially a primary school.[23]

The life and activities of the college culminated in the centenary celebrations of 1911. Kingsmill Moore with his knowledge of the history of Kildare Place wished to emphasise the roots of the college in the old pioneer training institution of the 1820s and to show that the taking over of the college in 1878 by the General Synod had been but a new step in a long-term development. By dating the college from 1811, it became one of the oldest training colleges in the British Isles contemporary with Lancaster's college at Borough Road.

Plans for the centenary celebrations were well under way by 1910. Professor Steele, using his college records, contacted all past students who were invited to attend. Kingsmill Moore wrote a short history of the college which was beautifully presented in *The Centenary Book of the Church of Ireland Training College 1811–1911* and which had photographs of the founder members such as Archbishop Plunket, the Recorder and W. G. Brooke and a complete list of past students and their current positions. Mr. Charles Grandison, the college organist, composed a 'Centenary Ode' to be sung at the celebrations:

> A Hundred Years! what mighty revolutions
> Have swept the world within their crowded span!
> Empires have fallen, and new powers uprisen,
> But never since this God-built world began
> Has knowledge so outpoured
> The treasures of her hoard,
> Nor Earth so graciously revealed her plan.[24]

The celebrations themselves were held on Friday 2nd and Saturday 3rd June 1911. A service of thanksgiving took place in St. Patrick's Cathedral at which the Reverend Bernard Reynolds, Prebendary of St. Paul's Cathedral and Inspector of the Church Training Colleges to the archbishops of Canterbury and York, was invited to preach. A garden party was held in the Iveagh grounds, St. Stephen's Green, and Kingsmill Moore gave a public lecture to a packed audience at the Royal Dublin Society on the history of the Kildare Place Society. Thanks to the work of Professor Steele and his hospitality committee, around 600 past students attended the festivities and were housed in Dublin overnight. The students marked the occasion by presenting the principal with a portrait of himself which was to be hung in the dining-hall. It showed Kingsmill Moore dressed in his red academic robes, seated, confident and proud of his college's achievements. The centenary book appeared on the table by his side. The portrait which was painted by Mr. Sydney Rowley was presented to the principal by

Mr. David Horgan, M.A., LLD., one of the first biennial students to enter the college in 1884, and then principal of Castleknock National School. The portrait hangs today in the board-room of the college.

The centenary celebrations marked the height of CITC's development since 1884. The newly completed buildings, the esteem in which the college was held, and the warm affection with which the past students expressed their appreciation, were all of great credit to the principal and his staff who had worked loyally with him since 1884. The Reverend Prebendary Reynolds writing in the 1911–12 report paid tribute to the achievements of the college:

> At Dublin I had the honour of attending really remarkable functions—it was the centenary of the Kildare Place Training College, the history of which is most instructive. The interest and keenness about the work of teaching shown there was inspiring to an Englishman, and I must confess that I was sorry at the large congregation in St. Patrick's Cathedral, and in speaking to the kindly Bishops and other ecclesiastical dignitaries, that I could not say that I was an Irishman. I never attended any function connected with Training Colleges which showed more life or zeal. The Principal of the College has shown force and determination, which reflect the greatest credit.[25]

However, the decade had brought serious disappointments, and there were further dark clouds looming which by 1914 had become apparent. The major disappointment was the failure of the men's department to expand and flourish. The numbers instead declined as the years went by. The gradual change of primary teaching to a women's profession was a national trend, and the growing number of alternative careers and the lack of a regular ladder of recruitment militated against the men's department. As early as 1904 the college was forced to offer places to male candidates without competition because there were insufficient applicants. The college blamed the new lower starting salaries and the decreased incentives to work in small rural schools. Although after 1900 all principal teachers had henceforth to be trained in a college, this rule did not increase the numbers. In 1905 the National Board itself drove a further 'nail in the coffin' of the male teacher. In an effort to reduce the number of small schools, Rule 127(b) of the Board's regulations was revised to read 'That boys under eight are ineligible for enrolment in a boys' school where there is not an assistant mistress unless there is not a suitable school under a mistress in the locality'. This new rule meant that in the future in a two-teacher school, with a male principal, the assistant would have to be a woman, and that in an all male school the number of boys would be reduced because the younger ones could no longer attend. This rule caused a furore in the Roman Catholic Church because it was seen as an effort to bring about co-education and the amalgamation of boys and girls schools. Bishop Foley of Kildare, a member of the National Board, protested vigorously and eventually the rule was modified, but not removed.[26] Professor Henly himself wrote a trenchant article 'The Passing of the Male Teacher' in the *Irish School Weekly*, in which he showed the fatal consequences which the rule would have for male teachers; and which he feared would deprive the national schools of male recruits. By 1914 the problem of male recruitment had become serious for CITC, and the college became very concerned about the loss of grants. In 1912–13 there were only 34 male students in residence and in 1913–14, 25. The college was licensed to hold 50 and had an expensive separate male department to maintain. In February 1914 a special open letter was sent to the clergy in Ireland urging them to encourage suitable men to apply, stressing the advantages which national teaching offered, and the opportunities which the college could provide:

> While the particular object of the College is to train for the service of National Schools, a large number of the students find that the education received here is such as enables them when they have taught the required time, to qualify with little difficulty for many other posts, and many of them subsequently add a University degree to their other qualifications.[27]

The college was pleased to receive a positive response to this letter though many clergy pointed out the lack of a ladder of recruitment for boys who left school at 13 but were unable to take the King's Scholarship examination until they were 18. For many of them the post of paid monitor in a national school was the only opening, so the college were pleased when the rates of payment for monitors were raised in 1914. But August 1914 brought the outbreak of the First World War and the young men were now called to serve in the armed forces.

Another disappointment of these years was the failure of the centenary chapel fund to raise sufficient money to build a college chapel. Sir Thomas Manly Deane had drawn up plans in 1911 whereby the gymnasium building in the Plunket Quadrangle was to be altered and extended to serve as a chapel. It had been estimated in 1911 that about £2,500 would be needed to carry out the project but by 1914 only £1,362 9s. 11d. had been collected and after the outbreak of war there was little hope of obtaining any more.[28] Perhaps this failure was a blessing in disguise because the college was beginning to be too large for its purposes and the upkeep and maintenance too costly. The men's department was only half full, and the women's department though fully occupied was housed in premises with many stairs and corridors, which were expensive to heat and light. In 1904, still in an expansionist mood, the college had attempted to purchase 3 Kildare Place but this had fallen through. Later that year it bought 34 St. Stephen's Green, the garden of which adjoined the college. This large house was seen as a possible residence for the principal but Kingsmill Moore preferred to live out at his own house, 'Cedar Mount' in Dundrum, from which he cycled in each day. The St. Stephen's Green house was let, and in 1922 was sold to the Girls' Friendly Society as a hostel. The building of the new Royal College of Science in Merrion Street had given the Kildare Place College a better back entrance through Merrion Lane, and while this was little used, the right of way was retained by using it once a year on the 15th October when the principal walked through.

The college also now had a staff of ageing men. It had, by choice or default, recruited few young men on to the staff since 1884. The principal, and Professors Cooke, Steele and Henly were all still in office. Professor Rea retired in 1913 owing to ill health and was succeeded by Mr. William Moore, B.A., a scholar and moderator of TCD. 'Billy' Moore taught mathematics for many years at the college and became like his predecessor a much loved figure, if something of a character. He along with John Perry and the other 'TA's' (training assistants) were the only young men on the staff.

The college also lost many of its original supporters and benefactors, and Kingsmill Moore sorely felt their passing. In 1907 W. G. Brooke who had been first manager of the Kildare Place model schools and had been so influential in the negotiations in the Synod and with the National Board, died at the age of 74. He had been a much admired figure in Church of Ireland circles and a tablet was placed in St. Patrick's Cathedral in the south transept beside that of his uncle Master William Brooke:

In memory of William G. Brooke,
Master of Arts of Trinity College, Dublin.
Born MDCCC XXXIII
Died MDM VII.

Farewell, beloved Brother, farewell until the Day.

Beloved at home, honoured abroad, a faithful friend, in converse gay, in work inspiring, a lover of justice, truth and beauty, he served the State and the Church and Education in Ireland from youth to old age with increasing devotion to the cause of God and Man.

In Christo vixit vicit nunc vivit.[29]

In 1908 the Recorder, F. R. Falkiner, who had guided the college through its early years, died while on holiday in Madeira, and in 1909 Lord Justice Fitzgibbon who had given so much of his legal wisdom to the college died. In 1914, Dr. Anthony Traill, Provost of TCD, who had been a governor of the college from the early days, also passed away.

Within the college itself the staff were saddened by the death of two of their oldest members. Mr. Charles Grandison, the organist, died just before the centenary celebrations in 1911 and did not live to hear his 'Centenary Ode' performed. In 1914 Miss Mary Jane Smith who had been on the staff of the college since the 1870s died in office. As head governess of the women's department she had been known to generations of students, and had provided under various lady superintendents loyal and dedicated service. Her love of music and her skill as a conductor were renowned, and her quiet, unselfish ways had been a stable and constant element in the women's department. A huge crowd gathered at her funeral at St. Ann's Church, Dawson Street, where her colleagues, friends and students paid tribute to her. The governors of the college founded a memorial prize for singing in her honour and a carved wooden plaque was hung in the dining-hall which read:

In Piam Memoriam
Mariae J. Smith
Quae per annos quadraginta quinque vim, virtutem, immo vitam totam,
Huic Collegio, ejusque Discipulis
Sedule ac laete dedicabat,
Amici et Discipuli
Praemia Perpetua
Pro Arte Canendi feliciter Tractata
Gratis Animis Instituerunt.
MCMXV.[30]

It was, however, on the political front in particular that the college was least prepared to meet the changes that lay ahead. In 1914 it was still a staunchly loyalist college, proud of the British and imperial connection. In 1903 the lord lieutenant, Earl Cadogan, had been invited to open the new Kildare Street front, and the following year he had unveiled the statue of Archbishop Plunket. In 1903 when King Edward VII and Queen Alexandra visited Dublin, the college had presented a loyal address, and the lord lieutenant, Lord Dudley and his wife visited Kildare Place. In 1911 at the time of the royal visit of King George V and Queen Mary, Kingsmill Moore had attended a garden party at the Viceregal Lodge and he was present at the official opening of the Royal College of Science. He himself was a strong loyalist and proud of his Oxford degree and English connections. Most of his students were northern unionists who strongly supported the Crown. Therefore, the Irish nationalist movement had made little impact on CITC and there had been little or no demand for the teaching or study of the Irish language or history as had happened at the the other training colleges. The effect of the Irish Literary Revival movement was being felt in the school curriculum and the teaching of Irish history in schools was becoming more common. Kingsmill Moore himself had responded to this need and had written *A History of Ireland for Young Readers* which was published in 1912 in a series by Macmillan and was designed for children in Church of Ireland national schools. Nonetheless, like many members of the Protestant community of the south of Ireland the college was taken by surprise by the impact of the nationalist rising in 1916 and by the demand for political independence for Ireland. The future of the college was to be much more difficult and much more traumatic than anyone envisaged in 1914. Kingsmill Moore's sadness and depression were reflected in his concluding words in the 1913 college report:

> Nearly 30 years ago when the college was reorganised, the necessity for its work was thoroughly understood and friends in many parts of Ireland made it a personal matter to watch over its interest. Since then a new generation has sprung up; the struggles which were necessary to insure not only the success but even the existence of the college, are largely forgotten and there is a tendency to forget also the responsibilities which the possession of such a College entails upon the Church. To be able to control the training of Teachers is a fruitful source of strength; but if the work is to be accomplished efficiently the Training College must be kept well supplied with capable and intelligent students and its finances must be well maintained.[31]

VI

The First World War and after, 1914–1927

The First World War and the subsequent political upheaval in Ireland changed the fortunes of CITC. That the college survived and emerged from these struggles, albeit much reduced in size and numbers but none the less a lively and active institution, was much to the credit of the governors and staff who carried it through. The political partition of Ireland into the Irish Free State and Northern Ireland in 1922 meant that the college lost its students from the northern counties who henceforth went to train in the new state college, Stranmillis, in Belfast, and CITC was reduced to serving the 26 counties only. The majority of students at CITC had come from the north so that this change was a serious loss to the college and the effects of 'Partition' were sorely felt. The Church of Ireland as a whole did not accept the division and continued to operate as a single administrative unit north and south of the border, but in the area of teacher training it was forced to recognise the reality of partition.

Through these difficult years the college was to be helped by its newly established link with the University of Dublin by which students attended lectures at Trinity College, and were eligible to continue for a degree. The prestige of the university link offered the college support and increased confidence when these were most needed. Early in the century two sub-committees of the governors had been formed, the Finance Committee and the House and Staff Committee. During the period 1918–22 Sir Robert Tate, FTCD, Canon F. C. Hayes, Canon R. A. Kernan, and Alfred Purser, chief inspector of the National Board served on both committees as did the principal, and the Reverend Richards Goff was on the House Committee. These men guided the college wisely through the crisis years.

The college survived the First World War fairly well. The number of male students declined as many men volunteered for the armed forces, but the number of women students increased to 115 so the overall size of the college was maintained at 135. In 1911 the National Board had ended the one year training course for experienced teachers so there were no more 'annuals' at the college. The Board had decided that the one year students had held back the general work of the senior divisions of the training colleges as they were often inferior in knowledge to the King's Scholars in their second year. From henceforth all the students at the colleges would be 'biennials'. This meant the loss of some of the older more experienced students, and though the National Board did discuss the introduction of a three year rather than a two year course of training for all teachers, this plan did not materialise. By 1918 the numbers in the college had dropped to 124, 21 men and 103 women. The governors were faced with the cruel dilemma of wanting young men to come to the college while being politically and morally committed to encouraging men to serve in the armed forces. The Education Office had granted special concessions to candidate teachers who joined the armed services and in 1917 Kingsmill Moore wrote to all male candidates and King's Scholars pointing out these concessions yet encouraging them to apply to the college:

> The Governors think it right to place these facts before you in order that upon due consideration, in view of these, wherein duty does not call upon you to serve your country in the field at this grave crisis in the history of the British Empire and of Ireland. Should you be physically disqualified from military service, there could be no question as to the propriety of your proceeding quietly with your studies, but should you be strong and vigorous the call of our Army and Navy is one which merits full consideration before it is rejected.[1]

The college supported the war effort in every way. In 1917 the college was used as an army recruiting centre for some months and the men students housed elsewhere. As the finances of the college declined economies became essential. The men students, under the supervision of Mr. Perry, cultivated a vegetable garden to provide produce for the college, and the meals were curtailed and the food poor. The weekly ration in 1918 was:[2]

	Men	*Women*
Sugar	½ lb	½ lb
Meat	3 lbs	2½ lbs
Bread	5½ lbs	4½ lbs
Margarine	1 lb	1 lb
Cereal	1 lb	1 lb
Milk	5 pts	5 pts

Food parcels from home became essential and dishes known as 'Resurrection Pie' (yesterday's left-overs) and 'Boiled Baby' (roly-poly pudding) became a common feature, as were visits to the nearby DBC café for buns and cakes. Heating and lighting were cut to a minimum. In 1918 the influenza epidemic swept the college and 50% of the students fell ill. The college was closed for five weeks and three deaths occurred. One past student remembers with gratitude how the principal and the lady superintendent both visited her when she was in hospital recovering from the 'flu and how Mrs. Moore sent her a loaf of wheaten bread. It has been said 'Anyone who survived the CITC of World War I, was hard to kill'.[3]

The toll on the staff was heavy also. Kingsmill Moore himself became ill in 1916 and had to have six months rest. Professor Henly who had been the strength and stay of the college throughout its existence lost his two sons, Fred Lewis and Ernest A. W. Henley in the War and became a broken man. Students who had admired and feared his sarcastic tongue and brusque manner were saddened to see him weep openly on Armistice Day. These last years in the college were very difficult for Henly, for in the light of his own loss, he resented the presence of the male students in the college who had not gone to the Western Front, and he was heard to remark bitterly 'There are no *men* in this college, only boys'. He struggled on until 1922 when after forty years of service he retired. The governors acknowledged their debt to him: 'In no part of its work has the college done better than in the Art of teaching; and the reputation which it has earned all over Ireland for sending out good practical teachers is chiefly due to Professor Henly's great experience and exceptional skill.'[4] As a founder member of the INTO Henly had seen national school teaching develop from an ill-trained poorly-paid subservient job to a fully qualified and confident profession with its own union and standard salary structure. He had devoted his life to the betterment of his fellow-teachers, and had been a wise friend and mentor to his colleagues and students. He died in 1926. In 1963 his daughter, Miss Florence Henley, presented a prize in natural sciences to TCD in memory of her two brothers.

The women's department also experienced major changes. Miss Elsie Tuckey the lady superintendent appointed in 1911, decided in 1916 to go abroad as a missionary in India. (She later became headmistress of the Masonic School for Girls, Dublin). Miss Eveline Welch B.A. who had been a senior lecturer at St. Mary's College, Cheltenham was appointed in her place. Unfortunately Miss Welch was not a success at CITC. She found the move to Dublin difficult and made the mistake of unfavourably comparing the facilities in Dublin with those she had been used to in Cheltenham. A more demanding and forceful person than the quiet Miss Tuckey, she tried to reorganize the women's department and caused much friction. 'She interfered with meals, timetables and everything' was the memory of one past student, and there was relief on both sides when Miss Welch decided to resign after two years and return to England. Miss Jeannie Beattie, who had been head governess, was appointed lady superintendent.

Miss Beattie, a native of Co. Down, had been a student at the college from 1905–07. She had taught at St. Luke's National School, Belfast, before returning to CITC as head governess in 1914. A forthright and strong personality with a northern directness, she gave the college the energetic leadership which it needed. An excellent teacher of music she built on the traditions of choral singing inherited from Miss Mary J. Smith, and she trained both the men and women student choir, an experience remembered with pleasure by many of her past students. Now, as sole head of the women's department, Miss Beattie had complete control of its running, and worked closely with Kingsmill Moore with whom she established a life-long friendship. A formidable authoritative woman 'Jane Anne' was admired and respected by all her students. Those called to her room for misdemeanours were said to be 'on the green carpet' which decorated her comfortable quarters. She entertained her students generously and a grand party was held to celebrate her new university degree.

Miss Heron, the longest serving member of staff of the women's department, died in 1918. She had taught in the Church Education Society college and had served CITC faithfully since 1884. A thorough teacher of needlework, she had, like her colleague Miss Mary Jane Smith, dedicated her life to the service of her students, and her quiet strict personality was missed in the corridors of Kildare Place. In 1918 Miss Agnes Brown, head of the girls' model school since 1884 also retired, and Miss Hilda McWhirter took her place. Miss Molly Maguire, the other assistant, herself became head in 1925. Miss Gertrude Houston, known affectionately as 'The Hawk' because 'she pounced', was also an able assistant.[5]

Although the war years at CITC seemed to be a holding operation and a period of economic stringency, there was one important development under way. This was the establishment of a formal link between the college and Trinity College, Dublin. Since the beginning of the century training colleges in Britain had been working more closely with universities and the establishment of 'Day Training Colleges' by the civic universities had led to increased opportunities for teachers. University departments of education began to be formed. At Trinity College the chair of education had been established in 1905. The first holder was Professor Edward Parnall Culverwell, who became known as an expert on Montessori. In 1913 he had published an authoritative book *Montessori Principles and Practice*, which was widely read. Since 1898 the university had offered an examination in the 'Theory, History and Practice of Education' which was open both to certificated national teachers and to graduate secondary teachers. By 1910 these courses had developed into a certificate in elementary education, and a diploma in education. No tuition was offered by the university but a course of set books was laid down and candidates were expected to prepare themselves for the examinations. In 1918 the set books in education included Domville's *Fundamentals of Psychology*, Bayley's *The Education Process*, Monroe's *Textbook in the History of Education*, and Culverwell's own book on the Montessori method.[6]

Though there had been no formal links between the university and the training college, many ex-CITC students had proceeded for degrees while working as national teachers, and it was this procedure as well as that of offering present students an opportunity of university life, that CITC was anxious to formalize. In October 1918 Professor W. E. Thrift of Trinity College, who was a governor of CITC, agreed to negotiate with the university regarding the establishment of a formal link. In December he and Dean Robert Miller of Waterford, another governor, presented a draft scheme under which CITC students would attend arts lectures at the university while receiving their practical training at the college:

> The Training College would be a Hall of Residence for the students under the control and supervision of the Principal. To enable the transition to be made the present Training College Professors and teachers in Arts subjects would if necessary, be taken over and appointed by TCD as members of staff.[7]

The governors agreed to the draft scheme and set up a sub-committee to negotiate with Trinity College, consisting of Bishop Maurice Day of Clogher, Dean Robert Miller of Waterford, Dean H. V. White of Christ Church Cathedral, Canon R. A. Kernan, Professor W. E. Thrift, and Dr. Kingsmill Moore. Both the bishop of Clogher and the dean of Waterford were members of the National Board and this proved a useful link. Professor Thrift (later Provost of Trinity College, 1937—42) played a central role in the negotiations and headed the TCD sub-committee consisting of Rev. W. R. Westropp-Roberts, SFTCD, Professor E. P. Culverwell, SFTCD, and Mr. Edward Gwynn, FTCD. The two sub-committees met in January 1919 in Professor Thrift's rooms in Trinity College, and by February an agreed scheme had been drawn up.[8] Discussion by the Board of Trinity College was delayed owing to the death of Provost Mahaffy in April 1919, but the appointment of Dr. J. H. Bernard as the new provost was of great advantage to CITC. Bernard as archbishop of Dublin had been manager of the training college, and had been privy to the negotiations from the outset. Therefore, by July 1919 the scheme had received the approval of both parties, and application was made to the National Board for permission to put the plan into immediate action. Alfred Purser, a chief inspector of national schools, who was also a governor of CITC, advised both Provost Bernard and Kingsmill Moore on the details. Purser foresaw that difficulties could arise where CITC students were unable to reach the required university standards and he did not approve of the idea of separate arts lectures being provided for training college students. He also considered that the CNEI would be most reluctant to approve a scheme if it entailed extra financial cost.[9]

CITC, however, had good reason to believe that the National Board would agree. In March 1919 the University Training of National Teachers Committee of the National Board had agreed to various proposals 'to consider the question of the relations (if any) which should exist between the training colleges and the universities.' This sub-committee of the National Board was chaired by the resident commissioner, Dr. W. J. M. Starkie, and both the bishop of Clogher and the dean of Waterford were members. The proposals discussed had included depositions presented by the principals of the training colleges and covered a variety of approaches to university teacher training such as a three year arts degree course followed by one year of professional training or a two year arts course and one year professional training leading to a diploma in education, and a three year concurrent arts and education degree course. Since 1913 there had been an arrangement between St. Patrick's College, Drumcondra and the National University of Ireland whereby a successful student could be accepted for a third year of training and attend lectures at the university leading to the award of the university diploma in education, and continue for a fourth year for a B.A. degree. The scheme, however, had been open to male students only and had proved very expensive.[10]

Therefore, when TCD and CITC sought approval for their scheme, the CNEI readily gave their support, and wrote to the chief secretary for his agreement. A supplementary grant was sought to enable the training college to pay the university tuition fees, but otherwise the scheme would not involve the Board in any expense.[11] However, sanction for the scheme was refused by the Treasury and it had to be postponed. In the autumn of 1919 the MacPherson Education Bill was under debate. This bill proposed to establish a central co-ordinating authority for Irish education and local education authorities which would control primary and secondary schools. A storm of criticism against the bill had been aroused, particularly by the Roman Catholic hierarchy, who feared a curtailment of Church power in education, and the bill was eventually withdrawn. CITC on the whole supported the bill because it would bring increased financial aid for education, but the delay over its passage meant that the college was not allowed to go ahead with its ambitious university scheme.[12]

By 1918 all the training colleges were suffering from financial shortages. In 1917 the CITC had had a deficit balance and though this was eliminated in 1918, by 1919 it had returned due to decreased income and increased expenses. While the 1919 bill was pending, the government was not prepared to grant extra finance to the colleges. The principals of the three male colleges, St. Patrick's, Drumcondra, De la Salle, Waterford and CITC sought meetings with the resident commissioner of the National Board. A deputation went to London to talk directly with a senior treasury official, Mr. Sydney Baldwin, and an audience was obtained at Dublin Castle with the chief secretary, Sir Hamar Greenwood. There seemed little hope of increased grants in view of the post-war shortages and the delay of the 1919 Bill. Eventually a special emergency grant of £13 per student was obtained for 1919–20 only. The CITC report for 1919–20 reflected the general gloom:

> The times are grave. The scarcity of properly qualified candidates, and financial pressure, present difficulties whose seriousness to the Training College and the Church of Ireland for which the college exists, is unmistakeable. The removal, or at least the lessening, of these difficulties will continue to engage the attention of the Board. Grave times are times for strenuous work and prayer; the Governors know that where these are present the help of God will not be withheld.[13]

Early in 1921 another deputation led by Archbishop John Gregg of Dublin went to the Castle where they were received by the treasury official, Sir John Anderson. At this meeting it was hinted to Kingsmill Moore that if the training colleges themselves were prepared to raise their fees which were at that time around five guineas a year, the Treasury would consider an increased grant. Kingsmill Moore took up this advice and three college principals wrote again to the chief secretary and published the letter in the press. In March 1921 a deputation travelled none too hopefully to London to press their case. It was the middle of the Irish political crisis, and Kingsmill Moore recalled the problems presented:

> We were determined to brave the Irish Office next morning, even though without an appointment. Arriving early we found the hall crowded with detectives. Evidently no unnecessary risks were being taken. The Archbishop's card secured admission; we were shown up to the little room where I had first spoken to Mr. Balfour.[14]

An audience was eventually secured with Sir Hamar Greenwood and a bargain was struck whereby the colleges would raise their fees and the government would increase its grant to the colleges by a similar amount. This meant that the future looked more hopeful and CITC could once again attempt to implement its university plan.

In April 1921 the college wrote to the CNEI seeking authorization for the university scheme. The Commissioners requested formal sanction from the chief secretary which was once again refused. The Treasury was not prepared to accept the scheme because it involved extra cost. The governors of the college were much dismayed to receive a letter from the CNEI on June 14th 1921 stating:

> The scheme was submitted to the Lord Commissioners of His Majesty's Treasury for approval of the financial proposals involved therein, but their Lordships have now notified the Commissioners that they are unable to sanction the scheme which involves additional state contribution amounting to £900 per annum. Their Lordships point out in their letter that the arrangement approved by them for the award of improved grants to training colleges, as recently notified to you, was based on the assumption that the course of education in the training colleges would be of a certain standard, towards the cost of which the students would be willing to make certain contributions. The present proposal however involves an elevation of that standard not by a modification of the curriculum within the college itself, but by giving the students the benefit of training at the senior university in Ireland.[15]

However, with the able assistance of the senior secretary of the National Board, Mr. W. J. Dilworth, the governors were able to persuade the government that no extra expenses would be incurred because the college intended to raise its fees to the maximum in order to obtain the full treasury grant and if the students were to be offered university tuition they would be much more willing to pay the increased fees. Moreover, the college would make a saving on the salaries of its staff who would henceforth become members of the university. Following a personal deputation to the Castle by Bishop Miller of Cashel and Mr. Dilworth, the Treasury agreed, and the scheme came into operation in September 1921.

Under the terms of the agreed scheme students entering CITC in 1921 were to become registered students of Trinity College, Dublin and would receive instruction in arts subjects at the university, and in practical and professional methods at the training college. At the end of their two years of training they would be eligible for the award of the university's diploma in elementary education, provided they successfully completed their two probationary years in a national school and were awarded their teaching diploma by the National Board. Another important part of the scheme stated that:

> Such students as wish to obtain a B.A. degree in the University may at any time after the conclusion of the two years' course, put their names on the College books as matriculated students of Junior Sophister standing by passing the Final Freshman Examinations in languages, and pay the Entrance fee of £15.[16]

This scheme meant a major reorganization in the teaching of the training college. In future the general education of the students would take place in the university and professors Cooke, Steele and Moore were to be recognised as lecturers of the university. The students were to attend lectures in the first year in English grammar, composition and literature, in history, geography, Irish, arithmetic, elementary algebra, geometry, physics and chemistry, and theory of education. In the second year logic and natural sciences were added as extra subjects. At the end of the two years, the students, both men and women, were to take a final examination of 'Little-go' standard ('Little-go' was the common name in TCD for the Final Freshman arts examination), and after a further two years were to be awarded the university diploma in elementary education, provided they had successfully completed their period of probationary teaching. Trinity College reserved the right to terminate the scheme 'at the expiration of any period of five years, upon giving notice of two years previously'. All future appointments to either institution, either in arts or on the teaching side, were to be ratified by both colleges, and it was anticipated that a closer integration of teaching would follow.[17]

Support for the scheme was wholehearted on both sides. Faced with the political uncertainties of 1921, and the approaching independence of the Irish Free State, Trinity College was anxious to strengthen its position and considered it wise for Protestant institutions in the south of Ireland to stand together. CITC saw that the possible political partition of Ireland would threaten its very existence and that it would need every support it could obtain. The other main gain for the training college was the broadening of its courses and the valuable opportunity of proceeding to a degree. However, the long-term effect of the scheme was to reduce its own full-time teaching staff to the minimum and to become dependent on part-time university teaching. The practical side of teacher training remained the most important function of the college, but the separation of it from the general arts courses and the theory of education, resulted in a division between the theory and practice of education which had not existed in the college in its earlier years when it had functioned as a self-contained unit. The link with TCD enabled the training college to save money on salaries, but integration with the university did not materialise and despite their physical proximity, the two institutions remained distant. There was little academic or social intercourse between them, and the provision of separate arts lectures for the training college students prevented them mixing with other students or participating in the broader university community.

Trinity College used the opportunity of the introduction of the training college scheme to create a university school of education and to appoint a new full-time professor of education. Professor E. P. Culverwell had retired in 1916 but had not been officially replaced. He had supported the training college link throughout, and was pleased to see his infant education department develop into a fully fledged school. In February, 1922 the Board of TCD advertised a new full-time chair of education at a starting salary of £500. The duties of the professor were to include 'the administration of his own department, lecturing in the theory and practice of education and in educational psychology to the King's Scholars both at TCD and at the Kildare Place College, as well as lecturing in the theory of education in the arts course at TCD, and on the higher diploma in education'.[18] One of the terms of the TCD-CITC link was that the training college would pay part of the salary of the new professor and in return he would undertake the supervision of teaching practice and give lectures in the theory of education to the Kildare Place students. The retirement of Professor Henly as the master of method had opened the way for this next development.

In May 1922 Professor Robert John Fynne was appointed to the chair of education. Fynne was a TCD graduate who had been a pupil of Culverwell, and had studied for an M.A. in London University under Professor John Adamson, one of the pioneer scholars in the academic study of education in Britain who was a specialist in the history of education. Fynne was, like his mentor Culverwell, an authority on Montessori and in 1924 he published a book *Montessori and her Inspirers* (London, 1924). He was an able, elegant young man full of enthusiasm and eager to build up the new TCD School of Education. Unfortunately for the future of the training college scheme he and Kingsmill Moore clashed at both the personal and professional level, and the relationship between the School of Education and the training college was not to be a happy one. Signs of strains were evident from the outset. Before accepting his appointment as professor, Fynne had written to the Provost of TCD, Dr. J. H. Bernard, stressing that his work at the training college would have to be kept to a minimum if he was to make full use of the new chair of education and develop the school. Fynne had had a discussion with Kingsmill Moore while in Dublin for his interview and the two men had immediately disagreed about Fynne's duties. Kingsmill Moore was used to managing his 'own' college and his domineering and dictatorial manner had obviously annoyed Fynne.[19] Realising that trouble might lie ahead the Board of TCD drew up an agreed schedule of duties of the professor in June 1922. The professor was expected to spend at least two hours per day at the training college during the term and 'to arrange his work at the Training College as seems most desirable in view of the requirements of the National Board of Education and of course having regard to the convenience of the staff at CITC'. The professor's work at the training college was to include lecturing in the theory and practice of education and in educational psychology, the supervision of the presentation of lesson notes and of the students' teaching practice. The schedule emphasised that the professor of education was to be subject only to the Board but while he was at the training college the principal's authority had to be recognised:

> The Professor (of Educ.) is not subject to any authority except the Board of TCD. But he may not enter the Practising Schools without 'the consent and good will of the Manager', although when he is there his actions are not open to criticism. The Professor may attend Criticism Lessons and give advice as the expert in charge of the class. The Principal, while there, shall be in the chair but will take no part except as a listener, when the Professor is present.[20]

The main area of conflict between the two men was the system of criticism lessons and the supervision of teaching practice. Professor Fynne represented the new developments in teacher training which emphasised an open and informal approach whereby a student was encouraged to develop his own individual style in the classroom and not to conform to an authoritarian and rigid pattern dictated by a master of method. The 'crit. lessons' had been a long established tradition at CITC and Kingsmill Moore himself had always presided. He resented both Professor Fynne's presence and his comments, while Fynne considered the whole procedure out-of-date and positively damaging to the students' self-confidence.

On February 2nd 1923 Provost Bernard wrote to Archbishop Gregg, as manager of CITC, to point out that while Professor Fynne had agreed to take over part of Professor Henly's work, he could not be expected to do it all, and that the training college should appoint another lecturer in teaching method. The Archbishop replied on February 7th saying that he had discussed the matter with the principal and that Professor Fynne's work at the training college could not be regarded as being equal to or 'even as a substitute for Professor Henly's work'. Professor Henly had not been 'full-time' for rather than lecturing in the theory of education, he had devoted himself to experimental teaching methods for 6—8 hours per week, and Professor Fynne's lectures could not be regarded as a substitute as these lectures were 'academic rather than experimental' and the principal felt very keenly on the matter. As these comments amounted to a direct criticism of Professor Fynne's work, the Provost suggested that a personal interview should be arranged. At the same time Kingsmill Moore himself also tactlessly sent a peremptory note to Fynne saying that since the professor was so hard worked he could have an hour off from teaching practice each week on Wednesdays and Fridays.[21]

Fynne reacted very angrily to Kingsmill Moore's note and wrote on 10th February saying that he himself would decide his own timetable in the practising school, and that the principal was not in a position to decide the disposal of his time. He went on to attack the training methods and organization of the training college as well as the personal style of the principal. He said that he had found the burden of the training college work 'almost unbearable in the University Term' but that he had been unable to lessen it because 'the need for careful supervision of teaching practice at Kildare Place where there are many rather weak students, has been so urgent and so obvious that I have felt free to absent myself on only two occasions when it was necessary to see the teaching practice of the diploma students'. He bitterly criticised the procedure of the 'crit. lessons' and Kingsmill Moore's own conduct of them. He considered that these sessions were 'not in keeping with an institution affiliated to a university' and discouraged the students from developing their own ideas. He concluded that 'the students should escape from the elementary atmosphere and enjoy greater freedom for the cultivation and expression of individuality', and that it was 'very regrettable that their increasing knowledge of Education and their rapidly developing powers of critical study must inevitably reveal to them that Kildare Place is being kept so very far "behind the times" in so many respects'.[22]

This harsh criticism of Kildare Place must have been very hurtful to Kingsmill Moore who had prided himself on the excellent standard of his training college. The conflict was not only personal but was one of difference between the university concept of a liberal education and the narrower applied methods of the teacher training college. The emphasis on the academic study of the theory of education was a feature of the new university education department, but was seen by the training college as being 'irrelevant' and of little practical value to the young teachers who needed to master the basic skills of school management. This dichotomy of aim was almost inevitable given the differing values of the two institutions, but the gap between the theory and practice of education was widened further by the personal conflict between the two men in the first year and by the failure to co-ordinate the work of the School of Education with that of the training college.

Kingsmill Moore tried to placate Professor Fynne and suggested he should appoint W. E. Bailie, the new headmaster of the boys' model school, as an assistant master of method but Fynne refused to accept this as his relationships with the practising school staff had been strained. They had refused to co-operate with him over the giving of 'demonstration lessons' which he much preferred to the old 'crit. lessons'. In June 1923 Fynne withdrew from his supervisory work at Kildare Place and henceforth lectured the CITC students in the theory of education only. The training college continued to pay £200 per year towards his salary but the relationship between the two institutions became formal and distant. The reason given for the decision was that the government Education Office had to be satisfied with the practical work of the training college and therefore the principal himself must have control: 'It is not necessary that the Principal and the Professor should agree on all subjects. Educational methods are many and various . . . But all matters with reference to the ordering of Criticism Lessons, the giving of Demonstration Lessons, the Supervision of Students in the Schools and the marking of students' work should be carefully discussed with the Principal'.[23]

Professor Fynne turned his energies to where his chief interests lay, namely the development of a secondary teachers' training course in the TCD School of Education. In 1924 a department for the training of secondary teachers was established and it offered a full-time lecture course leading to the university higher diploma in education. Lectures and tutorials were held in the afternoons and students were supervised by the university staff while doing teaching practice in schools in the city. The course was first open to men only but in 1925 was opened to women. Although it remained possible still to take the higher diploma by examination only, Fynne began to build up an effective though small education department. From 1937 all students were required to attend classes if they wished to qualify for the higher diploma and the elementary diploma continued to be offered not only to CITC students but to other qualified national teachers. Education became a popular subject in the general arts degree course. However, the link with the training college failed to develop into a more fruitful partnership and though the School of Education continued to service the training college little attempt was made to work closely together.[24]

Overall, however, CITC benefited from the university link. Once the initial difficulties had been overcome the college settled down well into the university routine. It became a less enclosed and confined institution. The men and women were able to mix freely both at lectures and in recreational activities. Many of them made full use of the opportunities offered by university life, and enjoyed the stimulus of Professor Fynne's lectures and the contact with other university staff. Some problems arose regarding the high standard of academic attainment required by the university and the compulsory logic examination in the second year proved a stumbling block. It was eventually agreed that CITC students could have two attempts at it during the second year but if they failed in the June examination they could resit the whole examination the following year. This allowed students to take up a teaching position and to study in their own time for the supplemental examinations. Another problem was the delay in the publication of the TCD examination results in June which prevented the Education Office from allowing students to be accepted for teaching posts. In 1923 Kingsmill Moore had to return hurriedly from his holiday in Wales to deal with the matter himself, and in his view 'the continuance of our connexion with the university stood in grave danger of being called in question'. Following this crisis it was agreed that in future all examiners of CITC students would be required to return their marks within six days of receiving the papers in June, and that the Senior Lecturer of TCD was to be responsible for conveying the marks to the government authorities and to CITC.[25]

The CNEI, and later the Department of Education, supported the university link, and facilitated CITC wherever it could. Under the terms of the scheme the chief inspectors of the National Board reserved the right to scrutinize the examination papers of the CITC students, and were to be allowed opportunities of access to the papers set in order to satisfy themselves that the standard of examination was maintained. The smooth running of the TCD-CITC link showed that such a partnership in teacher training had many advantages and it provided a useful prototype for the development of the full B.Ed. degree course in the 1970s.

One unexpected development at TCD was the demand by past students of CITC to be granted the right to proceed to degrees. The scheme had been set up for present and prospective students of the college but in November 1921, two months after the scheme had come into operation, Trinity College received a request from Mr. T. A. Spearman who had qualified from CITC in June 1921 to be allowed to avail himself of the 'new training scheme' and to proceed for a B.A. degree. The TCD Board was somewhat taken aback by this request as it had not been foreseen that such a privilege would be sought. The matter was referred to a sub-committee at the Board meeting on 26th November: 'The individual case of Mr. Spearman was not decided on; that the application was likely to constitute a precedent was referred for a report to a committee consisting of the Senior Lecturer, Professor Thrift and Dr. W. A. Goligher'.

On December 10th the Board having first passed a resolution supporting the 'Irish Settlement' which had been announced following the Treaty negotiations in London, and which 'it was hoped would bring peace to the country', turned its attention to the 'Spearman

Case' and agreed to the recommendations of the sub-committee that 'if Mr. Spearman paid the entrance fee of three half yearly fees before presenting himself for the 'Little-Go' examination permission should be granted to him to present himself for that examination and that if he be successful, he should be entered on the College books as a rising Junior Sophister'. Some members of the Board objected to the large amount of fees required prior to entry but the amendment was lost.[26]

This important decision meant that in future not only was the opportunity for proceeding to a degree to be offered to prospective CITC students but it was to be open to all who had qualified since 1900. Mr. Thomas Spearman, having successfully established the precedent, took his B.A. degree in 1926 and had a distinguished career as a much respected and admired principal of Greenlanes National School, Clontarf. He later obtained a M.A. and a higher diploma in education, and served as an active member of the General Synod and of its Board of Religious Education. He died in a tragic drowning accident in 1959. Next to make use of the new privilege was Miss J. Beattie of the staff of CITC who obtained her B.A. in 1924 and her M.A. in 1927. This was an important achievement for her as she was now working among graduate staff and needed to be able to hold her own position. Thus strong links were forged between the two institutions and CITC was to be most grateful for the support which the university gave it in the difficult days ahead.

The political partition of Ireland in 1922 into the Irish Free State and Northern Ireland resulted in the setting up of two education authorities; in the south the National Board was dissolved and a Minister and Department of Education established, in the north a Ministry of Education was established in Belfast. The National Board's training college, Marlborough Street, was closed and Stranmillis College was founded in Belfast as a non-denominational state training college. The majority of students at the Marlborough Street College had been northern Presbyterians and it was presumed that in future these students would train at Stranmillis.

The Church of Ireland Training College was faced with a most difficult situation. As a church college it hoped that it would be able to continue to train all Church of Ireland students albeit now for two education authorities. The college had always drawn the majority of its students from the north and it was reasonable to hope that this could continue. However, it was not to prove so. At first it seemed that the northern ministry was anxious to maintain the link, and early in 1922 an agreement was made with CITC whereby northern students would continue to receive grants to attend Kildare Place and be recognised for schools in the north. The northern ministry wrote on 24th March 1922 to ask CITC if it would continue to accept northern candidates, 'since regretfully a joint system of examining candidate teachers had been rejected by the southern government', and the northern ministry would be holding its own examinations. CITC invited a delegation from Belfast to visit Kildare Place and on 3rd April 1922 the two parties met in the library of the college. The northern delegation, consisting of Mr. L. M. McQuibban, secretary to the northern ministry, Mr. A. N. Bonaparte-Wyse, assistant secretary, who had transferred from the National Board, and John C. Smith, the chief inspector of Scottish Training Colleges, who was advising the new ministry, met with Archbishop Gregg of Dublin and Kingsmill Moore. An agreement was reached whereby the northern Ministry of Education would pay capitation grants and recognise students trained at CITC, provided the usual regulations were upheld and the college curriculum was approved by the northern authorities. The valuable new link with Trinity College was acknowledged as being a marked asset.[27]

This agreement seems to have been seen by CITC as permanent and in October 1922 a confident letter was sent by Kingsmill Moore to the Primate Dr. C. F. D'Arcy and the bishops of Clogher; Down and Connor and Dromore; and Derry and Raphoe, to their clergy and primary teachers confirming that these arrangements had been made:

> We would ask the clergy and teachers to remember that under the arrangements made with the Northern Ministry, the CITC is still training teachers for and from the North. We trust that teachers will continue to attend in the usual numbers and that clergy will fully consider the claims of the Kildare Place teachers in maintaining appointments.[28]

The letter enclosed a copy of the agreement made with the northern ministry, and stressed the value of the university connexion and the good religious teaching provided by the college. It was also emphasised that the study of the Irish language was optional.

The college viewed the 'northern arrangement' as a revival of the old non-Government department (closed in 1903) whereby a section of the students had been trained for church schools without government aid, and the Scottish education authorities also had a policy in operation whereby students were financed to attend training colleges in England when suitable facilities did not exist in Scotland.

Unhappily, however, for CITC, the northern ministry appear to have viewed the agreement as a temporary one only. In 1922–23 there were 61 northern students attending CITC of whom 31 were in their second year of training. In January 1923 the college received notification from the northern ministry stating that no further grants would be given to students to attend CITC. This was a severe blow to the college and a special deputation of Dr. D'Arcy, the Primate, and Bishop Grierson of Down tried unsuccessfully to persuade the northern government to alter its decision. There would seem to have been a change of policy in the north and the 1923 *Ministry of Education Report* confirmed this:

> The Ministry has found it advisable to enter into a temporary arrangement with the Church of Ireland Training College, Kildare Place, Dublin, whereby that college has undertaken to train a limited number of students from Northern Ireland for a period of two years from September 1922, pending the completion of the Belfast College.[29]

The reasons for the change were complex for it would seem that the 1922 agreement had been made in good faith by both sides. Undoubtedly one of the major influences was the views of the Pollock Committee on the Training of Teachers which had been established by the northern government in 1922. Its chairman was H. M. Pollock, Minister of Finance, and the members were H. Garrett, Senior Chief Inspector; W. Haslett, headmaster of the Belfast Model School; R. R. Jones, headmaster of the Royal Academical Institution, Belfast; Major Rupert Stanley, principal of the Municipal College of Technology, Belfast; A. N. Bonaparte-Wyse, assistant secretary to the Ministry of Education; and two members of Queen's University Senate. This committee favoured the establishment of a separate northern training college, and in June 1922 it had been offered the Stranmillis estate by Queen's University, Belfast. This ministry of education college was opened in October 1922. Since it was a state non-denominational institution few Roman Catholic students were to attend, and it was to be dependent on Protestants almost entirely. Stranmillis was seen as a replacement for the old Marlborough Street College, which had been closed by the southern government, and where the majority of northern Presbyterians had attended. In 1922–23, out of the 198 students at Stranmillis 64 had been transferred from Marlborough Street to complete their second year of training. 31 Church of Ireland students attended Stranmillis that year, but with the withdrawal of grants to CITC the number doubled the following year. Stranmillis had established close links with Queen's University and could offer degree facilities similar to CITC. The professor of education at Queen's, Professor W. J. McCallister, was entrusted with the management of Stranmillis and in 1926 was given the title of Principal. Thus 'Stran' was offering similar advantages to CITC and there was little argument to be made as to why the Church of Ireland should not support it.[30] Also there was a dislike of the compulsory Irish policy and fear of what CITC would become in the new Free State where Roman Catholic influence would be paramount.

The Church had political reasons also for accepting the situation. In 1923 the educational structure of Northern Ireland was under review. Lord Londonderry, the minister of education, had appointed the Lynn Committee to report on the development of education in the north and in the spring of 1923 the new Londonderry Education Bill was under debate. The bill proposed to establish local education authorities and the Church of Ireland was engaged in a struggle with the government over the position of religious teaching in the state primary schools. The Church eventually gained some concessions and although these were not as radical as the Church would have wished, they did result in the public education system becoming *de facto* a Protestant one. The Roman Catholic hierarchy had refused to sit on the Lynn Committee or to co-operate with the new education bill, and it may well be that acceptance of the training college issue and support for Stranmillis was the price paid for the Church of Ireland's gains in the 1923 Education Act. The minutes of CITC reporting the decision were bland and non-committal:

> The Primate and the Bishop of Down explained the steps taken by them to avert this decision; asked if it arose from any dissatisfaction with the work done at Kildare Place, they stated emphatically that nothing of the kind was felt, on the contrary the education officials had expressed much appreciation of the way in which their wishes had been met, and the way in which the work had been carried out at CITC . . .[31]

Thus CITC found itself abandoned by the northern dioceses and left to serve the small Church of Ireland population in the south. Some members of the Church were unhappy with the decision. The matter was raised at the General Synod in April 1923, and a resolution passed supporting CITC, but there was to be no change of policy by the northern ministry. The non-denominational status of Stranmillis troubled some members of the Church and there were various moves to set up a church college in the north. This idea was raised at the

General Synod in 1945 and again in 1948 when representations were made to the Gibbon Committee on Teacher Training but nothing further materialised. On the whole the Church was satisfied with Stranmillis College, particularly as after 1931 it increased its control over the management. In that year when the Pollock Committee which had been responsible for running the college was dissolved, the Protestant churches demanded representation on the new management committee. After a lengthy struggle with the government this was granted and the three major Protestant churches each obtained a seat on the board. Thus in this way, and by maintaining the right to appoint chaplains and by approving the appointments of lecturers in Bible Studies, the churches ensured that Stranmillis produced 'Protestant teachers for Protestant schools'.[32]

The alternative of moving CITC to Belfast in 1923 does not seem to have been considered. Its roots were in Dublin though the majority of its clientèle had been northern. The Church of Ireland was determined not to be forced into 'administrative partition'; it maintained a single headquarters, the Representative Church Body, in Dublin and the clergy continued to be trained in the Divinity School at Trinity College, Dublin. Thus the Church resolutely retained its north-south links. However, in the area of teacher training this unity was not possible and the opportunity of educating northern and southern teachers together was lost. The increasing divergence of the two education systems and the non-recognition of each other's teaching qualifications, prevented any interchange of teachers, and a rigid division between schools in the north and south developed.

Kingsmill Moore as principal of CITC had one final embarrassing episode with the northern ministry. In 1924 the Department of Education in Dublin demanded that the Ministry should pay its share of the repayment of the 'Free home' grants and of the ground rent of the college, since it had had students attending there for two years.

ILLUSTRATIONS:

9 *The College staff in 1911. The group includes the principal, Rev. H. Kingsmill Moore, Miss Mary Lloyd Evans, the lady superintendent, Professors J. Cooke, L. E. Steele and J. C. Rea, Miss Mary J. Smith, Miss Heron and the assistant secretary, Rev. P. Pirrie Conerney.*

10 *The College Chapel, opened in 1934, with the stained glass window 'Christ teaching in the Temple' by H. V. McGoldrick.*

9

10

11

12

Kingsmill Moore protested saying that the agreement with the northern ministry had covered capitation grants only. However, the Department were adamant and since relations between the two government education departments were not cordial, Kingsmill Moore found himself having to write humbly to the northern ministry to request the payment of these extra grants. To their credit the northern ministry paid up without argument, and thus ended CITC's contact with the government of Northern Ireland.[33]

The loss of the northern students meant that CITC had to come to terms with the new education system in the south if it was to survive. Given that the college had been staunchly loyalist and pro-unionist, this was to be a difficult task and it was greatly to Kingsmill Moore's credit that he determinedly set about adapting the college to the new political and educational demands of the Irish Free State. In these years he was helped by Miss Beattie who, despite her northern and unionist background, gave full support to the principal and provided strong leadership within the college. Like much of the Protestant community in the south the college withdrew into itself, continuing its life much as before, and attempting to ignore the political and social changes taking place outside it. However, Kingsmill Moore was determined that a Church of Ireland voice, however small, should be heard in the formation of the educational policy of the new state and he participated wherever he could in public debate and policy making.

The major problem for CITC was the introduction of compulsory Irish into the curriculum of the national schools and therefore into teacher training courses. The new government hoped that through the

---

ILLUSTRATIONS:

11 *Women students in 1922 with Miss Jane Beattie, the lady superintendent.*

12 *College students in 1939 with the principal, Rev. E. C. Hodges and the lady registrar, Miss E. F. Pearson.* Left to right, back row: *W. M. Kleinstuber, Aoife Ní Chogarain, I. Buxton (Mrs. de Renzy), C. G. H. Hyde, R. McC. Clark, S. Armour, G. M. Allen, V. J. Wheatly, M. M. Mitchell, M. Middleton, F. T. Peters.* Middle row: *A. R. Doherty, B. Q. J. Graham, E. C. B. Beamish, M. I. Cooper, I. J. Hunter (Mrs. Grace), F. M. Harley (Mrs. Lee), M. I. Griffin, S. J. Stewart (Mrs. Anderson), E. J. Morrow.* Front row: *M. J. Logan, D. M. E. Farnham, D. V. Hennessy (Mrs. Rickerby), D. R. Griffin, E. C. Hodges, E. F. Pearson, I. M. Donaldson, F. M. Stewart (Mrs. Johnston), E. Booth.*

schools the Irish language would be revived and would become the everyday language of the country. The National Programme of Primary Instruction was introduced into national schools in 1922. Irish was to be a compulsory subject throughout the school while infant classes were to be conducted through the medium. Irish history and geography were to be taught in senior forms and where possible also through the medium. The new teacher training programme introduced in 1923 made Irish a compulsory subject in the Easter (no longer called the King's Scholarship) Entrance Examination, and in the training programme itself. English became just one of the other optional languages along with French and German. Algebra and geometry were made compulsory for girls along with arithmetic, and CITC found that many of the women had difficulty with these subjects. The remaining compulsory subjects were drawing, rural science, music, physical training and education. Needlework and domestic economy remained compulsory for girls, while history and geography were to be studied by all in the first year only.[34]

CITC, therefore, was faced with the formidable task of teaching Irish throughout the training course, and of educating its students to become bilingual. Irish had never been taught at CITC, and the majority of candidates at entry had little or no knowledge. The Church of Ireland was critical of the compulsory Irish policy of the government, and vigorously protested against it. This made the task of CITC all the more difficult. Kingsmill Moore considered that if Church of Ireland national schools were to survive, the college must ensure that there were sufficiently qualified teachers to maintain them. The Church was not in a position in the 1920s to withdraw from the national system, and therefore the schools must be provided with the necessary standard of Irish teaching. The policy was supported throughout by Dr. John A. F. Gregg, archbishop of Dublin. Gregg, who had been translated to Dublin in 1920, emerged as the strong leader of the Protestant community in the south and defended their rights in the Irish Free State. He considered that 'if Irish was to be taught at all it should be taught well' and he gave every support he could to the college and encouraged it to adapt to the new situation.[35]

Seeing the goodwill, the new Department of Education assisted CITC as much as it could with the problems. In December 1922 a deputation led by Archbishop Gregg called to see the minister for education, Professor Eoin MacNeill, to protest about the compulsory Irish programme. The Civil War was at its height and Kingsmill Moore recalled the visit vividly:

> Passing many guards and coming at last literally to wire cages, we found our Minister of Education safe beneath the level of the ground. The Archbishop, Dr. Gregg, opened with a vigorous and at times indignant exposure of the way our children were being compelled to study Irish books, written for Roman Catholic pupils.[36]

MacNeill warmly reassured the delegation that no discrimination would take place, and that if there were any books on the Irish programme which were objectionable to Protestants, he was open to suggestions of alterations. The delegates left much heartened and relieved.

However, the compulsory Irish programme was a long term certainty, and the major problem for CITC was the high standard of Irish required for the training college entrance examination. The majority of Protestant schools had taught little or no Irish previously. In 1923 when the situation was becoming desperate CITC enlisted the support of TCD and of the Standing Committee of the General Synod to protest against the high standard of the Irish course. Kingsmill Moore wrote to request an interview with the Minister but instead received a friendly phone-call from Mr. J. O'Neill, secretary in the Education Office, who inquired what the problem was. He then suggested that CITC should itself draw up an Irish entrance programme 'which was practicable' and submit it to them. Kingsmill Moore whose Irish vocabulary could as he admitted 'be exhausted by my ten fingers', readily agreed and with the help of the professor of Irish in TCD, Dr. T. F. O'Rahilly, drew up a simple programme which was accepted by the Education Office for CITC students. Kingsmill Moore later received an informal congratulatory note from the chief of inspection Mr. T. P. O'Connor: 'You have got your own Irish Programme for Easter, and now we have Algebra and Geometry optional for girls: so you have won on all fronts'.[37] And two days later he was very pleased to receive an encouraging personal letter from the Secretary himself:

> Dear Dr. Moore,
>
> Many thanks for your letter. This is very good news that the change in the Irish course is helping you already. I do hope that when you have some parish or diocesan machinery in motion for bringing the advantages of the National Teacher's position to the attention of promising boys and girls. Kildare Place will get the pick of the population.
>
> With best wishes for a pleasant Xmas.
> Very sincerely yours,
> Signed *J. O'Neill.*

Thus encouraged by the supportive attitude of the government, CITC struggled ahead. It was, however, not the only institution to find the demands of the new programme too severe. Many teachers were experiencing difficulties with the amount of Irish required and so the INTO persuaded the government to call a national conference in 1925 to review the progress of the new curriculum. Kingsmill Moore was invited to represent the Church of Ireland school managers at the Second National Programme Conference. There were two other Protestant members, Henry Morris, divisional inspector of the Department of Education, and Professor W. E. Thrift who represented Dublin University in Dáil Éireann. The Church of Ireland General Synod's Board of Education submitted evidence to the conference stressing the difficulties which the Church's national schools were experiencing with the Irish courses:

> In regard to the question of compulsory Irish we desire in the first place to point out that the managers and teachers of the Church of Ireland schools in the Free State have made loyal and sincere efforts to carry out Irish teaching as directed in the programme; and that while there are among the members of our Church all shades of opinion as to the value of Irish, we recognise fully that a knowledge of the literature in all its branches of our country, is a very important factor in the national life. We hope, therefore that it will be recognised that it is in no spirit of hostility to Irish Studies that we feel compelled to enter the strongest protest against the inclusion at the present time of Irish as a compulsory subject at all standards.[39]

The Board of Education was also concerned that the standards of other subjects in the school would be lowered, and that the narrow nationalist approach to history and geography would have ill-effects on society in Ireland.

The meetings of the Second National Programme Conference ran for over six months and Kingsmill Moore as the Protestant 'elder statesman' was given a place of honour next to the chairman, Rev. Lambert McKenna, S.J. He participated fully in the discussions and questioned the witnesses closely on the Irish language policy, in particular Dr. T. J. Corcoran, S.J., professor of education at University College, Dublin who was one of its main advocates. The report of the conference was published in March 1926 and as a result the Irish courses were modified to allow for a wider range of ability. 'Higher' and 'lower' courses in Irish and English could be offered in schools, and in infant classes the use of Irish as the compulsory medium was reduced to the hours between 10.30 am and 2 pm. Both the Easter entrance scholarship and the teacher training programme itself were allowed to offer a 'higher' and 'lower' course in Irish and English and the Church of Ireland was much pleased with the outcome for CITC was able to offer the lower course in Irish until such time as the standard of its entrants improved.[40]

Having to some degree come to terms with the compulsory Irish problem CITC turned its attention to the second major difficulty which it faced, namely that of recruitment. With the loss of the northern counties which had traditionally been the main source of supply, the college had to try to establish new recruitment procedures within the southern dioceses. It first attempted to maintain its numbers at about a hundred, but since the Protestant population in the south declined the numbers inevitably dropped as did the demand for Church of Ireland national teachers. Between 1911 and 1926 the Church of Ireland population decreased to 85,000 in the twenty-six counties of the Irish Free State. By 1961 the Church of Ireland represented only 3.7% of the total population of the state. The three Ulster counties of Donegal, Cavan and Monaghan continued to be the main source of supply for the college. It was estimated in 1924 that there were about 800 Church of Ireland national schools in the Irish Free State and that around 20 new teachers per year would be required. In 1922 the college had launched a campaign to encourage candidates from the south and west to apply and a circular letter entitled 'A Very Grave Need' was sent out. It began:

> If Southern and Western Schools are to be preserved there must be MORE AND BETTER QUALIFIED CANDIDATES FOR TRAINING for the 26 counties.

It explained that since northern students could no longer train for schools in the south, the southern counties would have to supply their own: 'The Need is ACUTE and SPELLS DISASTER unless immediate steps are taken to find a remedy'.[41]

As a follow up to this letter CITC established a Candidate Teachers' Training Fund in 1924. It was inaugurated by Kingsmill Moore with the assistance of the Dublin and Glendalough and Kildare Diocesan Synod. In 1924 an appeal was made 'that the Diocesan Board be requested to open a special fund with the object of helping suitable candidates to qualify for the office of Primary-Teachers'. It was stressed that the already high standard of entry to the college had been accentuated by the addition of compulsory Irish, and that the cost of training had 'increased owing to the Government regulations with which the Training Colleges must comply'.[42]

A fund, therefore, was established whereby both candidate teachers and teachers in training could apply for loans to enable them to qualify as national teachers, and the loans were repayable over a period of years once the students had become fully qualified. The object was to assist students both to prepare for the training college entrance examination and to support them while in training. All applicants had to provide suitable guarantors who would undertake to repay the loans should the candidate default. Throughout the 1920s the fund provided a useful source of financial support for candidates who might not otherwise have been able to proceed for training. As soon as the first recipients became qualified and began to repay their loans, the fund became to some degree self-supporting and continued to prove a valuable asset to the college.

The other problem, however, for the college was not obtaining sufficiently qualified candidates who could pass the entrance examinations in Irish. In 1925 out of 100 applicants 19 only qualified, and the Department of Education had to agree to a certain number 'who had fallen below their standard' to be received into training. In 1926 the situation was no better with only 10 out of 115 candidates being declared qualified. Therefore it was with eagerness and relief that CITC welcomed the new government scheme of 'preparatory colleges' which was introduced in 1926. Traditionally, candidates for primary teaching had been drawn direct from primary schools, and the new preparatory colleges were designed to recruit pupils from these schools and 'prepare' them for the training college entrance. Pupils were to be offered a free secondary type education through Irish on condition that they agreed to enter the national teaching profession. The object was to provide better educated candidates who would be fluent in the Irish language before entering the training colleges. Seven such colleges were established by the government in 1926, three for boys, Coláiste Caoimhin, Glasnevin; Coláiste Einne, Galway, and Coláiste na Mumhan, Mallow; and three for girls, Coláiste Ide, Dingle; Coláiste Bhrighde, Falcarragh, and Coláiste Mhuire, Tourmakeady. Initially the government proposed that the Dublin college would be multidenominational but Archbishop Gregg objected so the minister for education, Professor John Marcus O'Sullivan, suggested that the Church of Ireland should have its own separate mixed college. Archbishop Gregg, while making it known that he favoured neither compulsory Irish nor teaching through Irish, agreed to this proposal and Coláiste Moibhí, so called from its first location in St. Moibhí Road, Glasnevin, came into operation in 1926. By accepting this offer of its own preparatory college, the Church of Ireland finally accepted the policy of compulsory Irish. Archbishop Gregg was undoubtedly the major influence in this decision. He was determined not to allow Protestant children to be 'second class' citizens in the Free State, and speaking at the Diocesan Synod in 1927 he stressed this:

> I do not pretend to like compulsory Irish in our National Schools. I think it is a bad policy, but as long as the Government requires it to be taught, I would rather it were taught well than ill . . . I want to see our young people holding Government positions, and if the path of those positions is along the thorny track of Irish grammar, Irish cannot be altogether an uneconomic subject of study, when it makes the difference between employment and unemployment.[43]

Dr. Gregg took a special interest in the preparatory college and in 1934 when, in the presence of Mr. De Valera, the President of the Executive Council, he opened the college's new spacious premises in the old Hibernian Military School in the Phoenix Park, he spoke again of the government's helpful support:

> The Education Department had agreed to its [Coláiste Moibhí] foundation with the greatest readiness and goodwill. He could not have expected anything more in the way of courtesy and goodwill than he had received from the government of the Irish Free State.[44]

In addition to the preparatory colleges, in 1926 the government introduced a Pupil-Teacher Scheme intended to draw recruits from the secondary schools into primary teaching. Scholarships were offered to pupils on the results of their Intermediate Certificate Examination results to enable them to continue their education until the Leaving Certificate examination. Candidates both from the preparatory colleges and the pupil-teacher scheme, were given priority over 'open competition' candidates who took the Easter Scholarship entrance examination. CITC received a steady number of recruits through this scheme, though the low standard of Irish in the Protestant secondary schools prevented it from becoming fully effective. Celbridge Collegiate School continued to be the best source of well-qualified students.[45]

Thus by 1927 when Kingsmill Moore retired after 43 years as principal, he left a college whose morale and hopes had been restored. It had survived the political crises of the early 1920s and had established a recognised university link. The staff appreciated the status which this link gave to the college and Professor John Cooke had been honoured by the appointment to a lecturership in geography at Trinity College. Miss Beattie organised the women's department with efficiency and confidence and her college choir won first prize at the Feis Ceoil in 1922 and again in 1925. She herself had been appointed by the Department of Education as examiner in vocal music for both the training college and preparatory college entrance examinations. Irish was taught by Rev. Paul Quigley, B.A., and Rev. James O'Connor, M.A., and the standard was rising each year. The numbers at the college had been maintained at an average of 90–100, helped by the fact that after the closure of Marlborough Street College, Presbyterian and Methodist students from the south of Ireland now attended CITC. The men averaged around 16 and the women 80 so each department had an active life of its own. Even a serious fire in 1927, which extensively damaged the men's department, had done little to affect morale. An active ex-students' association which had been formed in 1922, maintained contacts between students from the north and south and a special reunion song 'In Gremio Matris Salus et Solatium' had been composed for the annual meetings.

Therefore, Kingsmill Moore could look back with pride at his achievement. He had guided CITC from its foundation in 1884, through the heady days prior to the 1914–18 war, and along the difficult path of post-war retrenchment. He had been the leading Church of Ireland spokesman on education, and had upheld the rights of the Church through the vicissitudes of the Balfour 'Free Home' scheme and the 1892 Education Act. He had advocated the cause of the small school and had striven to make the position of Church of Ireland national schools secure. He had been a vigorous spokesman for the denominational teaching colleges and had built up cordial relationships between CITC and the government education department. His autocratic and forceful personality had been at its best in a crisis and he had made many friends and enemies during his long career. His attitude to teacher training had been paternalistic, which by the 1920s was becoming an anachronism. He regarded the establishment of the university link as the high point of his achievement and in 1928 he presented a prize to the college to be awarded to the student who obtained the highest marks in the first year university examinations. He remained a governor of the college and continued to serve on the finance committee which made life difficult for his successor. 'The old principal', as he liked to be called, retained a great interest in the college and he resented the radical changes required in the 1930s.

In 1937 Kingsmill Moore published an autobiography *Reflections and Reminiscences* (London, 1937) which covered his long career in education in a lively and personal style. He maintained a keen interest in education, particularly in Celbridge Collegiate School and in the Incorporated Society for Promoting Protestant Schools. His life-long interest in gardening gave him continuous pleasure at his home, 'Cedar Mount' in Dundrum, and he was a Fellow of the Linnean Society (named after the pioneer Swedish botanist) and often used the letters F.L.S. after his name. His work on the history of the Kildare Place Society was continued by Miss Beattie and the archives which he sorted were carefully preserved in the college. He died in 1943 at the age of 89 and was widely honoured. His son, Justice T. C. Kingsmill Moore, presented a prize to the college in his memory called 'The Old Principal's Prize' which was awarded to the best first year student in practical teaching. 'Ball' had created a college; his successors had to reform and reorganise it in the decades ahead.

VII

The 1930s: Retrenchment and reform

The Reverend Canon Evelyn Charles Hodges, M.A., B.D., who became principal of CITC in 1927, was very different from his predecessor both in personality and background. Educated at Mountjoy School and Trinity College, Dublin, he had graduated in 1910 with a degree in mental and moral philosophy. He had served first as a curate in Drumcondra and North Strand and in 1924 had been appointed incumbent of Rathmines Church where he was a popular pastor and preacher. He was keenly interested in education and was an active member of the Sunday School Society for Ireland. He served on the Dublin Diocesan Board of Education and in 1920 obtained a diploma in education from TCD. A handsome, charming man, he was much admired for his excellent sermons and for his beautiful voice and delivery. He could talk himself and others out of difficult situations and his powers of persuasion were widely acknowledged. Known as 'Darby' to his friends, E. C. Hodges was a man of talent and enterprise.

In 1927 he inherited what was to all intents and purposes, a Victorian training college. The men's and women's departments still functioned separately though since 1922 there had been more social contact between them. Relations between staff and students were still formal, the rules restricting and the discipline rigid. While the existence of the Irish Free State had been accepted, the college had remained largely unionist and loyalist in outlook, and still culturally identified with England.

Hodges was to change all this and was to turn the college into a liberal open co-educational institution integrated into the Irish Free State and bilingual in Irish and English. This was achieved at a high cost to himself and to the college and his years as principal were difficult due to pressures both within and without. Yet his achievement was to be equal to that of his predecessor in his day, and is remembered by his staff and students with admiration and affection.[1]

In the 1930s he was ably assisted by the governors, particularly by the Finance and House and Staff Committees. Canon J. W. Crozier, later archdeacon of Dublin; Canon A. E. Hughes, M.A.; Rev. J. H. Yates, B.D.; Mr. R. H. Ryland, B.L.; Mr. T. J. Smalley and Mr. S. D. Budd served on both committees. In 1934 Mr. R. Meredith, C.S.I., C.I.E., and Mr. Seacome Mason both joined the board and became active members of the sub-committees. Archbishop J. A. F. Gregg continued as manager of the college and his firm and realistic guidance was of great assistance to the new principal.

The first major problem which the college faced in the decade was the change in the system of government financing of the training colleges. In 1928 a departmental committee on teacher training recommended that the payment system of capitation and bonus grants, which had been in operation since 1892, should be ended, and instead a fixed payment based on a 'licensed number' should be given to each college plus a capitation grant per student in residence. The licensed number for CITC was fixed in 1928 at 102, but as the demand for Protestant teachers declined this was reduced in 1934 to 75 and again in 1937 to 55. Hodges estimated in 1929 that the college stood to lose about £500—800 per annum, and this trend continued as the decade went on. The Department of Education assisted the college where it could by fixing a 'notional' licensed number for CITC which was usually above that of the actual number in residence. In 1935 the licensed number was 75, the actual number in residence 52; by 1939 the licensed number was 35, the actual number in residence 28. Despite this help by 1939 the college debt stood at nearly £8,000.[2]

This depressing decline in student numbers was not due to mismanagement on the part of the college authorities, but rather to external forces at work. The primary teaching profession overall was depressed in the 1930s and a surplus of teachers existed. This surplus was particularly acute in the Protestant community because of the decline in the population. In the early days of the Free State some Protestant teachers had obtained employment in the north but by the 1930s this had ceased. In the south between 1926 and 1936 the Church of Ireland population fell by over 11%, the Methodists by 9.5% and the Presbyterians by 13.5%. Emigration affected the whole population but the birth rate among the Protestants did not compensate for the loss as occurred among the Roman Catholic population. Also since many Protestant schools in the south were one-

or two-teacher the demand for male teachers was very low, and in 1936 Coláiste Moibhí stopped recruiting boys and in 1940 there ceased to be any men students at CITC.

The Department of Education itself took steps to reduce the teacher supply. In 1933 'the marriage ban' was introduced whereby a woman teacher was required to resign her post on marriage, and in 1936 the Department made a rule whereby a training college student who failed the final examinations was ineligible for a permanent appointment to a school. Teachers' salaries had been reduced by 10% in 1923 from their 1920 level and again in 1934, and despite vigorous protests from the INTO were to remain at this low level until after the 1946 INTO teachers' strike and the recommendations of the Roe Committee on Teachers' Salaries in 1949. Thus the general depressed state of the teaching profession and the necessity of training only the number of teachers required made the existence of CITC very difficult indeed.[3]

To deal with these problems of grave financial shortage and reduced student numbers, Hodges and the governors of CITC embarked on a policy of retrenchment and reform. The buildings of the college had been designed to house over a hundred students and now the number in residence had been halved. Therefore, it was decided to sell or lease parts of the college. In 1929, 34 St. Stephen's Green, which had been purchased in 1904 as a possible principal's residence, was sold to the Girls' Friendly Society. The bookshop in 10 Kildare Street, The Educational Depository, was closed and the premises rented to the Guardian Assurance Co. Since the death of the general manager, Mr. J. M. Quinn, in 1921, the shop had been losing money, and the demand for books and school supplies had dwindled. Its closure marked the end of an era of bookselling in Kildare Street which had commenced with the Kildare Place Society in the 1820s.

In addition the principal began to rationalise the internal organization of the college to make it more compact and less costly to run. Many of his changes and ideas were resented by the older staff who felt that he was 'destroying' the college and its traditions. In 1930 the separate men's department which had had its own diningroom and staff was closed, and the students all ate together in the dining-hall. Hodges abolished the old 'high table' and encouraged the staff and students to mix at meals, and the standard of food and service was improved. The men's department, which had been repaired at great expense after the fire in 1927, had proved too costly to run for only twenty men, and in any case changing attitudes encouraged the open mixing of men and women. As a further economy it was decided that the practising school staff who had from the foundation of the college been resident in the college, would in future live out. The decision was bitterly resented by the school staff, particularly by the head of the boys' school, W. E. Bailie. 'Paddy' Bailie who had been appointed in 1922, had presided over the men's department with vigour and style. A shrewd, tough, northern man, he had been a student at the college in 1909–11 and had taught at Howth Road National School, Clontarf. A strict disciplinarian, he ruled his school with an iron rod. He was an outstanding teacher of English and introduced his pupils early to Shakespeare and poetry. His hobbies were fishing and shooting and his nature study classes gave much pleasure to his city-bred pupils. He lived in bachelor quarters in the men's department where he entertained the men students listening to music and smoking his pipe. He was assisted usually by a resident 'supernumerary', one of the senior men students who stayed on at the college. In 1930 Bailie therefore lost not only the superintendence of the men's department but also his home and a way of life which he had much enjoyed. Relations between him and the new principal became strained, particularly since Bailie had been a great admirer of Kingsmill Moore. The other practising school staff, Miss Maguire and her assistants, Miss Houston and Miss Butler, and the head of the infant model school, Miss Morrison, also became non resident and the community life of the college was impoverished.[4]

This 'demotion' of the school staff, as it was seen by those involved, was to some extent justified by the decision of the Department of Education in 1931 no longer to confine the teaching practice of training college students to the practising schools but instead to send them out to ordinary national schools in the city. The Department considered that such a change would give the students a wider experience of teaching:

> The Practising School did not give sufficient scope for the further practical training which is necessary. The students' work has been done frequently under conditions which are not obtaining for the class teacher in an ordinary school. Teachers trained in the Practising School have constantly urged that the practice was marred by certain unreal or artificial elements attached to the conduct of lessons; they felt that they were at all times in touch with a particular type of organization dealing with a special class of pupils whose frequent contact with student-teachers rendered them somewhat precocious or sophisticated for normal class-work; they needed, they said, an experience more akin to the actualities of ordinary school work, and a wider experience.[5]

This decision marked a radical change in the pattern of teacher training. Since the early nineteenth century model schools had been the central focus of a training institution and had been seen by some as a most important part of the establishment. Many girls from the Kildare Place schools had themselves become teachers, encouraged by their early contact with the students. Now the model schools were to become ordinary national schools, serving the surrounding area, but with no particular training function other than to provide teaching practice facilities for student teachers as would other national schools. Despite the sense of loss and the resentment caused, the Kildare Place schools contined to flourish and maintain high standards. Bailie served as principal until 1953 and he trained under him many able young masters, among whom were Mr. George Clarke, later principal of Zion National School, Rathgar; Mr. R. W. Smyth, later principal of Taney National School, Dundrum; Mr. F. T. Peters, later of The High School, Dublin; and Mr. George Fitch who himself became head of the school when Bailie retired. Miss Mary Maguire continued as head of the girls' school until her death in 1944. She was the active president of the Ex-CITC Students' Association which flourished in the 1930s and 1940s. Miss Gertrude Houston also served the school for many years and became head in 1944.

The staff of the training college itself was also reduced in the 1930s following the retirement of the 'old guard'. Professor John Cooke and Professor L. E. Steele both retired in 1931 after a life-time of service to CITC. The governors acknowledged their debt to these men: 'The Governors recognise that much of the success which has given prominence to the college is due to their culture, their acquirements and their skill as teachers.'[6] Professor Cooke died a year later aged 81, and Professor Steele in 1944 aged 90 years.

Professor 'Billy' Moore also retired in 1933 as lecturer in mathematics and Rev. P. Pirrie Conerney, who had been bursar and assistant secretary in the college since 1910, retired the same year. He had been an able administrator and had served both principals well. In his first year of office he had undertaken the organization of the centenary celebrations of 1911 and had been immediately recognised for his administrative skills. Miss Jane Beattie also retired in 1933 as lady superintendent of the college. As an admirer and loyal friend of Kingsmill Moore she had not found the rule of the new principal easy to accept. She resented the changes which he was introducing, and also with her northern loyalist outlook she resented the growing emphasis in the college on the Irish language and culture. She was unable to give this policy whole-hearted support and so, after much discussion, she agreed to accept early retirement with a good pension. She returned to live in Hillsborough, Co. Down, but she maintained contact with her past students for the rest of her days. CITC had been the centre of her life and 'my girls' were to remain a constant interest, particularly those who lived and worked in the north. Subscriptions were received from as far afield as America and India. In May 1934 at a formal ceremony, a solid silver inscribed tea and coffee service, a silver fruit dish, and an album of the subscribers' names were presented to Miss Beattie at the college. The 'old principal' presided and tributes were paid to Miss Beattie by him and by two past students, Miss Constance Hewitt on behalf of the northern students, and Mrs. Lily Spearman on behalf of the southern students. Each expressed the high regard in which Miss Beattie was held and hoped that, though retired, she would keep in close touch with the college and her students. The ceremony concluded with a rendering of the college song 'We Saw a Mighty River' conducted by Miss Beattie herself.[7]

In 1936 the northern students, encouraged by Miss Beattie, formed their own Kildare Place Ex-Students' Association which held regular meetings and social outings up to the 1970s. Past students kept in touch with each other and with 'Our Miss Beattie' who, on Kingsmill Moore's death in 1943, became president of the association until her own death in 1971. One of the important decisions of the association was to found a special CITC prize at Queen's University to perpetuate the memory of the college and its contribution to education in the northern community. In later years the association made further presentations, one to St. Ann's Church, Dawson Street, where the students had attended Sunday worship, and another to St. Anne's Cathedral, Belfast. In 1970 when the new college chapel was built at Rathmines the association presented a solid silver bread box, a chair and a prie-dieu for use in the chapel. Miss Edith E. Gillespie of Belfast who had been a student at the college 1917–1919, was honorary secretary and treasurer of the association for many years and she retained a close friendship with Miss Beattie. Canon W. J. Whittaker, rector of St. Columba, Knock, Belfast was also an active member and he preached at Miss Beattie's funeral at Hillsborough in 1971. The association only closed down in 1979 when the members had become too old to attend regular meetings. It had not been easy for northern students to accept the radical changes which had taken place at Kildare Place as it adjusted to meet the demands of the educational system in the south, but none the less the old loyalty was very strong.[8]

Miss Beattie herself retained a keen interest in the history of the college and in 1942 she published a short outline history of the college based on a paper read at the annual meeting of the ex-students' association. She remained a life-long friend of the Kingsmill Moore family and on her death in 1971, the Hon. Justice T. C. Kingsmill Moore, son of the 'old principal' paid tribute to her:

> She was a northerner with all the fine qualities of the North. Shrewd, staunch, uncomplicated and when once she had given her trust, loyal to death . . . She was the best Lady Principal the Church of Ireland Training College had ever known. Others had been more distinguished academically. Thoroughness and conscientiousness rather than brilliance were the characteristics of her mind. Yet she was capable not only of training her pupils but of inspiring them with her own single-minded devotion. She drew out their capabilities to the full as anyone who heard the performance of her choirs at the Feis will appreciate . . . Men and women all over Ireland will be remembering her with love this week.[9]

Thus the resident staff of the college in the 1930s was reduced to the minimum. Canon Hodges and his family lived in at first but later found accommodation elsewhere. Miss Eileen Pearson, B.A., a graduate of TCD who had been appointed assistant to Miss Beattie in 1931, became resident Lady Registrar in 1933 and assumed responsibility for teaching practice and the daily organization of the college. Though young and shy, she gave devoted and loyal service to Canon

---

ILLUSTRATIONS:

13 *College students in 1947 with the Chaplain-secretary, Dr. G. O. Simms, and the lady registrar, Miss E. F. Pearson.* Left to right, back row: *H. A. Bagnall, V. M. Dagg (Mrs. Despard), M. S. McMurry, E. M. E. Bright (Mrs. Fisher), M. J. Breakey, E. M. Williams (Mrs. Taylor), E. G. Dobbs (Mrs. Boyd), M. M. Carberry (Mrs. Henderson), J. J. Willoughby.* Front row: *I. M. Jamieson, E. S. Wolfe (Mrs. Ralph), G. O. Simms, E. F. Pearson, V. H. Manning (Mrs. Taylor), B. L. Gibson (Mrs. Beattie), M. A. Delahunt (Mrs. Tyrrell).*

14 *College students in 1960 with the principal, Rev. R. J. Ross and the lady registrar, Miss E. F. Pearson.* Left to right, back row: *V. Jermyn, A. Buchanan, M. Moore, B. Muir, S. Pratt, M. Marshall, A. Hay, H. Griffin.* Middle row: *A. Elliott, S. Larke, R. Doherty, M. Kingston, J. Taylor, J. Henry (Mrs. Foster), M. Billingsley, O. Lowry.* Front row: *M. McGirr, M. Patterson, M. Allen (Mrs. Magee), R. J. Ross, E. F. Pearson, V. Walker, J. Scott, M. Somers.*

13

14

15

16

Hodges during the difficult years and she encouraged and supported the development of the Irish language and the new approaches which he introduced. Known affectionately as 'Judy' by the students, Miss Pearson was strict and stern yet gave for over thirty years a rigorous and inspiring training to her students. She carried the heavy burden of responsibility with a quiet sense of duty and served under three principals until her retirement in 1967.

Two new members of staff at CITC were appointed jointly by Trinity College and the training college, Mr. Frank Stephens to teach Irish and history and Dr. W. F. Pyle to teach English and geography.[10] Stephens was a member of the talented Synge family and a nephew of John Millington Synge the dramatist. With a deep interest in history and archaeology he encouraged a love of Irish history and culture among his students, and organized regular outings to places of historical interest. He was equally effective working with school children and when visiting schools 'could stir the interest of a class of city boys by producing from his pocket an ancient axe-head and in a few graphic sentences carry them back to very, very early times.'[11] Stephens died suddenly in 1948 and was a loss to the college. Dr. William Fitzroy Pyle, a graduate of Trinity College with a double first class degree, was appointed to teach English and geography. His quiet courtesy and inspired teaching were much appreciated by the students who gained from him a knowledge and understanding of English literature. Dr. Pyle became a distinguished member of the English department at Trinity College but retained a deep interest in the training college and in 1954 became a governor.

At the college itself, Mr. W. S. E. Hickson was appointed house-master and lecturer in mathematics, but he stayed only a couple of years before moving on to technical college work. Mr. George Harrison continued to teach instrumental music and the organ. 'Daddy' Harrison who was organist at St. George's Church, had succeeded Mr. C. O. Grandison in 1911 and had maintained the high standard of music in the college, and was a much loved figure. Mr. J. F. Gillespie continued to take the drill classes, and Dr. H. T. Bewley,

---

ILLUSTRATIONS:

15 *Kildare Place in the late 1960s.*

16 *The Church of Ireland College of Education, Rathmines, Dublin 6, in the 1970s. From a watercolour by Mr. Tom Nisbet, R.H.A.*

who had been 'Visiting Physician' to the college since 1884 also continued his services. Thus some ties with the past were maintained though the organization and style of the college radically changed.

The reduction in the need for residential accommodation allowed the college to continue the policy of leasing out its premises. In 1936 the men students (six only) moved out of the men's department building and resided in Kildare Street. The old model schoolrooms at the back were closed off and let to the Office of Public Works which was entered from Merrion Street. The men's residence rooms were converted into classrooms for the practising schools, and the children clattered noisily up and down the stone staircase. A new modern infant classroom was built in the yard and was fitted out with up-to-date equipment. The Kildare Street buildings were modernised, the dormitories divided to give more privacy and classrooms reconstructed there. Other rooms were let out to the Sunday School Society for Ireland of which Canon Hodges was Honorary Secretary and to the Transport Sub-Committee of the General Synod Board of Education which was assisting Church of Ireland children in isolated areas to travel to a nearby school. Finally, in 1938 the large dining-hall, and the ground floor of 11 Kildare Street were leased to the Agricultural Credit Corporation, and in future all students entered the college through the Kildare Place gates. The loss of the fine Deane dining-hall was deeply regretted but it was now too big for the college's needs. A smaller dining room was erected by building an extra floor into the old gymnasium building thus leaving a gym hall underneath which had little air or light. So, working in cramped quarters, the college strove to make itself more compact and economic, and the rents from the leased premises helped to reduce the college debts.[12]

Despite the many difficulties CITC in the 1930s was a place full of interesting developments. Canon Hodges strove to change both the curriculum and the attitudes of the college. He realistically accepted the Irish language policy and was determined that CITC as the 'minority' training college should have a standard of Irish second to none. Students who worked under him were inspired by his courage and enthusiasm, and he treated them as mature adults, encouraging them to have self-confidence in their own ideas and ability. For some the newly found freedom of the college was too much but most appreciated the opportunities which Hodges' policy created.

In the 1920s the Department of Education had been lenient on CITC regarding the standard of Irish obtained but in the 1930s after the advent of the Fianna Fáil government under the leadership of De Valera, this leniency ended. Mr. Tomás Derrig, the new minister for education, was determined to strengthen the language revival and renewed pressure was placed on the schools. In 1934 the Revised Programme of Primary Instruction for National Schools was issued, and the 'lower course' in Irish which had been introduced in 1926 was abolished and all schools had to take the 'higher course'. Irish once again became the compulsory medium throughout the infant day. The success of this programme depended on the training colleges producing fully qualified teachers. By 1932 the majority of training college students were not only fluent in Irish but were taking their college examinations through the medium. The Department of Education report in 1932 was pleased with this progress:

> The Irish language has now become the everyday language of the Catholic Training Colleges. Both inside and outside the Colleges it is noted that the students use Irish as a matter of course. Practically all the work in the Training Colleges is done through the medium of Irish.[13]

CITC was not able yet to reach such standards and the Department Report politely acknowledged this:

> At the Church of Ireland Training College, owing to the lack of Irish of many students entering training, the teaching of subjects through the medium of Irish is not undertaken but there is a marked improvement from year to year in the students' ability to use Irish fluently.[14]

In 1932 the Department announced that a student would have to qualify in the oral and written Irish proficiency certificate before being eligible for a permanent appointment to a school. CITC protested about this rule and was granted a concession whereby a student could qualify for the bilingual certificate during the first year of teaching. However, by 1937 this concession was to be withdrawn and Hodges saw that if the Church of Ireland national schools were to survive, CITC must produce the qualified teachers. The attitude of the Protestant community to the Irish language had remained in some areas antagonistic, in others simply resigned. The *Irish Times* in November 1931 expressed its critical views of compulsory Irish policy and of the Church's lack of opposition to it:

> The compulsion of the Irish language is playing havoc with education throughout the Free State. In the national schools the claims of Irish are so insistent that even "the three R's" have fallen into neglect . . . The Irish Secondary Schools educate largely for export, and now under the pressure

> of compulsory Irish, the Free State Schools are turning out an inefficient article . . . In a word compulsory Irish is not only a denial of intellectual freedom but is a material menace to the Church of Ireland youth. Yet on this vital matter the Church's leaders . . . are dumb.

Archbishop Gregg took little heed of such views and he fully supported CITC in its 'Gaelicisation' policy. In 1935 at the college's annual general meeting he declared 'we must give nobody the chance to say that they who belonged to the ancient Church of Ireland were foreigners in their own land'. Hodges did all he could to encourage the students to become bilingual and appreciate Irish studies. Regular céilís and Irish dancing classes were held in the college and for several summers special holiday courses in Irish were held in Furbough in the Connacht Gaeltacht. The college moved to a large country house there, and the course was a most enjoyable social gathering for staff and students alike. The principal, Miss Pearson, and Frank Stephens participated, the Irish classes were attended by all and a strong sense of common purpose prevailed. The *Irish Times* commented:

> A regular course of lectures in Irish pronunciation and grammar, as well as in methods of teaching school subjects through Irish was provided close by under the auspices of Mr. Thornton, Principal of the National School at Furbough. In the evening a local 'story teller' was a constant visitor and recounted Irish folktales of the district . . . In undertaking such a practical scheme for improving the students' knowledge of Irish, the Governors of the College have initiated a movement which should have far reaching results in the Protestant national schools in the Free State.[16]

However, the problem of the standard of Irish in CITC was solved by the success of Coláiste Moibhí, the preparatory college. From its foundation in 1926 this college began to provide recruits for the training college who were already fluent bilingual speakers and came to CITC well equipped to undertake the training course. The preparatory college was served by a group of talented and dedicated teachers and soon became renowned for the high standard of its achievement. The first head, Mr. Seoirse de Ruit, seconded from the Civil Service, along with his wife May established a happy mixed community in which Irish became the everyday language of the pupils. He was soon succeeded as head by Mr. John Andrew Kyle, an inspector in the Department of Education who was given the task of developing the college. An Ulsterman and Trinity graduate, Kyle had a strong, stern personality and a vision of what the college could achieve. One ex-student of the college remembered:

> (John Kyle) had to overcome our comparative ignorance of the Irish language and culture; he had to see that we could do as well in the public examinations as those pupils from English speaking schools. (This we did not only in Irish but in English and other subjects as well). He had also to introduce us to other cultures so that, in doing everything through Irish, we should not become narrow and insular. This he also did. He quietly encouraged us to be discriminating and adventurous in our reading and we had a very good library.[17]

The other members of staff were equally committed. Miss Eileen Penrose, 'a charming dainty little lady', taught Anglo-Irish poetry and music; Mr. Liam Condell, a stylish man, gave classes in both classical and Irish folk music; Máire Ní Neill, 'an exciting teacher', passed on her love of literature both Irish and English, and Seán Mac Eachain, an ardent nationalist, presented history in a lively manner. The most colourful figure was Oscar Diarmuid MacCarthy Willis who taught history and offered his pupils a wide knowledge of languages and travels. A barrister by profession, he had given up a lucrative career to foster the Irish language and culture. Seen by some as a fanatic, he was devoted to traditional music and song and on his death, his friends established a competition for the harp in the Oireachtas.

These staff all made Coláiste Moibhí an unusual and exciting place in which to work. Kyle encouraged his pupils, both boys and girls, to think for themselves and to be proud of their Irish heritage. There was plenty of freedom and extra-curricular activities. An ex-student recalled:

> We were allowed to experiment with drama; we were taught to play Bridge; we were taken on outings; we entertained some well-known people. We played tennis and a kind of baseball; we had a lot of fun. I remember that at the end of term we were almost reluctant to go home.[18]

In 1934 the college moved into new premises in the old Royal Hibernian Marine School, in the Phoenix Park. Miss Lilian Duncan succeeded Mr. Kyle as principal and the college continued to flourish and produce a high standard of scholars.

Entrance to the college was obtained by the Department of Education preparatory colleges' competitive examination, which could be taken between the ages of 13–16. The examination was based on the seventh class programme as most of the recruits came from the senior classes of the national school. Irish, English, arithmetic, history, geography and singing (for girls) were compulsory and three additional subjects could be offered from a list of six: algebra, geometry, drawing, rural science, natural science and needlework. All candidates had to obtain a 50% pass grade in both oral and written Irish, and those who answered the question papers through Irish were offered bonus marks. In the other preparatory colleges, 50% of the places were reserved for candidates who gained 85% in oral Irish but at Coláiste Moibhí this rule did not apply. In fact each year a number of the entrants to Coláiste Moibhí were unable to reach the required standard in Irish because the teaching of Irish was still inadequate in Protestant national schools, so the Department of Education sensibly agreed to allow a certain number to be declared 'eligible exceptionally' each year. Seeing that there was goodwill, the Department showed a wise tolerance in its dealing with the Protestant college, and Kyle himself helped to ease the college through the initial difficult years. Even in the 1930s when the entrance examinations to all the other preparatory colleges was taken through Irish, the Department continued to present a special set of papers in English for the Coláiste Moibhí candidates.[19]

Therefore, Coláiste Moibhí came to be seen as a successful pioneer venture, making a marked contribution to the life of the Church of Ireland. In 1938 an article in the *Irish Times* entitled 'Reconcilers of the Past and Present' eulogised it showing how far the Protestant community had come to accept the Irish language policy:

> In the west of the old Royal Hibernian Marine School 'Reconcilers of the Past and Present' keep the 'lonely flame' of Protestantism alive. If the Church of Ireland and other Protestant churches are to survive at all it will be because the primary schools of their denominations have willed it to be so. It will rest with the pupils of these schools to accept the full privileges of citizens.[20]

The article went on to describe the excellent premises and facilities of the preparatory college in the Phoenix Park, the spacious classrooms, the gymnasium, and the swimming pool and then concluded:

> These happy clever-looking girls in their pretty uniform and their fine carriage look at us straightly and independently. Do they know how much depends on them? At least they are enjoying life at present. They soon become fluent in Irish, the language used in college life, and can presently say, as one of them expressed it, 'All we need to say and more' . . . These are 'Reconcilers of the Past and Present' and as such are called to play an unusual part . . . a part of heroic responsibility and inspired courage. They defend and uphold the faith of their forefathers in a new spirit.[21]

Thus Coláiste Moibhí and CITC between they produced fluent

Irish speakers to teach in Church of Ireland national schools, and while the Protestant community remained socially isolated, its youth became slowly integrated into the life of the Irish Free State. A knowledge of Irish ceased to be a barrier, and the young entered fully into the professional and economic life of the new state. Both the preparatory college and the training college made a marked contribution to this successful integration.

In addition to the challenge of the Irish language policy, in the 1930s CITC had to face major changes in the general teacher training programme, and in the method of recruitment. In 1931 the Department of Education ended the Easter Scholarship entrance examination and in future all training college candidates were selected on the results of the Leaving Certificate examination. It was now envisaged that all candidates would have received a full secondary education either at a preparatory college or at an ordinary secondary school prior to entry. 'Open competition' candidates still had to take a special oral Irish examination at Easter along with oral English, vocal music and needlework for girls.

The Department planned to reduce the quantity and improve the quality of future training college students. The change was serious for CITC because recruits other than from the preparatory college would have to be drawn from the Protestant secondary schools where the standard of Leaving Certificate honours Irish was often not high. Canon Hodges visited some of the leading secondary schools to encourage able pupils to apply to CITC and stressed the need to obtain a high standard in Irish. In 1931 4 men and 14 women only of the 'open competition' candidates obtained the necessary standard in Irish, but the Department of Education once again assisted by allowing some of the candidates to proceed provided they made every effort to reach the required standard before the end of the course. However, as the demand for teachers declined and preference was given to preparatory college pupils, no 'open competition' pupils were admitted. The pupil-teacher scheme inaugurated in 1926 had not proved successful owing to the lower standard of Irish in secondary schools, and in 1936 the government had ended it. It was considered that the preparatory colleges were now sufficiently developed to provide the necessary candidates.[22]

Therefore, CITC found that by the end of the 1930s its entry was restricted to Coláiste Moibhí students only, and in the long term this had a narrowing and impoverishing effect on the college. From 1936 Coláiste Moibhí admitted no boys so by 1940 there were no male students at CITC. Most of the girls were recruited at the early age of $13\frac{1}{2}$ and spent their formative years in an enclosed community. There was little opportunity to mix with other young people and the students lived and worked for eight years in a group of the same sex, religion and outlook. Some of the girls, attracted to the preparatory college by the offer of a free secondary education, felt at eighteen that they had little motivation to become teachers but found it very difficult to withdraw at that stage. Other girls who were at secondary schools, if at the age of 16 or so they had a desire to train as teachers, often were unable to proceed owing to the limited entry. The INTO began in the late 1930s to protest about the narrow formation of primary teachers, and strongly criticised the preparatory college system. The governors of CITC were well aware of the ill-effects of the policy and in 1937 issued a pamphlet entitled 'Teachers in Training', criticising its effects. The governors were anxious to recruit the best possible candidates to the preparatory college and offered a bonus of £5 to any primary teachers who successfully prepared candidates for the entrance examination. In February 1938 a special meeting was convened at CITC to which representatives of the General Synod board of Education and the Diocesan Board of Education of Dublin and Glendalough and Kildare were invited. A resolution was sent to the Department of Education requesting, in view of the serious limitations of the policy of recruiting only through the preparatory college, that CITC should be allowed to allocate at least 20% of its places each year to open competition candidates and in addition that Coláiste Moibhí should be allowed to recruit pupils at 16+ after the Intermediate certificate as well as at 13+. The governors considered that these changes would allow CITC a much wider pool of resources to draw on, and that girls from rural national schools who often were not sufficiently advanced to reach the standard of the preparatory college entrance at 13+ could have another attempt at 16.

The Department would not agree to alter the entry age to Coláiste Moibhí but it did agree to allow a given number of 'open competition' places each year. In 1939–40 there was only one open competition candidate admitted and it was not until 1944 that the number of open competition candidates began to rise. The governors' own pamphlet did have some success in encouraging candidates of better calibre to apply to the preparatory college, and the training college began to be less concerned about the quality of its recruits.[22].

The new training programme which the Department of Education introduced in 1932 required a number of major changes at the college.

After 1932 all future training college students would have received a full six years of secondary education, so that the new training programme placed increased emphasis back on to professional studies and reduced the amount of general education. The course was divided into three sections, (A) Professional Course, (B) General Education Course and (C) Optional Course, and students were required to take all three. The professional course, which was the most important, consisted of the principles and practice of teaching plus the methodology of the primary school subjects, and drawing, music, rural or domestic science, physical training, hygiene (personal and school), and needlework (for girls). The students were examined in each area in two years. The general education course was reduced to a minimum and students were required to take only Irish, Irish history and one other subject from a list of English, mathematics, history and geography. The emphasis on Irish and Irish history was reflected in the school teaching programme, and it was possible for a student to study no English or mathematics or history other than Irish while at college. The optional subjects offered of which the student had to select one were Latin, French, history, geography, mathematics. In the first year examination the students had to obtain pass marks of 35% in all subjects of the professional course and 50% in oral Irish.[24]

The practical training of the students was extended to include teaching in local national schools. At CITC the model school continued to take a number of students but the majority went out to surrounding schools for a minimum of six weeks practice each year. This new system required much liaison work with school principals and Miss Pearson, the lady-registrar, undertook this responsible work. She visited all the schools and arranged the student placements, and then prepared the classwork with them prior to their appointment. This new system offered the students a greater variety of experience and an opportunity to see both large and small schools at work.

Canon Hodges abolished the old system of 'crit. lessons' and inaugurated a scheme of 'a model one-teacher school'. This was the same idea that the old Church Education Society college had had back in the 1860s. Since most of the students would be teaching in one- or two-teacher rural schools the big city schools were often untypical, and therefore Miss Pearson adapted two rooms in the college and borrowed some children from the model schools each week to make up a small all-age school where the students could learn to organize and run their own small school. The students were encouraged to plan and develop their classes based on the needs of their pupils and to learn to adapt and innovate accordingly. The old system of rigidly planned lesson notes was abandoned and a series of lessons based on themes and integrated subjects was favoured. Educational theory developed rapidly in the 1930s and the students studied child psychology and learning development as well as the principles of school organization. The national schools were becoming better equipped and activity and heuristic methods were possible.[25]

Canon Hodges was anxious to develop the girls' self-reliance and independence. All of them had received a secondary education and had had wider experience than their predecessors. Many were destined to work in remote parishes in the country where they would need to be self-sufficient and self-reliant. Hodges attempted to make the college less 'paternalistic' and to allow the students much more freedom. The senior students appreciated the privacy of the new single study bedrooms and the courteous informal manner of the staff: 'We were no longer treated as charity children; we were now ladies and gentlemen.' The new dining arrangements, and the ending of the domestic duties of the women students also helped. However, despite these changes the college was unable to prepare the students for the lonely and arduous life which awaited many of them on leaving. In isolated Protestant communities they were still expected not only to run the school, but to teach in the Sunday school, to sing in the choir or play the organ, and support numerous parish functions. Relationships between teachers and their clerical managers were formal, and the young teacher often found herself required to act as an 'unpaid curate' but not accepted as a social equal. Expected to live in a lonely, cold teacher's residence and to conform to a strict code of behaviour, the young teacher had little or no social life among her own age group. The college was fully aware of the hardship faced and encouraged the Church of Ireland community to support and assist its young teachers as much as possible. The college report in 1931 stressed that the students required 'not only the mental training needed to prepare themselves for their profession, but also the environment most suitable for young people embarking on a career dependent for its success upon a sufficient sense of responsibility and self-respect', and it was to be hoped that 'when these young people undertake their difficult task perhaps in some outlying parish in the Free State, they will receive a cordial welcome from the Church people of the district, and will be made to feel at home in their surroundings'.[26]

Throughout the 1930s Trinity College offered much support to CITC. The training college was able, despite the cutbacks, to maintain a high standard of general education and to offer its students a wide range of opportunities. The changes in the new teacher training programme required some alterations in the university courses, and at times CITC found it difficult 'to serve two masters' when the academic and professional interests clashed. In 1932 TCD agreed to changes in the programme for training college students, which allowed for increased time to be spent on Irish and reduced the other general education subjects. Junior year students were required to attend lectures in Irish (4 hours per week), in mathematics (with junior freshman arts students) and in English, history or geography. The students had more opportunity to mix with other undergraduates and to attend arts lectures with them. However, this caused problems as often the academic university courses were not suitable for prospective primary teachers. The School of Education continued to service the training college and Professor Fynne's lectures in psychology were appreciated. But the relationship between the two institutions remained distant and little was done to bridge the gap between the theory and practice in education. CITC students attended Trinity College chapel on Sundays and enjoyed the social contacts but, unfortunately, for many the university link seemed 'a waste of time'. Much of what was taught appeared to be irrelevant to the trainee teacher, and while valuable time was spent going up and down Kildare Street to lectures, the training college students did not feel really part of the university, particularly as they had little time available for the average undergraduate pursuits.[27]

The relationship between CITC and the university was strained at times by the failure of students in the senior year examinations. While the university demanded a sufficiently high standard of academic performance, the training college often considered that a student's attainments in practical work was more important. In the early years it was possible for a student to take up his or her first appointment and to return to the university later to sit the supplemental examinations. For instance in 1930 five junior year students and 24 senior year students had to take supplemental examinations, and in 1931 while all the junior year passed, 14 senior year students failed. In 1936 the Department of Education introduced a rule whereby a student who failed in the final examination was ineligible for a permanent appointment so it became essential for all students to pass at the end of their finals. Hodges was very pleased when this was achieved in 1936, particularly when, for the first time, all the students also obtained their bilingual Irish certificates. His efforts and all those of his new young staff were rewarded by these results, and the university also adopted a realistic attitude to the peculiar needs of the training college.[28]

The other valuable development of the 1930s was the increasing number of the ex-CITC students proceeding to TCD degrees. In the early years these had been about five or six a year but in 1933 this had risen to 18. Both men and women used this route to obtain a B.A. degree. Although all students had to undertake a minimum of two years service in a national school after leaving the college, some had hopes of entering secondary teaching or, for the men, holy orders. Among ex-CITC graduates of these years who became clergymen were Rev. G. S. Nowlan (1926), Rev. E. N. Rowe (1929), Rev. R. H. Boyle (1931), Rev. C. G. Gregory (1930), Rev. J. J. A. Hodgins (1933), Rev. W. J. Whittaker (1933), Rev. F. Phillips (1937) and Rev. R. E. Pritchard (1938). Among those who entered secondary teaching were Miss E. Heatley (1928), headmistress of the French School, Bray, Mr. James Goulden (1932) of The High School, Dublin, Mr. V. Wheatly (1944) of Mt. Temple Comprehensive School (formerly Mountjoy School) and Mr. F. T. Peters (1943) of The High School, Dublin. While these men and women were a loss to the primary teaching profession, CITC did offer the opening to a graduate career and many students made use of this opportunity over the years. Most of those who obtained degrees remained in primary teaching and brought enrichment to it.

Of all the achievements which Hodges executed at CITC in the 1930s the one for which he was most admired was the building of the college chapel. In 1911 at the time of the centenary celebrations, a fund had been established for a college chapel, and Sir Thomas N. Deane had produced a plan to extend and convert the gymnasium building. However this fund had been insufficient and the onset of the First World War had put an end to the project. In 1932 Hodges proposed to convert the old model classroom in the men's building into a small chapel and the governors applied for permission to use the 1911 chapel fund for this purpose. Reaction to the plan was mixed. For many the model classroom built in the 1890s, with its sloping floor, pine desks and range of educational fittings had been the college's pride and joy and it seemed near sacrilege to dismantle it. However, by the 1930s the room was too formal and severe for teaching purposes, and the decline in male students and the ending of 'crit. lessons' had further reduced its use. The old staff were sad to see the solid furniture and effects auctioned off and one was heard to say grimly that since the 'new chapel would be built on litigation it would not prosper'.

In 1933 the governors were granted permission by a decision of the High Court to use the existing chapel fund for the conversion so work began.[29] The organ was removed from the dining-hall and installed in the new chapel, and a beautiful stained glass window was commissioned from 'An Túr Gloine' workshops in Upper Pembroke Street. The window, designed by Herbert V. McGoldrick, a distinguished Irish stained glass artist, portrayed Christ Teaching in the Temple. The upper panels contained the arms of the sees of Armagh and Dublin with the college crest in the centre. The chapel was opened in 1934 by Archbishop Gregg and was acclaimed by all to be a most lovely place with its oak panelled pews and splendid east window. The prayer and hymn books were presented by Celbridge Collegiate School, an altar book by Bishop R. T. Hearn of Cork, and the communion plate which had been given in 1911 by Rt. Rev. A. G. Elliott, sometime Bishop of Kilmore, was put to use. Services were held morning and evening and the students gathered there daily for a time of quiet and refreshment. It was remembered as a place apart and it became the centre of the religious life of the college although the students continued to attend TCD chapel on Sundays. Dr. G. O. Simms in an article on the chapel in the *Irish Times* wrote:

> The early morning sun has lit up for recent generations of teachers in training the deep jewel-like colours of green, rich red and golden amber which fill the window with an unforgettable beauty. The theme of this simple yet profoundly devotional poem in glass is the temple scene at Jerusalem in which the Christ-child is the central figure.
>
> Such a scene lends a permanent inspiration to teachers and learners in their ever-living, ever-changing deeply enriching quest for meaning and truth.[30]

Both the organ and the stained glass window were removed to the new college chapel built in Rathmines in 1969 and were installed in fine new surroundings, but many past students regretted the passing of the old chapel. The oak stalls were transferred to St. Mary's Church, Donnybrook.

By the end of the decade, however, Hodges was beginning to lose heart and momentum in his drive to maintain and develop the college, and the onset of the Second World War and the 'Emergency' made the situation more difficult. Despite all his efforts the numbers at the college continued to fall and the financial debt to rise. In 1938 there were 28 students only in residence (23 women and 5 men), and in 1940 20 women only. Despite the retrenchment and the curtailment of the college premises, the financial situation continued to deteriorate, and in 1939 the college debt stood at nearly £8,000. The lack of male students and the increasing narrowness of the college life as an all-female institution made a depressing picture. Hodges found that he had many critics who, saddened by the closure of the college buildings, blamed him and his policies for the sorry state in which the college found itself. In 1939 he missed the strong support of Archbishop Gregg who as manager of the college had been a staunch ally and advocate of the Protestant college coming to terms with the changes in the Free State. Archbishop Gregg was translated to Armagh where he led the Church as Primate with vigour and wisdom, but his regular contact with the training college was ended. In addition Hodges lost two of his most active governors, Archdeacon J. W. Crozier and Canon A. E. Hughes who were appointed in 1939 to the bishoprics of Tuam and Kilmore respectively. Therefore, by 1943 Hodges himself was ready to accept the see of Limerick where he was to serve as a much loved bishop for seventeen years until his retirement in 1960. He became a governor of CITC and retained his keen interest in education particularly in the Sunday School Society of which he became president in 1943. He died in 1980 and a memorial service was held in Christ Church Cathedral to which his many friends and past students gathered to pay homage to a life of service and achievement.

Hodges' contribution to CITC was immense, though it may have not seemed so to his critics and indeed even to himself in 1943. He had inherited in 1927 a conservative and traditional college which had been dominated for forty years by a powerful leader, and he had forced the college, often against its will and that of other churchmen, to change in order to meet the challenges of the new era. Hodges made CITC a college in which the Irish language and culture had an honoured place, and whose students went out confident and equipped to take their place in the education system.

In 1932 in an address to the Church of Ireland Conference commemorating the 1,500th anniversary of the Church, he had spoken of the changes in Irish primary education north and south and while 'the intensive study and teaching of the Irish language had been the order of the day' the 'very heavy burden almost too great to be borne' had in fact been carried. The teachers deserved much credit and 'kudos' as they had 'tried not only to maintain the level of their schools in many subjects of the programme, and at the same time to make the necessary advance in the knowledge and teaching of the Irish language'. Hodges had stressed that the Church of Ireland was gradually adjusting to the new policies and that 'it was not for the Church of Ireland to oppose or disapprove of these conditions'. They had arrived and if the Church of Ireland was to take part in the national system of education 'it must arrange its machinery to meet the conditions honourably and efficiently'. The duty of the training college itself Hodges regarded was to serve candidates 'who can enter the College on their merits, reaching the required standard, to train them to give loyal service to the Church, and to equip them to teach the programme of the Department of Education without fear or favour, fully qualified in Irish as in other subjects, owing no man anything either by way of concession or favour'.[31]

This realistic and brave objective Hodges had attempted to achieve. To a generation of students he had been an inspiring teacher and friend. They had admired his intellect, his enthusiasm and his ability to achieve the impossible by persuasion and persistence. Although they recognised that it was nigh impossible to refuse 'Darby' Hodges anything he asked, and that all arguments 'fell by the wayside', they knew he had given them ideals to follow.

For Hodges the leaving of CITC was a sad occasion, since the future of the college looked bleak, and in the report which he wrote for the governors in 1943, he felt that he had to defend his actions and justify his policies, showing how he had tried to reorganize the college both in its premises and its attitudes, and how the new type of secondary education student could be treated in a more adult and open manner. He had worked to raise the standard of Irish and of the general education of the students to meet the requirements both of the Department of Education and of the university.[32]

However, circumstances had worked against Hodges, and the decline in the Protestant population, the depressed state of the primary teaching profession, and the difficult financial situation of the 1930s had reduced CITC to its lowest ebb and its very survival seemed in question. The governors recognised the difficulties which Hodges had had to face and paid tribute to his achievements:

> The Governors of the Church of Ireland Training College convey to the Bishop of Limerick their appreciation of the services which he has rendered to the Training College, and in the realms both of secular and

religious education to the Church of Ireland during the fifteen years in which he held the post of Principal of the College. They express their appreciation of the unfailing courage and self-sacrifice with which he faced a long series of reverses in the fortunes of the college.[33]

VIII

The 1950s and 1960s: Recovery and expansion

In 1943 the governors of the college were faced with the difficult decision of whether to close the college down or to appoint a new principal and hope that the college would survive the war years and revive. There were only 17 students in residence that year, and the college's income which had been £16,610 in 1927 had dropped to £1,720 per annum and the debt stood at over £8,000. Various alternatives were considered. One was to move the college to the north of Ireland and to attempt to have a church college which would serve the whole of Ireland. CITC could look with envy at the well-equipped and flourishing college at Stranmillis, where the northern Protestant students were trained, though some churchmen were not wholly satisfied with the non-denominational nature of that college. The matter was to be raised in the General Synod in 1945 but was not given serious consideration as the cost to the Church would have been too great and the majority of northern clergy were satisfied with Stranmillis for training their teachers. It was unlikely that the Department of Education in the south would agree to recognise teachers trained outside the state and the Irish language requirement would have meant having to offer two different training programmes.

In 1939 CITC had sought legal advice regarding the transfer of the college to the north and had been informed that this would not be possible:

> Investigations were made as to the possibility of assisting in providing Church of Ireland teachers trained in Northern Ireland for Church of Ireland schools situated there. However the Governors were legally advised that as at present constituted, the Church of Ireland Training College must operate in Kildare Place, Dublin, and its funds must be restricted to Students in Training in connection therewith.[1]

Therefore the governors in 1943 decided on a 'stop gap' solution. Rev. G. O. Simms who was chaplain and dean of residence at Trinity College, was invited to become chaplain-secretary of the college and to act as principal until such time as a further decision regarding the future of the college could be made. By offering the new chaplain-secretary residential accommodation, thus saving on the principal's salary, the governors hoped that the college finances would improve and a reduction in costs be achieved. Dr. George Otto Simms, one of the most distinguished young churchmen of the 1940s and destined to become dean and bishop of Cork, archbishop of Dublin and archbishop of Armagh, accepted the offer and with his wife and family moved into the college. He combined his duties there with those of chaplain and dean at Trinity College. Having a thorough knowledge and love of Irish, he gave to the college the leadership and intellectual stimulus which it needed. Miss Pearson continued as lady registrar, and was in charge of the day-to-day running of the college and the supervision of the students. The Professor of Education at TCD took over responsibility for the supervision of the students' teaching practice. The only other residential staff were the matron, and the cook; Mr. James Burns the gate porter, who served the college with great devotion from 1931 to 1947, was non-resident. University staff continued to give lectures and in 1947 Mr. Victor Graham, M.A., was appointed lecturer in mathematics; in 1949 Rev. A. E. Stokes was appointed to teach history.

Thus from 1943 to 1952 the college survived, its numbers not rising above 30 but none-the-less a happy and close-knit community. Dr. Simms and his young family brought renewed life and vigour to the college and the links with TCD were strengthened through the daily contact of the chaplain. Dr. Simms lectured to the students in religious knowledge and took the daily services in the chapel. Despite the hardship and the shortages the students enjoyed the family atmosphere and the friendship of their chaplain-secretary. 'Daddy' Harrison continued to play and teach the organ and the musical life of the college flourished.

In 1943 the governors' finance and staff committees were amalgamated and became one single executive committee. New members were co-opted and gave gladly of their time and talents. The bishop of Limerick and the bishop of Kilmore remained active members, and Mr. F. La Touche Godfrey of Trinity College; Mr. E. N. Edwards, B.A., LL.B.; Archdeacon E. G. Sullivan of Dublin; C. E. Riley, M.A.; W. Power-Steele; H. H. Wells and H. R. Chillingworth, M.A. all served on the finance committee. The problem of recruitment to the college remained serious and the bishops of Kilmore and Limerick visited secondary schools encouraging able pupils to apply. However, the high standard of Irish required for entry remained a stumbling block. In 1950 the situation was so serious that a bishops' pastoral letter was issued to which the response was encouraging, and a wider range of secondary schools began to send pupils. Eight or nine different schools were represented among the entrants in 1951.[2]

The college, however, continued to depend on Coláiste Moibhí for the majority of its recruits. In 1941 the preparatory college had lost its extensive premises in the Phoenix Park which were required by the government and for one year had to be housed in Kildare Place. It then moved to Merrion Square and finally to Shanganagh Castle in Shankill. In 1951 Miss Gladys Allen was appointed principal, and the college continued to maintain its long tradition of a high standard of Irish and of solid foundation work for the training college. Entrants to CITC were drawn about half from Coláiste Moibhí and half from 'open competition' candidates and this provided a good mix within each year. There were no men students except in 1946–50 when three Presbyterian students from the preparatory college were admitted as non-resident students. The Presbyterian Church, anxious about the future of its few primary schools, had requested that these men be allowed to train as a special concession.[3]

The model schools continued under the headship of W. E. Bailie and Miss Maguire, while Mrs. Whitten, assisted by Mrs. Jenkinson, ran the infant school. A high standard of work was maintained despite the cramped quarters and ageing buildings. Many pupils won scholarships to secondary schools, and senior pupils from other schools used to come to Kildare Place to be prepared for the scholarship examinations. The majority of the pupils, however, still went straight into employment, and Bailie used his contacts to obtain jobs for the boys in Dublin firms like Dockrells, Parkes, Heitons and Henshaws. One ex-pupil remembers with gratitude and pleasure his school days spent in Kildare Place—going for nature walks in St. Stephen's Green, keeping watch on a magpie's nest in a tree in the school yard, being in awe of Miss Pearson (nicknamed 'fairy feet' because she moved so quietly), and much enjoying 'fire drill' when the door at the back of the schools was unlocked and the children went out, down a ladder and into the Government buildings at the back where there used to be an armed military police guard on duty.[4]

Miss Maguire died suddenly in 1944 and was succeeded as head of the girls' school by Miss G. Houston who had been her assistant for many years. Bailie retired in 1953 and his ex-pupil and assistant, George Fitch, took over. Fitch was a keen sportsman, and he started a soccer team in the school which had a very successful record. In 1948 Miss F. W. Robinson, B.A., was appointed as the first graduate member of the model school staff and the girls' school again had three woman teachers.

In 1951 Dr. Simms was elected dean of Cork and in 1952 terminated his work at CITC and TCD. The governors considered that the future of the college looked much brighter than it had ten years previously. The war years were over, and shortages eased. The demand for Protestant teachers had begun to rise and after the 1946 INTO strike and the recommendations of the Roe Committee in 1949 national teachers' salaries had begun to improve. Numbers at CITC had risen and there was renewed confidence in the Church as a whole. Opposition to the Irish language had declined, and for the rising generation who had learnt the language from infancy at school it ceased to be a serious problem. Dr. Simms, through his tact and diplomacy, had established excellent relations with the Department of Education which itself was anxious to see CITC survive.[5]

Therefore, the governors decided to appoint as full-time principal, Canon R. J. Ross, M.A., B.D., who had been headmaster of Christ Church Cathedral Grammar School. A native of Dublin, he was an excellent musician and organist and an energetic administrator and scholar. He was to lead the college for the next 25 years and was to see it established in its fine, new premises in Rathmines before his retirement in 1977. One possible alternative considered in 1952 was that the college should be integrated into the university education department and Professor E. A. Crawford who had succeeded Professor Fynne in 1950 as professor of education was interested in the idea. However, the governors decided to continue the separate college while encouraging closer links with TCD wherever possible.

The numbers and confidence of the college began to rise again. In 1952–53 there were 40 students in residence, and by 1954–55 the number had increased to 54. Some of the accommodation which had been leased out had to be regained and the college became somewhat crowded in the Kildare Place premises. With 11 Kildare Street let to the Agricultural Credit Corporation and the ground floor of No. 10 to the Guardian Assurance, the students themselves resided in the upper part of No. 10, and the chapel, library and model schools still functioned across the Plunket quadrangle.

Canon Ross took over responsibility for the supervision of the students and their teaching practice. Ably assisted by Miss Pearson he encouraged the cultural and musical life of the college and maintained the devotional tradition of the chapel. In 1956 changes were made in the university programme for the training of college students which it was considered 'would enable the students to make the best use of the opportunity provided by a two-year course at the university'. In 1963 the Department of Education itself introduced a new programme which reduced the general subjects and placed more emphasis on education as the central study. Irish and English were both now obligatory subjects in each year but only one other academic subject was necessary. The practical subjects, art and craft, elementary science, rural science, physiology and needlework were reduced to one-year courses. The CITC students attended lectures in English, Irish and education at the university and took all their other subjects at the training college.[6]

In 1961 the college celebrated the 150th anniversary of its foundation in Kildare Place. A special thanksgiving service was held in the college chapel which was attended by past and present staff and students. The Most Rev. G. O. Simms, archbishop of Dublin preached, and the Most Rev. A. W. Barton, former manager of the college and Rt. Rev. E. C. Hodges, bishop of Limerick attended. The Hon. Justice T. C. Kingsmill Moore, son of the first principal, and Miss J. Beattie were both invited to speak, and an evening concert concluded the day of celebrations. The next day, a special service was held in St. Patrick's Cathedral where Very Rev. E. S. Abbott, dean of Westminster preached the sermon.[7]

Therefore, by the 1960s the college restored with life and vigour was expanding beyond the accommodation available in Kildare Place. The old eighteenth century buildings were run down and dilapidated, and what had seemed in the 1890s a fine modern college was by the 1960s a cramped and depressing place in which to work. Kildare Street had grown noisy with traffic, and Kildare Place itself served as a car park. Thus the governors began to look for an alternative site. The economic expansion of the country and the increased government investment in education meant that capital building grants would be available, and the central city site in Kildare Street would be a much coveted purchase for building developers. Canon Ross was ably advised by the governors throughout these important years of decision. F. La T. Godfrey, SFTCD was the chairman of the Finance Committee and Dr. W. F. Pyle, M.A., FTCD; R. Mitchell; John N.

Ross, LL.B.; W. H. H. Cooke, F.R.I.A.I.; Benjamin Plunket, M.V.O.; J. A. Kyle and John Wilson-Wright were all active members. Canon J. W. Armstrong, dean of St. Patrick's (later archbishop of Armagh) also served on the Finance Committee.

In 1963 the college received an unexpected offer for the Kildare Place site from a London construction company (Messrs. Laing). At the same time the residence and extensive ground of Rathmines Castle became available on the market, and the owner, Mrs. Jobling-Purser, was prepared to give the college the first offer. In April 1963 a contract for the sale of Kildare Place was signed and the purchase of Rathmines Castle was made for a sum which allowed the governors to plan and build a spacious and well-equipped new college. A government grant was received from the Department of Finance. The architects Downes, Meehan and Robson were engaged to design the new buildings which had to meet the strict requirements of the Department of Education. Rathmines Castle was demolished but the outhouses and stables were renovated for residential use and the walled gardens and trees were preserved. The main college block had single study bedrooms for the students and a small separate bungalow for the men students was provided. A principal's residence, a gymnasium, a lecture theatre, a swimming pool, practising schools and a beautiful chapel completed the facilities which were in marked contrast to the dark cramped quarters of the old college. To quote Miss Pearson who experienced both:

> It seemed to me like the release of the old spirit of CITC from surroundings which had become restrictive, and so to speak imprisoned it.[8]

One of the arrangements made for the new college was the integration of Coláiste Moibhí into the training college. In 1961 the other preparatory colleges had been closed by the government. They had been very expensive to run and the INTO had criticised the narrow education which these colleges offered to prospective teachers. Moreover, since the secondary schools had now attained the necessary high standard of Irish teaching, the preparatory colleges were no longer necessary. However, for the Church of Ireland the situation was different, for Coláiste Moibhí was the only 'A' School (that is one where subjects were taught through Irish) which Protestant pupils could attend. Insufficient students in the Protestant secondary schools were taking Irish at honours level and if the preparatory college should close it was feared that the training college would be deprived of qualified recruits. Therefore, an appeal led by the principal of Coláiste

Moibhi, Miss Gladys Allen, successfully persuaded the Department of Education to allow Coláiste Moibhí to continue. In 1968 it was agreed that the preparatory college would be housed at Rathmines along with the training college and would offer a two year senior cycle leading to the Leaving Certificate. The pupils, both boys and girls as the years went on, became part of the community life there and added a youthful and eager Irish speaking element to it. Pupils, about 25 per year, from rural and city schools came to the preparatory college to benefit from the rigorous education in the Irish language and culture offered there.

The new college was opened in March 1969 by the Minister for Education, Mr. Brian Lenihan and the official ceremony was attended by the President, the Taoiseach and representatives of the Churches in Ireland. Mr. Lenihan spoke of his pleasure at 'the commitment of our Protestant people to participate in the life and institutions of the country' and of the 'State's commitment to that community'. The new college represented these substantial commitments, not only financial but in terms of the co-operation and mutual support which existed between the State and the Protestant community.. To all who attended the opening ceremony that day, the new buildings symbolised the achievement of long years and the hope for the future.[9] From the early days of the pioneer Kildare Place Society institution, through the dedicated work of the Church Education Society, by the difficult decision to accept the State aid and by a stubborn determination to survive against the odds, the Kildare Place college had upheld its traditions and educated teachers to serve the community in Ireland. It had seen teacher training develop from the simple monitorial system where the trainee teachers were themselves only senior primary school children drilled in the mechanics of school management to a fully developed college, where all students were receiving a third level education taught by a graduate staff. From the practical pioneer work of John Veevers in the 1820s, through the innovative lecturing of W. T. Wilkinson in the Church Education Society College of the 1850s and by the professional knowledge and skill of Jeremiah Henly and his colleagues, Kildare Place had contributed to the overall development of primary education in Ireland and had met the challenges of evolving methodology and ideas. Canon Kingsmill Moore had inherited in 1884 from Canon Alexander Leeper a church college in which a tradition of dedicated service had been established and he had integrated this into the state national system of education and had given the Church of Ireland primary school teachers second to none.

He had been in the forefront of the struggle to develop the denominational training colleges and he had been spokesman for his church's rights in education. His successors Canon Hodges, Dr. Simms, and Canon R. J. Ross had upheld these traditions and had brought the college through the difficult days of retrenchment and adjustment until it emerged strong and renewed in the 1960s.

Conclusion

Thus established in its new premises, the Church of Ireland College of Education as it now became known rapidly developed in the 1970s into a confident and expanding third-level institution. The introduction of the three year Bachelor in Education degree for primary teachers was for CICE a natural development of its long standing links with Dublin University. The college of education students became fully registered university students at Trinity College throughout their three years, attending lectures there in education. A fourth year for the honours B.Ed. degree was also offered.

A new curriculum has been introduced into national schools which places increased emphasis on the creative and artistic potential of the child and allows for much more individual and group learning in the classroom. The colleges of education played a leading role in preparing their students to undertake this new curriculum and its successful implementation depended much on their ready co-operation and enthusiastic response. Miss Millicent Fitzsimons, the vice-principal of CICE (1967—1977), played an important part in encouraging her students to adapt to the new approaches in practical teaching and to understand the underlying principles of the new curriculum. The college met the needs of the new situation by the development of the library and audio-visual resources with professional staff. In terms of staffing and facilities the college is well placed to meet the inevitable demands that micro-technology will make on those engaged in teacher training.

CITC also began to develop a research area to further the study of education and under the firm guidance of the new principal, Dr. Kenneth Milne, has built up a collection of printed and manuscript materials which contains many of the official education reports of the nineteenth and twentieth century. It is hoped to develop a museum of Irish education on the premises and already the nucleus of a historical text-book library is in being.

Thus in 1984 when the Church of Ireland College of Education celebrates its hundred years as a national teacher training college, it can look to the past with pride and to the future with confidence. It was appropriate that in the year leading up to the celebrations of the centenary, a Past Students' Association came into being by the spontaneous action of those of many generations who wished to keep alive their association with Kildare Place at Rathmines.

NOTES

Chapter I (pp.17–36)

1 Regulations of the Society for Promoting the Education of the Poor in Ireland (S.P.E.P.I.), *4th Annual Report*, 1816. Also H. Kingsmill Moore, *An Unwritten Chapter in the History of Education* (London, 1904).
2 *Fourth Report of the Commissioners of the Board of Education in Ireland*, p.6; H.C. 1812–13, (21.) VI.
3 *Ibid.*
4 *First Report of the Commissioners of Irish Education Inquiry*, pp.40–47; H.C. 1825 (400.) XII.
5 *Letter from Lord Stanley, Chief Secretary for Ireland to His Grace the Duke of Leinster, on the formation of a Board of Commissioners of Education, October 1831*; H.C. 1831–32 (196.) XXIX. 757.
6 D. Salmon (ed.), *The Practical Parts of Lancaster's "Improvements" and Bell's "Experiments"* (London, 1922), p.3.
7 *4th Annual Report of S.P.E.P.I.*, 1816.
8 Kildare Place Society Archives, Box I, General Correspondence, No. 46.
9 See Carol Revington, 'The Kildare Place Society, its principles and policy', unpublished M.Ed. thesis, University of Dublin, 1981.
10 K.P.S., MS.680, Male Teachers' Register, 1814–25.
11 K.P.S., Box 36, Model School, No. 1.
12 *5th Annual Report of S.P.E.P.I.*, 1817, p.22.
13 K.P.S. archives, Box 16, Inspectors' Correspondence I, No. 3. See also E. O'Heideain, *National School Inspection in Ireland: the Beginnings* (Dublin, 1967).
14 *5th Annual Report of S.P.E.P.I.*, 1817, p.22.
15 *First Report of Irish Education Inquiry*, 1825, p.58.
16 *10th Annual Report of S.P.E.P.I.*, 1822, p.23.
17 *6th Annual Report of S.P.E.P.I.*, 1818, Appendix IV, p.43.
18 *Ibid.* p.56.

19 *First Report of Irish Education Inquiry*, 1825, Appendix 203, p.449.

20 *First Report of Irish Education Inquiry*, 1825, p.41.

21 K. Silber, *Pestalozzi, the Man and His Work* (London, 1960).

22 P. C. Williams, 'Pestalozzi John', unpublished Ph.D. thesis, University of Dublin, 1965. Also P. C. Williams, 'Pestalozzi and John Synge', *Hermathena*, cvi, (1968), pp.23-39.

23 *The School Master's Manual* (Dublin, 1825), p.67

24 *18th Annual Report of S.P.E.P.I.*, 1830, p.38.

25 *First Report of Irish Education Inquiry*, 1825, Appendix 207, pp.470-83.

26 *First Report of Irish Education Inquiry*, 1825, p.42.

27 K.P.S., Box 2, General Correspondence, No. 80.

28 *Ibid.*, No. 85.

29 K.P.S., MS.684, Female Teachers' Register, 1824—55.

30 *12th Annual Report of S.P.E.P.I.*, 1825, Appendix VI.

31 K.P.S., MS.688, Observation Book of Martha Donaldson, MS.688a, Observation Book of Elizabeth Crowther.

32 K.P.S., MS.691(3), Terms for receiving female teachers into training schools.

33 *12th Annual Report of S.P.E.P.I.*, 1825, Appendix IX.

34 *9th Annual Report of S.P.E.P.I.*, 1821, Appendix VII.

35 *Report of the Select Committee appointed to take into consideration the State of the Poorer Classes in Ireland*, p.601; H.C. 1830 (667.) VII.

36 *29th Annual Report of S.P.E.P.I.*, 1842.

37 Taylor, W. Cooke, *Notes on a visit to the model schools* (Dublin, 1847), p.49.

38 K.P.S., Box 36, Model School, 1814—53, No. 51.

39 *Report from the Selection Committee of the House of Lords appointed to inquire into the Practical working of the system of National Education*, Part II, pp.382—6; H.C. 1854 (525.) XV, pt.II.

Chapter II (pp.37—56)

1 D. H. Akenson, *The Irish Education Experiment* (London, 1970), pp.187—202.

2 *1st Report of the Church Education Society*, 1840.

3 *11th Report of the Church Education Society*, 1850.

4 Representative Church Body Library, Church Education Society records, MS.19, Sub-Committees Rough Proceedings Book.

5 *2nd Report of the C.E.S.*, 1841.

6 C.E.S., MS.19.

7 C.E.S., MS.47, Applications for Admission, 1855—81.

8 *15th Report of C.E.S.*, 1855.

9 Archdeacon of Emly, *An Address Delivered to the Schoolmasters and Schoolmistresses under the Church Education Society* (Dublin, 1850).

10 *Royal Commission on Primary Education (Ireland)* (*Powis*), Vol. VIII, *Returns of the Church Education Society*, pp. 947–1000; H.C. 1870 (C.6VII), XXVIII, Part V. Also G. D. Burtchaell and T. U. Sadleir (ed.), *Alumni Dublinenses (1593–1846)* (London, 1924).

11 'Obituary of Miss Jane Lewis', *Church of Ireland Training College Magazine*, July 1889.

12 *16th Report of the C.E.S.*, 1856.

13 C.E.S. records, MS.49, Applications for Schoolmasters and Schoolmistresses.

14 *13th Report of the C.E.S.*, 1852.

15 *Powis Commission, 1870*, Vol. VIII, *Returns of the C.E.S.*, pp.986–99.

16 *Ibid.*

17 C.E.S. records, MS.48, Register of Male and Female Teachers, 1855–83.

18 *Powis Commission, 1870*, Vol. VIII, *Returns of the C.E.S.*, p.994.

19 K.P.S. archives, C.E.S. college examination papers, 1864, 1867.

20 W. T. Wilkinson, *The Training of Teachers—a course of Lectures on Education* (Dublin, n.d.).

21 S. Sadie (ed.), *The New Grove Dictionary of Music and Musicians* (London, 1980), Vol. 5, p.103; Vol. 19, pp.61–5.

22 *Powis Commission, 1870*, Vol. VIII, *Returns of the C.E.S.*, p.995.

23 *Ibid.*

24 Akenson, *The Irish Education Experiment*, pp.285–94. Also D. H. Akenson, *The Church of Ireland, ecclesiastical reform and revolution, 1800–1885* (New Haven and London, 1971), pp.201–6.

25 *40th Report of C.N.E.I. for 1873*; H.C. 1874 (C.965).

26 *Powis Commission, 1870*, Vol. VIII, *Returns of the C.E.S.*, p.949.

27 *Powis Commission, 1870*, Vol. III, *Minutes of Evidence*, pp. 282–310; H.C. 1870 (C.611), XXVIII, part iii.

28 *Powis Commission, 1870*, Vol. I, Part I, *Report of the Commissioners*, p. 421. Also Vol. II, Part II, *Special Reports*, pp. 800–25.

29 *Report of C.E.S.*, 1872. Also *Journal of the General Synod of the Church of Ireland*, 1872.

30 *Letter of November 1874 by the Chief Secretary to the Lord Lieutenant in Ireland to the Commissioners of National Education in Ireland, and their reply*; H.C. 1875 (70.) LIX, 489.

31 *Memorials from the Council of the National Education League for Ireland . . . and from the Elementary Education Committee of the General Assembly of the Presbyterian Church in Ireland on the subject of non-vested training colleges*; H.C. 1875 (210.) LIX, 509.

32 *Reports of C.E.S.*, 1875, 1876.

Chapter III (pp.57–85)

1 *Journal of the General Synod of the Church of Ireland*, 1878, p.29.
2 *Journal of the General Synod*, 1879, Report of the Board of Religious Education, pp.222–5.
3 F. D. How, *William Conyngham Plunket* (London, 1900). See also W. C. Plunket, *A Short visit to the Connemara Missions* (London, 1863).
4 W. G. Brooke, *Statement of the Proceedings from 1892–1895 in connection with the admission of women to Trinity College, Dublin* (Dublin, 1895). Also *Alexandra College Magazine*, June 1907.
5 *Who was Who, 1897–1915* (London, 1967), p. 247. Also W. S. Churchill, *Lord Randolph Churchill* (London, 1951); L. Whiteside, *A History of the King's Hospital* (Dublin, 1975).
6 *30th–50th Reports of the CNEI*, 1870–83.
7 *Journal of the General Synod*, 1882, p.x.
8 *Journal of the General Synod*, 1883, Report of the Recorder's Committee, pp.99–104.
9 *Correspondence between the Irish Government and the Commissioners of National Education on the Subject of Training Schools in Ireland*; H.C. 1883 (144.) LIII 471.

It has not proved possible to locate the specific file of correspondence in the Chief Secretary's Office Registered Papers. One file located CSORP 1883 24758 would suggest that the Lord Lieutenant, Earl Spencer, himself played an active part in working out the details of the scheme.

10 *Journal of the General Synod*, 1884, Report on the Standing Committee, pp. 108–14.
11 Minute Book of the Church of Ireland Training College Management Committee, June 1884.
12 *Report of the Organising Committee of CITC*, September, 1884.
13 M. Hurley (ed.), *Irish Anglicanism, 1869–1969* (Dublin, 1969), p.52.
14 H. Kingsmill Moore, *Reminiscences and Reflections* (London, 1930).
15 T. J. O'Connell, *One Hundred Years of Progress 1868–1968* (Dublin, 1968), pp.4–8. Also *Vice-Regal Committee of Inquiry into Primary Education (Ireland), 1913*; H.C. 1913 (Cd.6838) XII; 1914 (Cd.7235) XXVIII.
16 *Queen's University Bulletin*, No. 82 (February, 1982). I am grateful to Mr. D. H. Wilson, Administrative Services Secretary, Q.U.B., for information.
17 'Obituary', *Irish Times*, 5th August 1931. Also *CITC Report*, 1930–31.
18 'Obituary', *Irish Times*, 11th October 1944.
19 'Funeral Notice', *Irish Times*, May 1914. I am grateful to Mrs. Dona Mollan, niece of Miss Mary Jane Smith, for information.
20 *Report of the Organising Committee of CITC*, 1884.

21 Minutes of the Board of Governors of CITC, July 1884.
22 *CITC Report*, 1884–85.
23 *Educational Endowments (Ireland) Commission, Scheme 2*, 1887.
24 CITC, Programme of the 'Great Bazaar', 1886.
25 *CITC Reports*, 1884–90.
26 *54th Report of CNEI*, 1887, pp.21–5.
27 CITC, Register of Students, 1884–1910.
28 *CITC Report*, 1886–87.
29 Robinson, B., *The Kindergarten Practice for the use of teachers* (Belfast, 1887), p.1.
30 CITC, copy of College Song.
31 CITC, Minute Book of the Church of Ireland Training College Students' Association and Mutual Improvement Society, 1885–1891.
32 *CITC Report*, 1886–87.
33 CITC archives, *Church of Ireland Training College Magazine, 1886*–92.
34 *CITC Reports*, 1888–1905. A list of prize-winners is given in the appendix.
35 See J. McIvor, *The Presbyterian Church and Education* (Dublin, 1968).
36 *CITC Report*, 1886–87.
37 *54th Report of CNEI*, p.25.
38 *CITC Reports*, 1884–90.
39 *CITC Report*, 1888–89.

Chapter IV (pp.86–103)

1 F. O'Dwyer, *Lost Dublin* (Dublin, 1980). Sir T. N. Deane was knighted in 1890 and his son, Sir T. M. Deane, in 1911.
2 *CITC Report*, 1888–89; 1889–90.
3 Letter from Lord Spencer, October 1883, CSORP 1883 24758.
4 P. J. Walsh, *William J. Walsh, Archbishop of Dublin* (Dublin, 1928), pp.473–77.
5 *57th Report of CNEI*, 1890–91, pp.19–28.
6 H.C. 1890–91 (391.) X.421.
7 Kingsmill Moore, *Reminiscences*, pp. 158–60.
8 *Our Lady of Mercy College Centenary Booklet, 1877–1977* (Dublin, 1977). Also *St. Patrick's College, Drumcondra Centenary Booklet, 1875–1975)* (Dublin, 1975).
9 CITC, Kingsmill Moore Correspondence.
10 *CITC College Magazine*, October 1892, October 1893.
11 CITC, T. N. Deane and Son, Building Plans, 1900.
12 *Report of Mr. F. H. Dale, His Majesty's Inspector of Schools, Board of Education, on Primary Education in Ireland*; H.C. 1904 (Cmd. 1981) XX.947.

13 *Bill for the distribution and application of certain duties of Customs and Excise: and for other purposes connected therewith*; H.C. 1890 (244.) V.245.

14 *Journal of the General Synod of the Church of Ireland*, 1891 Report of the Standing Committee, p.170.

15 *Bill to Improve National Education in Ireland*; H.C. 1892 (234.) IV.635.

16 CITC, Minute Book of the Free Education Sub-Committee of the Standing Committee of the Church of Ireland, 1891–92. Also H. Kingsmill Moore, *£200,000 a year for Irish Education, How may it best be spent?* (Dublin, 1892).

17 *Correspondence between the Irish Government and the Commissioners of National Education for Ireland . . . in relation to certain proposed changes under which grants are made by Parliament for Elementary Education in Ireland*; H.C. 1893 (55.) LXVIII.637. See also H. H. Dickinson, *The Present Crisis in Elementary Education in Ireland* (Dublin, 1896).

18 *CITC Reports*, 1890–99.

19 H. Kingsmill Moore, *A History of the Incorporated Society* (Dublin, 1938). Also K. Milne, 'Irish Charter Schools', *Irish Journal of Education*, viii, 1 (1974), pp.3–39.

20 E. Cholmondeley, *The Story of Charlotte Mason* (London, 1960).

21 CITC; a photograph of the scroll was kindly presented by Major J. B. Condon of Surrey in 1980.

22 Letter from E. Cholmondeley to the author, August 1979.

23 J. O. Browne and S. M. Parkes, 'Annie Lloyd Evans', *History of Education Society Bulletin*, No. 29 (Spring 1982), pp.36–40. Also records of Furzedown College, Greater London Record Office.

24 CITC, Minute Books of the Educational Research Club, 1891–99.

25 *CITC Reports*, 1895–99.

26 H. Clayton, *To School Without Shoes—a brief history of the Sunday School Society for Ireland* (Dublin, 1979).

27 CITC, Church of Ireland Educational Association Scrapbook, 1891–96.

28 *Select Committee on Teachers' Registration and Organization Bill*, pp.509–20; H.C. 1890–91 (335.) XVII. Also *Commission on Intermediate Education in Ireland, Minutes of Evidence*, pp.439–45; H.C. 1899 (C.9512) XXIII.

29 Kingsmill Moore, *Reminiscences*, p.197.

30 *Irish Church Hymnal* (Dublin, 1960).

31 *CITC Report*, 1903–04.

32 *CITC Report*, 1897–98.

Chapter V (p.104–124)

1 *Rules and Regulations of CNEI*, 1902 (Dublin, 1902), Appendix, pp.15–56.
2 *Royal Commission on Manual and Practical Instruction in Primary Schools under the Board of National Education in Ireland, Minutes of Evidence*, pp.55–61, 379–408; H.C. 1897 (8383.) XLIII.
3 *Rules and Regulations of CNEI*, 1898 (Dublin, 1898), Appendix, pp.132–40.
4 T. J. O'Connell, *One Hundred Years of Progress* (Dublin, 1968), pp.335–7.
5 CITC, Newspaper Cutting Book, *Freeman's Journal*, 2nd February 1903.
6 Minutes of CITC, 18th March 1903.
7 *Vice-Regal Committee of Inquiry into Primary Education*; H.C. 1913 XXII; 1914 XXVIII.
8 See A. Hyland, 'Educational Innovation – a case history. An analysis of the Revised Programme of 1900 for national schools in Ireland', unpublished M.Ed. thesis, University of Dublin, 1973.
9 *CITC Reports*, 1901–03.
10 CITC, NCB, *Irish Independent*, 30th March 1904; *Irish Times*, 4th April 1904.
11 T. J. O'Connell, *op. cit.*, pp. 151–54.
12 CITC, Kingsmill Moore Correspondence.
13 *Irish Times*, 25th April 1900.
14 CITC, Kingsmill Moore Correspondence. Also Kingsmill Moore, *Reminiscences*, pp. 245–9.
15 *Report of the Standing Committee of the General Synod of the Church of Ireland*, Appendix, Statistics of Schools in the Province of Dublin (Dublin, 1903).
16 Kingsmill Moore, *Reminiscences*, pp.249–52; also *CITC Report*, 1927.
17 CITC, *Resolution of the Conference of Church of Ireland Managers of National Schools*, 1903. Also D. H. Miller, *Church, State and Nation, 1898–1921 (Dublin, 1973), pp.80*–86, 118–24.
18 *Rules and Regulations of CNEI*, 1898 (Dublin, 1898), Appendix, pp.132–40.
19 CITC, NCB, 'Hints to Students Seeking Admission', 1904.
20 *CITC Report*, 1912.
21 CITC archives, NCB, 1904.
22 *CITC Reports*, 1900–20.
23 *CITC Report*, 1903–04.
24 *The Centenary Book of the Church of Ireland Training College* (Dublin, 1911).
25 *CITC Reports*, 1910–12.
26 *Proceedings of the Commissioners of National Education relating to*

Rule 127 (b) of the Code of Regulations; H.C. 1905 (184.) IX.371. Also T. J. O'Connell, pp. 138–40.

27 *CITC Report*, 1913–14.
28 *Ibid.*
29 Tablet in St. Patrick's Cathedral, Dublin.
30 *CITC Report*, 1914–15.
31 *CITC Report*, 1912–1913.

Chapter VI (pp.125–153)

1 *CITC Report*, 1917–18.
2 Minutes of CITC, 17th April 1918.
3 Notes from Miss Edith E. Gillespie (1917–19), February 1981.
4 *CITC Report*, 1921–22.
5 *CITC Report*, 1917–18.
6 *Dublin University Calendar*, 1918–19.
7 Minutes of CITC, 18th December 1918.
8 Minutes of CITC, 28th February 1919.
9 TCD, J. H. Bernard Correspondence, MS.170.
10 Bernard Correspondence, MS.173.
11 Minutes of CITC, 15th July 1919.
12 John Coolahan, 'The Education Bill of 1919—Problems of Educational Reform', *Proceedings of the Educational Studies Association of Ireland Conference, Dublin 1979.* (Officina Typographica, Galway, 1980).
13 *CITC Report*, 1919–20.
14 Minutes of CITC, 20th April 1921. Also Kingsmill Moore, *Reminiscences*, p.306.
15 Minutes of CITC, 15th June 1921. Also Trinity College Board Register 22, 21st June 1921.
16 Minutes of CITC, 15th July 1919.
17 Trinity College Board Register 21, 24th June 1919. Also D.U. Calendar, 1923–24, p.76.
18 TCD Board Register 23, 11th March 1922.
19 Bernard Correspondence, MS.343.
20 TCD Board Register 23, 3rd June 1922.
21 Bernard Correspondence, MSS.385, 387, 388.
22 *Ibid.*, MSS.390, 396.
23 Minutes of CITC, 4th June 1923.
24 *D.U. Calendar*, 1923–24, pp.304–5.
25 Bernard Correspondence, MSS.444, 450, 451.
26 TCD Board Register 22, 26th November 1921, 10th December 1921.
27 Minutes of CITC, 5th April 1922.
28 Minutes of CITC, 18th October 1922.

29 *Northern Ireland Ministry of Education Annual Report*, 1922–23, p.57.
30 *N.I. Ministry of Education Annual Report*, 1923–24, pp. 25–28. Also R. Marshall, *A History of Stranmillis College, Belfast* (Belfast, 1972).
31 Minutes of CITC, 21st February 1923. (The final paragraph of the draft minutes was deleted). Also D. H. Akenson, *Education and Enmity, The Control of Schooling in Northern Ireland, 1920–50* (Newton Abbot, 1973).
32 Marshall, *History of Stranmillis*, pp.10–12.
33 Minutes of CITC, 30th May 1924.
34 Department of Education, *National Programme of Primary Instruction* (Dublin, 1922).
35 George Seaver, *John Allen Fitzgerald Gregg* (Dublin, 1963).
36 Kingsmill Moore, *Reminiscences*, p.288.
37 Minutes of CITC, 19th December 1923.
38 *Ibid.*
39 Evidence of the Church of Ireland General Synod Board of Education to the Second National Programme Conference, 1926.
40 *Report of the Second National Programme Conference* (Dublin, 1926).
41 Minutes of CITC, 13th December 1922.
42 CITC, Candidate Teachers' Training Fund Minute Book, 1924–31.
43 Seaver, *Gregg*, p.190.
44 *Ibid.*
45 *Department of Education Report*, 1925–26, p.22.

Chapter VII (pp.154–176)

1 'An Appreciation', *Irish Times*, 24th April 1980.
2 *CITC Reports*, 1928–1939.
3 See T. J. O'Connell, *One Hundred Years of Progress* (Dublin, 1968), pp.199–273.
4 *CITC Report*, 1930–31.
5 *Department of Education Report*, 1931–32, p.15.
6 *CITC Report*, 1929–30.
7 *Belfast Telegraph*, 21st May 1934. I am indebted to Miss E. E. Gillespie of Belfast for details of Miss Beattie's career.
8 Notes of Kildare Place Ex-Students' Association in Northern Ireland sent to the author by Miss E. E. Gillespie in 1981.
9 Newspaper cutting sent by Miss E. E. Gillespie.
10 *D.U. Calendar*, 1930–31, p.35.*
11 *CITC Report*, 1947–48.
12 *CITC Report*, 1938–39.
13 *Department of Education Report*, 1931–32, p.15.
14 *Ibid.*
15 CITC, NCB, *Irish Times*, 23rd November 1931.

16 *Ibid.*, *Irish Times*, 2nd August 1933. I am grateful to Miss E. Pearson for details of these activities.
17 'An Appreciation' by A. Phillips, *Irish Times*, 25th March 1980.
18 CITC, 'Notes on Coláiste Moibhí, 1927.
19 Department of Education, Examinations for Preparatory Colleges, 1929–39.
20 CITC, NCB, 14th February 1938.
21 *Ibid.*
22 *CITC Reports*, 1931–36.
23 *CITC Reports*, 1937–39.
24 Department of Education, *Programme for Students in Training*, 1933–34.
25 Interview with Miss E. Pearson, January 1981.
26 *CITC Report*, 1930–31.
27 *D.U. Calendar*, 1932–33, p.81.
28 *CITC Report*, 1935–36.
29 CITC, Chapel Trust 1933, Saorstát Éireann, High Court of Justice.
30 CITC, NCB, 14 November 1961.
31 *Report of the Church of Ireland Conference Commemorating the 1500th Anniversary of the Church of Ireland* (Dublin, 1932).
32 *CITC Report*, 1942–43, E. C. Hodges, 'A Review of the Church of Ireland Training College, 1927–43'.
33 *CITC Report*, 1942–43.

Chapter VIII (pp.177–185)

1 *CITC Report*, 1938–39.
2 *CITC Report*, 1950–51.
3 *CITC Report*, 1940–41.
4 Notes sent by Mr. Joe Williams, pupil at the Kildare Place Model Schools, 1949–53, to the author in 1983.
5 *CITC Report*, 1951–52.
6 John Coolahan, 'Education in the Training Colleges', in *Two Centenary Lectures—Carysfort College, 1877–1977* (Dublin, 1981).
7 *CITC Report*, 1960–61.
8 C. Revington, 'Developments within the Church of Ireland Training College in the 1950s and 1960s', unpublished M.Ed. paper, TCD, 1979.
9 *Irish Times*, 14th March 1969.

APPENDIX A

Prize Winners

List of prize winners at the Church of Ireland Training College (compiled from the college annual reports).

Kingsmill Moore Prize

Founded in 1928 to commemorate the devoted services to the college of the Reverend Henry Kingsmill Moore D.D., F.L.S., Principal of the college from 1884 to 1927, and awarded to the student of the college who at the end of the first year obtained the highest marks at the Trinity College Examinations.

1929	Elizabeth Jane B. Griffin, Charlotte Noreen Quigley
1930	Thomas Groves
1931	Eamonn Cristóir de Bhairéad
1932	Vera Glansford, Bláthnaid M. Ní Mhuilleóir
1933	Mary Seymour
1934	Máire Nic Uilcin
1935	Doireann Tate
1936	Eric Mac Seartha
1937	Ida Mary Warren
1938	Margaret Mitchell
1939	Victor S. Mac Cruithneachtáin
1940	Carthannacht Ní Fhuarthain
1941	Anna Ní Longaigh
1942	Dóirin M. Ní Bhreághdha
1943	Maighréad S. Ni Laoghaire
1944	Siobhán Máire de Brun
1945	Eibhlís Ní Thréanlámhaigh
1946	Pádraicin M. Nic Gabhann
1947	Violet H. Manning

1948 G. Langrell
1949 Seoirse A. Mac Aoidh
1950 Florence R. J. Walsh
1951 Glaidis Ní Shluáin
1952 Doreen Armstrong, Olive M. Groves
1953 Gladys Dalton
1954 Elizabeth M. Stanley
1955 Euphemia M. Martin
1956 A. N. A. Poynton
1957 A. M. Ferguson
1958 V. M. Barkman
1959 Rita Adamson
1960 M. J. Allen
1961 E. A. Griffin
1962 I. A. Colhoun
1963 M. Kenny, M. S. Stephenson
1964 H. M. Dempsey
1965 D. T. D. Colhoun, L. J. Warren
1966 K. P. Russell
1967 P. C. Long

Old Principal's Prize

Founded by Senator Kingsmill Moore in 1945 in memory of his father Reverend Canon Henry Kingsmill Moore D.D., F.L.S., Principal of the College from 1884 to 1927, and awarded to the student or students of the College who at the end of the first year of Training showed most promise as teachers.

1946 Pádraicín M. Ní Gabhann
1947 Violet M. Dagg
1948 Maedhbh O. Ní Chonlocha
1949 Seoirse A. Mac Aoidh
1950 Máighréad Nic Aoidh
1951 Sinéad Ludgate
1952 Doreen M. Armstrong
1953 Mary Isobel Peoples
1954 Sarah E. Bonar
1955 Elizabeth J. Schofield
1956 A. G. Kee
1957 W. A. Wright
1958 H. P. Clinton, M. B. McConkey, M. S. Langley
1959 E. M. McCutcheon, I. E. Neill
1960 M. J. Allen
1961 I. G. Wright

1962	A. M. Beamish, F. M. Kelly
1963	B. M. Sweetnam
1964	F. M. Atkinson
1965	R. E. Davidson
1966	E. J. Morrow
1967	H. S. Smith

Wilson and Suffern Medals

Founded by Mr. and Mrs. R. M. Wilson (née Suffern), 1905, for the best teacher of the year. Open to women students only.

	GOLD	SILVER
1905	Alice M. Wright Mary F.Lindsay	Mary E. Adams
1906	Mary E. Warren	Elizabeth Orr
1907	Achsah L. Crampton	Mary Mohan
1908	Gladys Carter	Olive Iris Kidd
1909	Kathleen J. Orr Annie B. Douglas	Agnes J. Cumming
1910	Jenny Wilson	Isabella M. MacNamee Fanny Sullivan
1911	Elizabeth M. M. Flavelle	Mary Anne Boardman
1912	Jessica Monica Adkins	Violet Leckey
1913	Jeannie Yarr	Eileen Graham
1914	Mary Jane Hanlon	Elizabeth Maud Stafford
1915	Thomasina Longmore	Jane Gordon Magill Grace McKeown Watson
1916	Rachel England	Ellen Jane England
1917	Theresa Wilson	Elizabeth Dawson Olivia M. Rogan
1918	Florence M. Horner	Mabel B. Ireland
1919	Alexandra E. MacWilliam	Edith M. Parkinson Susanna P. Stuart
1920	Stella E. Bracegirdle	Mary A. McA. Barton
1921	Katherine Landon	Martha D. Walker
1922	Evaline M. Gransden	Rachel J. McCreery
1923	Grace Anna Winter	Emily Letitia Hall
1924	Elizabeth Heatley	Helen M. Connellan
1925	Helen Irvine	Elizabeth Alexandra Leadbeater
1926	Elizabeth Lalor	Hazel Campbell Margery Jane O'Brien
1927	Jessie A. Lowry	Violet J. Gordon
1928	Frances Elizabeth McQuade	*no award*
1929	Muriel Collier	Marie Elizabeth Burns

	GOLD	SILVER
1930	Mabel Irene Connell	Elizabeth F. Empey
1931	Moireen F. V. Wall	*no award*
1932	Roise Ní Dheaghain	Evelyn Elizabeth Matthews
1933	Bláthnaid M. Ní Mhuilléoir	Ailís E. de Brun
1934	Elizabeth Stuart	Salcuach Nic Aodha
1935	Ethel Wildman	Irene Ní Thomáis
1936	Oilbhe Nic Aodha	Edith Lilian Knott
1937	Lilian Margaret Johnson	Geraldine Margaret Griffin
1938	Maisie E. Kilroy	Mary Ann Barlow
1939	Máighréad Ní Mhistéil	Gladas M. Ní Allmhuin
		Elizabeth Beamish
1940	Isibéal Bucston	Doireann Ní Fharannáin
1941	Nóra Ní Shaoibhriuch	Síle Ní Thréanlámhaigh
1942	Salchuach S. de Carraig	Máire Nic Annraoi
1943	Dóirín M. Ní Bhreághdha	Eilís M. de Bhulf
1944	Máighréad S. Ní Laoghaire	*no award*
	Sinéad E. Nic Liam	
1945	Áine Ní Dhucló	Louisa M. Mistéal
		Caitlín Nic Pháidín
1946	Eibhlis Ni Thréanlámhaigh	Oilbhe M. Ní Thionael
	Máire P. Ní Bhromhnaill	
1947	Máigréad S. Ní Shiubhlaidhe	Una P. Sheartha
1948	Hilda A. Bagnall	Eilís Ní Ghibhealltáin
1949	Oilbhe P. Ní Mhistéal	Maedhbh O. Ní Chonlocha
		Proinnsias M. Ní Shluagháin
1950	Rhona Donaldson	Máighréad M. Ní Dhuinn
1951	Máighréad Nic Aoidh	Phyllis Somers
1952	Sinéad Ludgate	Áine Beula Ní Mhórdha
1953	Martha Hepburn	Mabel C. Johnston
		Phyllis E. I. Broomfield
1954	*no award*	Kathleen S. Hughes
		Gladys A. Dalton
1955	A. E. Johnston	E. M. C. Stanley
1956	V. G. Gilmour	E. J. Judge
1957	M. V. Roycroft	D. Hill
		A. G. Kee
1958	E. Killen	W. Wright
1959	M. S. Langley	H. P. Clinton
		D. A. Siney
1960	M. E. Layng	M. J. Steele
1961	M. N. McGirr	M. E. Somers
1962	M. Fannin	S. Lyttle
1963	D. Hillis	J. Eastwood
		C. A. E. Ruttle

	GOLD	SILVER
1964	M. Kenny	F. M. Dowse
	B. Sweetnam	M. E. Stephenson
1965	*no award*	M. E. J. Wallace
		E. M. Adair
1966	*no award*	I. E. McKinley
		L. M. Noble
1967	K. P. Russell	D. T. S. Colhoun

Mackay Wilson Medals

Founded by Mr. and Mrs. R. M. Wilson, 1894, for the two best lessons in Holy Scripture or Church Formularies. Open to men students only.

	GOLD	SILVER
1895	Frederick Martin	Thomas Storey
1896	*no award*	Walter Crane
		Samuel Mayes
1897	Samuel Bryson	Robert Gurd
1898	James G. Boyd	John Whisker
1899	R. H. Egar	J. C. C. Oliver
		Wm. Macourt
1900	J. H. Crane	F. P. Dodd
1901	Arthur G. Camp	Wm. C. Bradley
		Chas. H. Glasgow
1902	Duncan Anderson	Robert M'Ilroy
		James Vizard
1903	Ernest W. Thomson	James B. Daly
1904	Thomas Chapman	Thomas Guy
1905	John Cambridge	John C. Nelson
		George Pollock
1906	John J. Bradley	Joseph N. Coghlin
1907	Joseph Bradford	James D. Steen
1908	Alfred J. MacGowan	William Hall
1909	John J. V. Boyd	John W. Diver
		David P. Figgins
1910	John W. McMurray	George Power
1911	Henry John Gracey	David Blair Elliott
1912	Alfred W. Steen	James McFadden
1913	Charles Huston	William A. Kirkwood
1914	John Henry West	William H. M. Flanagan
1915	Walter Chiddick	George Blacker
1916	Samuel John Simpson	William Humphrey Harding
1917	Harry D. McCormack	William Crowther

	GOLD	SILVER
1918	William H. Claythorne	William Henry Gordon
1919	*no award*	Robert James Burgess Herbert S. McConnell
1920	Cecil R. J. Anderson	Thomas T. Taggart Robert Wallace
1921	Isaac Dalton	Thomas Spearman
1922	John Alex Williamson	G. Sheridan Jones
1923	*not listed*	*not listed*
1924	Matthew Dickie	Moses R. W. Gillespie
1925	*no award*	David Henry Kenny William J. Whittaker
1926	Edward N. Rowe	Cecil R. D. Abbott James McVeigh
1927	*no award*	William Fell
1928	*no award*	Robert E. Pritchard
1929	*no award*	Albert J. J. Hodgins
1930	George Clarke	*no award*
1931	Thomas Groves	*no award*
1932	Alfred Newburn	Eamonn C. de Bhairead
1933	Robert Smyth	Feardorcha Mac Philib
1934	George Armstrong	Proinnsias Ó Colmain
1935	Frederick Foster	Somhairle Mac Adhaimh
1936	Liam L. S. de Cleir	Proinnsias L. Mac Domhnaill
1937	Archibald G. Adhaimh	Eric Mac Seartha
1938	Fred Stephenson	Riobárd E. O Miurghaile
1939	Proinnsias T. Mac Pheadair	Liam Kleinstuber
1940	Victor Wheatly	Cecil Hyde
1941	*no award*	*no award*
1942	*no award*	*no award*
1943	*no award*	*no award*
1944	*no award*	*no award*
1945	*no award*	*no award*
1946	*no award*	*no award*
1947	*no award*	*no award*
1948	*no award*	*no award*
1949	*no award*	*no award*
1950	*no award*	Seoirse A. Mac Aoidh
1951	*no award*	*no award*
1952	*no award*	*no award*
1953	*no award*	*no award*
1954	*no award*	*no award*
1955	*no award*	*no award*

Lewis Memorial Medals

In memory of Miss Lewis, Vice-Principal of the Women's Department, who entered into her rest, June 1889. Given for the best two lessons in Holy Scripture or Church Formularies. Open to women students only.

	GOLD	SILVER
1891	Louisa Alexander	Emily Savage
1892	Sarah Grant	Margaret H. Staveacre
1893	Kezia Corr	Janet Brandeth
1894	Annie Willis	Mary E. Williamson
1895	Mary Henry	Alice McCombe
1896	Frances S. Warren	Caroline Bradshaw
1897	Mabel A. Hudson	Sarah E. Campbell
		Elizabeth Reid
1898	Annie Bell	Sarah Mac Manaway
1899	Matilda Mac Henry	Harriette F. Ensor
		Mary E. Morton
1900	Frances Hall	F. M. Wray
		H. de Ceise
1901	Mary A. Gilmore	Annie E. Campbell
1902	Annie M. P. Magahy	Florence Roden
1903	Elizabeth M. P. Ribton	Dora Landon
		Rebecca Newel
1904	Charlotte Mc Ilroy	Elizabeth J. Barnett
1905	Mary E. Adams	Alice A. Wright
		Mary F. Lindsay
1906	Elizabeth N. Hamilton	Gertrude Clarke
1907	Achsan L. Crampton	Alice Heaney
1908	Gladys Carter	Margaret Barnett
		Olive Iris Kidd
1909	Kathleen I. Orr	Annie B. Douglas
		Matilda M. Ebbitt
1910	Jenny Wilson	Ellen F. Cambridge
		Jessie Blaney
1911	Mary Anne Boardman	Clara Louisa Griffin
1912	Violet Leckey	Emily McCordick
		Margaret Eleanor Semple
1913	Sarah McKeown	Dora Elizabeth Woodman
1914	Ellen Dickson	Eleanor Sargent
1915	Eileen Georgina Kane	Margaret Lauretta Greene
		Annie Morrison
1916	Florence Bunting	Rachel M. K. England
1917	E. Pollard	Patricia E. Carroll
		Theresa Wilson

APPENDIX A

	GOLD	SILVER
1918	Mabel B. Ireland	Sarah E. McMillan
1919	Alexandra MacWilliam	Katherine A. R. J. King
1920	Nessie MacHenry	Doris Heenan
1921	Constance I. Hewitt	Katherine Landon
1922	Constance Eva Butler	Evaline M. Gransden
1923	Anna Mona Perdue	Isabel Hawkins
1924	Kathleen O'Donnell	Helen Connellan
		Elizabeth Heatley
		Frances E. Leckie
1925	Ruby Giltrap	Ellen E. Barrett
		Elizabeth A. Leadbeater
		Helen Irvine
1926	Bertha Margaret MacDonagh	Elizabeth Clarke
		Dorothy A. V. Walker
1927	Eleonore E. R. Connor	Kathleen Giltrap
1928	*no award*	Mary Stewart Christie
1929	Elizabeth Pollock	Lena F. Christie
1930	Charlotte Noreen Quigley	Elizabeth J. B. Griffin
1931	Elizabeth Empey	Lillian D. M. Wright
1932	Joan Ella Burns	Sarah E. Foster
1933	Olga McIlveen	Vera Glansford
1934	Kathleen Maybury	Elizabeth Craven
1935	Mide Nic Pheadair	Pádraicín Ni Cleirigh
1936	Doireann Tate	Gladys Hunter
1937	Kathleen Louisa Burrows	Eibhlín Ní Irbhin
		Elizabeth Jane Moore
1938	Maisie E. Kilroy	Margaret E. Wilson
1939	Gladas M. Ní Allmhuin	Máighréad Ní Mhistéil
1940	Doireann Ní Fharannáin	Isibéal Bucston
1941	Bhera Ní Chonchubhair	Nóra Ní Shaoibhriuch
1942	Linéad Ní Chinnéide	Salchuach S. de Carraig
1943	Eilís M. de Bhulf	Dóirín M. Ní Bhreághdha
1944	Aoife Ní Dhuacháin	Sorcha Ní Longaigh
1945	Louisa M. Mistéal	Áine P. Ní Dhucló
1946	Eibhlís Ní Thréanlámhaigh	Oilbhe M. Ní Thionael
1947	Máighréad S. Ní Shiubhlaidhe	Una Turner
		Muirgheal L. C. Exell
1948	Eilís Ní Ghibheallháin	Violet H. Manning
1949	Prionnsias M. Ní Shluagháin	Caitlín M. Nic Ghiolla Coinnigh
1950	*no award*	Annie M. Jones
		Doireann Ní Airt
1951	*no award*	Phyllis Somers
1952	*no award*	Jeanette Ludgate

	GOLD	SILVER
1953	*no award*	Olive M. Groves
		Gladys Kee
1954	*no award*	Adelaide A. Walker
1955	*no award*	A. E. Johnston
1956	*no award*	

Smyth Memorial Prizes

For Ancient and Modern History, founded by Mrs. Brien, in memory of her brother, W. T. Smyth, 76 Pembroke Road, who died 8th November, 1884.

1888	Hugh C. Atkinson, Marion Henchy
1889	Marion Henchy, Lucinda Lendrum, Edward Hogan
1890	Joseph J. Crane, Caroline Alcock
1891	Frederick Gibson, Annie Landon, Robert Turner
1892	Henry Atkinson, John Muller, Emily Warren
1893	Daniel Rice, Annie R. Travers
1894	Andrew Pilkington, Eliz. McMeekin, Marg. Walmsley
1895	George C. Keegan, Margaret H. Walker
1896	Frances Warren, William F. Willis
1897	Margaret J. Procter, William Warmington
1898	H. W. Buchanan, Edith Collins
1899	J. Thompson, Agnes McAteer, Harriette Ensor
1900	J. T. Daly, F. M. Wray
1901	Alexander Kilpatrick, Mary J. McKew
1902	James Vizard, Mary J. Young
1903	Alexander White
1904	James Gillespie, Mary Leech
1905	Mary F. Lindsay, William Victor Wray
1906	John J. Bradley, Charlotte Reburn
1907	Robert J. Fannon, Margaret Bond, Charlotte Ruttledge, Harriett Green
1908	Alfred J. MacGowan, Harriett Law
1909	Fredk. W. Date, Rebecca C. Crampton
1910	Maxwell Gillespie, Sophia M. Synnott
1911	Sarah Pilgrim
1912	Violet Leckey, Maud Stevens, Nancy L. Coulter
1913	Robert Scott, Violet A. Campbell, Mary Agnes Ferris
1914	William T. H. Robinson, Margaret H. M'Whirter
1915	Harley Lisle Smith, Winifred Kathleen Smyth
1916	William Humphrey Harding, Louisa Kathleen Stuart
1917	Annie Baxter
1918	Reginald Anketell, Sara Jane Hobson
1919	Adaleen Gallagher

1920	Mary Price
1921	*no award*
1922	John C. Butler
1923	Mary Langley
1924	Sarah A. Davidson, Clifford E. F. Reynolds
1925	Elizabeth Boyle, Aileen Gow Smith
1926	Susan Gertrude Pollock
1927	Richard H. Boyle, Eleonore E. R. Connor
1928	Samuel Ernest McMillan, Jane Chalmers Alexander
1929	John Charles Brennan
1930	James A. McMillan, Helena E. Blennerhassett
1931	Hubert A. Weir, Irene Jane Boyle
1932	Eamonn C. de Bhairead, Ivy Marion Simmons
1933	Evelyn Curry, Annie Groves
1934	Muriel Kelly, Robert Bennett, Elizabeth Craven, Kathleen Maybury
1935	Una Montgomeri, Ella Beamish, Frederick Foster, Constance Dillon, Irene Ní Thomáis
1936	Mary McClure, Doireann Tate, Una Hilton, William Boland
1937	Elizabeth Jane Moore
1938	R. S. Morrow, Eileen F. Hunter
1939	Proinnsias T. Mac Pheadair, Elizabeth Beamish, Margaret Mitchell, Sarah J. Stewart.
1940	Victor Wheatly, Sadie Armour, Dorothy Farnham, Beryl Graham, Alan Doherty.
1941	Carthannacht Ní Fhuarthain, Sile Ní Thréanlámhaigh, Nóra Ní Shaoibhriuch.
1942	Máire Evadine Ní Mhórdha, Seóirsín Nı Fhorbhais Siubhán M. Nic Roil.
1943	Dóirín M. Ní Bhreághdha, Proinnsias Ní Ghúd
1944	Sinéad E. Nic Liam, Aoife E. Ní Dhuacháin, Márta S. Ní Chonlocha
1945	Áine P. Ní Dhucló, Siobhán Máire de Brun, Louisa M. Mistéal.
1946	Eibhlís Ní Thréanlámhaigh, Nuala Ní Ghallchobhair
1947	*no award*
1948	*no award*
1949	Rosaleen G. Langrell
1950	Sorcha G. Nic Chárthaigh
1951	Phyllis Somers
1952	Daphne Free
1953	Gladys Kee, Doreen Armstrong
1954	Mary I. Peoples
1955	A. W. Bryan
1956	H. Sullivan
1957	M. F. Taylor

1958 M. F. Moore
1959 V. M. Barkman
1960 M. J. Steele
1961 E. M. Moore, J. Taylor
1962 M. Fannin
1963 I. Colhoun
1964 S. Blain
1965 G. A. Stanley
1966 D. T. S. Colhoun
1967 C. E. Lee

Mary Smith Memorial Premiums

For singing, founded by the staff and students, past and present in memory of Miss Mary J. Smith, Head Governess from 1884 to 1914.

1916 Florence Bunting, Alice Mary Rumball
1917 Sarah Dennison, Olivia Mary Rogan
1918 Reginald Anketell, Winifred V. Boardman
1919 Robert J. Burgess, Elizabeth S. Robinson
1920 Cecil R. J. Anderson, Victoria P. Boyd
1921 Annseley Tate, Essie G. Graham
1922 John A. Williamson, Dorothy Hill
1923 Matthew Shields, Florence Ferguson
1924 Ethel M. Willis, Alfred M. Clarke
1925 Ruth Savage, David Henry Kenny
1926 Barbara L. McEachern, Cecil R. D. Abbott
1927 Jessie A. Lowry, Kenny Mooney
1928 Florence W. Robinson, John Lusk Brown
1929 Laura E. Patton, George K. Langley
1930 Helena Blennerhassett, William David Boyd
1931 Margaret R. E. Clarke, John C. Kearon
1932 Francis Parke, Roise Ní Dheaghain
1933 Samuel Atkinson, Amy S. Hempenstall
1934 Annraoi O h'Annagain, Sibéal Ní Ruaidh
1935 Somhairle Mac Adhaimh, Máighréad Nic Dhiarmada
1936 Liam L. S. de Cleir, Charlotte G. Joynt
1937 Archibald G. Adhaimh, Annie Deacon
1938 Riobárd E. O Miurghaile, Mary Ann Barlow
1939 William Kleinstuber, Maureen Griffin
1940 Cecil Hyde, Dorothy Farnham
1941 Sile Ní Thréanlámhaigh
1942 Linéad Ní Chinnéide
1943 Fiona E. Ní Dhochartaigh
1944 Sorcha Ní Longaigh

1945	Caitlín Ní Chaidich
1946	Sylvia J. Sargent
1947	Una P. Nic Sheartha
1948	Hilda Bagnall
1949	Bhiola B. Nic Eoghain
1950	Rhona P. Donaldson
1951	Phyllis Somers
1952	Sinéad Ludgate
1953	Doreen Armstrong
1954	Kathleen Ludgate
1955	L. Johnston
1956	S. P. McCarthy
1957	A. M. Draper, A. G. Kee, A. N. A. Poynton
1958	W. A. Wright, S. Farrell
1959	M. A. Jackson, M. I. E. Stewart, M. E. Skelton, I. M. E. Woodhouse.
1960	E. A. Colhoun, O. W. D. Moore, R. Adamson
1961	S. A. V. Larke, E. M. Moore
1962	D.Gow
1963	Teresa Tinkler
1964	M. E. Rogers, Y. Stewart
1965	I. F. E. Lyons, T. F. Deacon
1966	S. J. Millar
1967	C. E. Lee

APPENDIX B

Church of Ireland Training College,
KILDARE PLACE

HINTS TO STUDENTS SEEKING ADMISSION

Candidates for admission to the College are invited to read, and earnestly meditate on, the following Hints as to the disposition and tone of mind necessary for those who hope to become useful and successful teachers:—

I. Cultivate an humble, teachable disposition. Come to your work as *learners*. Consider the importance of the charge you propose to undertake,—to sow the first seeds of Divine truth in immortal beings, and to watch over their opening characters and minds, rooting out the evil and implanting good. *Who is sufficient for these things?* No one in his own strength: seek therefore, earnestly, God's help in prayer; address yourself to every occupation in the spirit of prayer, and of dependence on the Divine blessing.

II. Keep your thoughts steadily fixed on the *one* object that you have in view; let your minds be unembarrassed from every other care and anxiety; recollect that the opportunity which you now seek will, if attained, be a talent which you must diligently husband: learn to be careful not to waste the minutes that may intervene between your stated employments, but to gather up the fragments, that nothing be lost.

III. Endeavour every evening to review and sum up all that you have observed and gained during the day. Unless you carefully endeavour to fix the knowledge you acquire in your minds, it will be either altogether lost, or become too vague and indistinct to be of much use to you in future.

IV. Avoid all negligence in your personal appearance. Let your manners be cheerful, sober, and decorous. Remember that you are to be as lights set on a hill that cannot be hid; that you are expected to exemplify in your conduct all that you teach. We would attach high importance to your office; not that you should be exalted thereby, but that you may seek a strength not your own, and in that strength be careful to maintain good works.

V. Live as brethren. Let Christian courtesy mark your intercourse with your fellow-labourers; show a modest willingness to communicate any knowledge you may possess, and what you freely receive, be ready freely to give. Remember that the God you serve is a God of love; that the lives of the first Christians were eminently marked by love; that the work you propose to engage in is peculiarly a work of love; and let your conduct be a continual exhibition of this distinguishing Christian grace.

[Suggestions for candidates seeking admission to the college, 1904. From a newspaper cuttings book in the college archives.]

APPENDIX C

Church of Ireland Training College,
KILDARE PLACE

Male Students are requested to bring the following articles of apparel:—

2 Suits of Clothes.
1 Outside Coat.
1 Pair of House Shoes.
1 Umbrella.
At least *four* Day Shirts.
2 Night Shirts.
4 Pairs of Socks.
6 Pocket-handkerchiefs.
2 Flannel Vests (if worn).
1 Hair Brush.
1 Comb.
1 Tooth Brush.
6 Collars.
2 Pairs of Cuffs.

All washing apparel must be plainly marked (the name in full) with Marking Ink.

N.B.—Students are required to wear house Shoes in the house.

Church of Ireland Training College,
KILDARE PLACE

Female Candidates are requested to bring the following articles of apparel:—

1 Shawl or Wrap.
2 Hats.
1 Jacket or Mantle.
1 Waterproof or Ulster.
2 Dresses.
2 Outside Petticoats.
2 Flannel do.
6 Pairs Drawers.
6 Chemises.
4 Nightdresses.
4 Pairs Stockings.
4 Bodices.
4 Coarse Aprons.
4 Pairs Cooking Sleeves.
2 Pairs Boots, or 1 Pair Boots and 1 Pair Walking Shoes.
2 Pairs House Shoes.
1 Pair Felt Slippers.
1 Dozen Collars.
8 Pairs Cuffs.
1 Dozen Pocket-Handkerchiefs.
1 Umbrella.
1 Tooth, Nail, Hair, and Clothes Brush.
1 Coarse and 1 Fine Comb.
1 Clothes Bag.
1 Comb Bag.
1 Nightdress Bag.
1 Gymnasium Blouse, dark blue material.

All washing apparel to be marked with name in full with Marking Ink.

All questions relating to the above List to be addressed to the Lady Superintendent.

(From newspaper cuttings book, 1904, in College archives)

SELECT BIBLIOGRAPHY

The records of the Society for Promoting the Education of the Poor in Ireland (The Kildare Place Society) are deposited in the research area of the Church of Ireland College of Education, Dublin 6, and recently have been sorted and listed. The records are extensive and include the Society's minute books, general correspondence, account books, registers of teachers at the training institution and inspectors' reports on the Society's schools. The first principal of CITC, Rev. Canon H. Kingsmill Moore, boxed and numbered most of the Society's correspondence at the beginning of the century when he was working on his book *An Unwritten Chapter in the History of Education*. The content of these boxes was listed in the 1940s by Dr. J. G. Simms and as a tribute to their work the boxes of correspondence have been retained and named the Moore/Simms Collection.

The records of the Church of Ireland Training College are also deposited in the research area and have been sorted but not yet formally listed. They contain minute books, account books, registers of the students in training, photographs, and a small collection of correspondence. The archives also include the printed publications of the Kildare Place Society and many of the education books which were in the training college library. Further purchases of official reports and of text books have been made and it is hoped to create a historical text-book collection and a museum of the history of Irish education on the premises. Permission to consult the records of the Kildare Place Society should be obtained in writing from the Principal, Church of Ireland College of Education, Rathmines, Dublin 6.

I MANUSCRIPT SOURCES

A. Church of Ireland College of Education

1. KILDARE PLACE SOCIETY RECORDS

MSS. 100–111 (Committee minutes and resolutions 1811–87.)
MS. 122A(1–104) (Quarterly reports of the model school sub-committee, 1817–53.)

MS. 680 (List of masters instructed in the Education Society's model school, February 1814–January 1825.)
MS. 681 (List of masters instructed in the Education Society's model school, January 1825–May 1833.)
MS. 682 (List of masters instructed in the Education Society's model school, February 1825–February 1854.)
MS. 684 (List of mistresses instructed in the Education Society's model school, December 1824–February 1834.)
MS. 685 (List of mistresses instructed in the Education Society's model school, December 1824–March 1855.)
MS. 688 (Description and observation written in the model school, Dublin by Martha Donaldson, 9th May–15th July 1836.)
MS. 688a (Description and observation written in the model school, Dublin by Elizabeth Crowther, 9th March–14th July 1838.)
MS. 691 (1–43) (Miscellaneous papers relative to Inspectors' reports of the model school, 1840–43.)
MS. 826 (Original draft plan of schools and buildings for the Kildare Place Society, at Kildare Place by William Farrell, n.d., *c.*1820.)
Kingsmill Moore/Simms Collection:
Box 1–4 (General correspondence, 1811–40.)
Box 16 (Inspectors' correspondence I.)
Box 36 (Model school.)
Box 38 (Teacher training.)

2. CHURCH OF IRELAND TRAINING COLLEGE RECORDS

Board of Governors minute books, 1884–1930.
Training College Management Committee minute book, 1878–1883.
Recorder's sub-committee of the Board of Religious Education minute book, May 1882–April 1884.
Training College sub-committee of the Standing Committee of the Church of Ireland minute book, April 1884–September 1885.
Educational Endowments sub-committee of the Standing Committee of the General Synod minute book, 1885.
Free Education sub-committee of the Standing Committee of the Church of Ireland minute book, 1891–92.
Registers of male and female students, 1884–1930.
Candidate Teachers' Training Fund minute book, 1924–31.
CITC Education Research Club minute books, 1891–99.
Church of Ireland Educational Association scrapbook, 1891–96.
Newspaper cutting-books, 1897–1904, 1922–1967.
Kingsmill Moore correspondence.
T. N. Deane & Son, plans for CITC, 1890–1900.
Chapel Trust, 1933, Saorstát Éireann High Court of Justice.
Programme of the 'Great Bazaar', 1886.

'The Centenary Ode' (1911), C. O. Grandison.

Copy of the college song 'God's Work is Ours' (words by the Rev. H. Kingsmill Moore M.A., Principal, music by Charles O. Grandison, professor of instrumental music) (London, n.d.).

College photographs.

B. Representative Church Body Library

CHURCH EDUCATION SOCIETY RECORDS

MS. 8 (Committee proceedings book, 1873–1901.)

MS. 19 (Sub-committees rough proceedings book, 1839–1854.)

MS. 47 (Applicants for admission to the training school, 1855–81.)

MS. 48 (Register of male and female teachers, 1855–83.)

MS. 49 (Applications for schoolmasters and schoolmistresses.)

C. Trinity College, Dublin Library

MSS. Mun V/5 21–23 (T.C.D. Board registers, 1921–23.)

MSS. 2388–93 (J. H. Bernard correspondence.)

D. Public Record Office, Dublin

MS. 5626 Kildare Place Society. Documents relating to the Educational Endowments (Ireland) Act, 1885.

F. Unpublished theses

Coolahan, John, 'Curricular policy for the primary and secondary schools of Ireland 1900–35', Ph.D. thesis, University of Dublin, 1973.

Hyland, A., 'An analysis of the administration and financing of National and Secondary education in Ireland, 1850–1922', Ph.D. thesis, University of Dublin, 1982.

Hyland, A., 'Educational innovation—a case history. An analysis of the revised programme of 1900 for national schools in Ireland', M.Ed. thesis, University of Dublin, 1973.

Parkes, S. M., 'Teacher training in Ireland, 1811–1870', M.Litt. thesis, University of Dublin, 1970.

Revington, C., 'The Kildare Place Society, its principles and policy', M.Ed. thesis, University of Dublin, 1981.

Wilkinson, W. R., 'Educational Endowments (Ireland) Act and its implementation in intermediate schools of public foundation in Ulster, 1885–1900', M.Ed. thesis, University of Dublin, 1982.

Williams, P. C., 'Pestalozzi John', Ph.D. thesis, University of Dublin, 1965.

II PRINTED SOURCES

A. Official Publications

Bill to amend the law relating to the Buildings of National Schools, Industrial Schools and Training Colleges in Ireland; H.C. 1884 (45.) VII. 55.

Bill to provide for the reimbursement to Training Colleges in Ireland of certain past expenditure on their Sites, Buildings, Appurtenances, Premises and Fixtures; H.C. 1890–91 (391.) X. 421.

Bill to improve National Education In Ireland; H.C. 1892 (234.) V. 645.

Bill to make further provision with respect to Education in Ireland; and for other purposes connected therewith; H.C. 1919 (214.) I. 407.

Fourteenth Report of the Commissioners of the Board of Education in Ireland; H.C. 1812–13 (21.) VI. 221.

First Report of the Commissioners of Irish Education Inquiry; H.C. 1825 (400.) XII. 1.

Second Report of the Commissioners of Irish Education Inquiry; H.C. 1826–27 (12.) XII. 1.

Report from the Select Committee of the House of Lords appointed to inquire into the practical working of the system of national education in Ireland; with minutes of evidence; Part I; H.C. 1854 (525) XV. Part I.i., Part II; 1854 (525.) XV. Part II.i.

Report of the Commissioners appointed to inquire into the nature and extent of the instruction afforded by several institutions in Ireland for the purpose of Elementary or Primary education; also into the practical working of the system of National Education in Ireland; Vols I–III; H.C. 1870 (C.–6VII) XXVIII. Parts I–V.

Report of the Commissioners on Intermediate Education (Ireland); with Appendix; H.C. 1899 (C.9116, C.9117) XXII. 175; 1899 (C.9512) XXIII. 1; 1899 (C.9513) XXIV. 1.

Royal Commission on Manual and Practical Instruction in Primary Schools under the Board of National Education in Ireland; H.C. 1897 (C.8383) XLIII. 1; 1898 (C.8928) XLIV. 77.

Report of Mr. F. H. Dale, His Majesty's Inspector of Schools, Board of Education on Primary Education in Ireland; H.C. 1904 (Cd.1981) XX. 947.

Report of the Vice-Regal Committee of Enquiry into Primary Education in Ireland; H.C. 1913 (Cd.6828) XXII. 231; 1914 (Cd. 7228) XXVIII. 1.

Report of the Vice-Regal Committee of Enquiry into Primary Education (Ireland), 1918; H.C. (Cmd.60) XXI. 741; 1919 (Cmd.178) XXI. 789.

Letter from the Secretary for Ireland to his Grace the Duke of Leinster, on the formation of a Board of Education; H.C. 1831–32 (196.) XXIX. 757.

Correspondence between the Government and the Commissioners of National Education on the subject of the organization and government of training and model schools; H.C. 1866 (456.) LV. 213.

Correspondence between the Government and the Commissioners of National Education upon the subject of the proposals with respect to the training and model schools contained in the letter of the Rt. Hon. C. P. Fortescue M.P., to the Commissioners, dated 19th June, 1866; minutes and memorandum upon the subject; 1867 (225.) LV. 747.

Letter from the Lord Lieutenant of Ireland to the Commissioners of National Education in Ireland, relating to the salaries, pensions and residences of the national teachers, and their reply; 1857 (70.) LIX. 489.

Memorials from the Council of the National Education League for Ireland . . . and from the Elementary Education Committee of the General Assembly of the Presbyterian Church in Ireland on the subject of non-vested training colleges; H.C. 1875 (210.) LIX. 509.

Correspondence between the Irish Government and the Commissioners of National Education on the subject of Training Schools in Ireland; H.C. 1883 (144.) LIII. 471.

Memorial from the Elementary Education Committee of the Presbyterian Church in Ireland on Training Schools; H.C. 1883 (181.) LIII. 465.

Correspondence between the Irish Government and the National Education Commissioners for Ireland, with Proceedings of the Commissioners, in relation to certain proposed changes in the Rules (relating to Religious Instruction) under which Grants are made by Parliament for Elementary Education in Ireland; H.C. 1893–94 (55.) LXVIII. 657; 1895 (324.) LXXVII. 527; 1896 (89.) LXVI. 1.

Returns relating to Training Colleges aided by the Board, for each year since their opening showing length of Course of training, grants expenditure, number trained, average cost of each Queen's Scholar who completed the course, and the number who have since obtained charge of Public Elementary Schools in Ireland; also the titles, functions, salaries, etc. of the professional staff: similar return for the Marlborough-street Training College for the five years ending 1890, with the religious denominations of the Queen's Scholars in residence there; with summaries and averages; H.C. 1892 (260–Sess.1.) LXI. 1.

Return showing the total cost to the state of the following Training Colleges, viz. Kildare Place, Dublin; Drumcondra, Dublin; Baggot Street, Dublin; Waterford Training College; Belfast Female Training College; Limerick Female Training College, for the five years ended 31st December, 1904; H.C. 1904 (152.) LX. 501.

Return giving the names of the training colleges in Ireland, on behalf of which application was made to the Commissioners of National Education within the last three years to sanction an increase in the number of King's Scholars which each such college was authorized to admit to training; the number of King's Scholars in each such case; the increased number of King's Scholars asked to be authorized for admission in each case; the decisions of the Commissioners, and the increase authorized; H.C. 1902 (288.) LXXI. 73.

National Programme of Primary Education (Dublin, 1922).
Report of the Second National Programme Conference (Dublin, 1926).
Revised Programme of Primary Instruction (Dublin, 1933).
An Roinn Oideachais, Programme for Students in Training, 1927–28.
An Roinn Oideachais, Programme for Students in Training, 1933–34.
Final Report of the Departmental Committee on the Educational Services in Northern Ireland (Belfast, 1923).

B. Annual Reports

Annual Reports of the Society for Promoting the Education of the Poor in Ireland, 1812–50.
Annual Reports of the Church Education Society, 1839–1900.
Annual Reports of the Commissioners of National Education in Ireland, 1831–1921.
Annual Reports of the Department of Education, 1922–63.
Annual Reports of the Northern Ireland Ministry of Education, 1922–30.
Journal of the General Synod of the Church of Ireland, 1870–1960.
Dublin University Calendar, 1898–1960.

C. Newspapers

Irish Times.
The Irish Independent.
Freeman's Journal.
The Irish Teachers' Journal.
The Irish School Weekly.
Church of Ireland Gazette
Church of Ireland Training College Magazine

III CONTEMPORARY BOOKS AND PAMPHLETS TO 1920

Bell, Robert, *National education in Ireland, some thoughts on the past history and present position of the question at issue between the adherents of the government system and the supporters of Scriptural education* (Dublin, 1850).
Brooke, W. G., *Statement of the proceedings from 1892–1895 in connection with admission of women to Trinity College, Dublin* (Dublin, 1895). 1895).
Cooke, J., *Elementary geography for Irish Schools* (Dublin, 1900).
Cooke, J., *Murray's handbook for travellers in Ireland* (London, 1896).
Cooke, J. (ed.), *Wakeman's handbook of Irish antiquities* (London, 1903).
Cooke, J. (ed.), *Meiklejohn's English literature—a new history and survey from Saxon times to the death of Tennyson* (Dublin and London, 1904).

Cooke, John (ed.), *The Dublin book of Irish verse* 1728–1909 (Dublin and London, 1909).
Culverwell, E. P., *Elementary Mechanics* (London, 1890).
Culverwell, E. P., *The Montessori principles and practice* (London, 1913).
Curwen, John, *Singing for schools and congregations* (London, 1843).
Curwen, John, *The Pupil's Manual of the Tonic Solfa method of teaching to sing* (London, 1852).
Dickinson, H. H., *Primary education in Ireland, the present crisis* (Dublin, 1896).
The Dublin spelling book (Dublin, n.d.).
The Dublin reading book (Dublin, n.d.).
The Education Controversy "Who should throw Stones?" (Dublin, 1860).
Elrington, C. R., *A few suggestions addressed to the clergy upon the present state of the question of National Education* (Dublin, 1847).
Emly, Archdeacon of, *An address delivered to the schoolmasters and schoolmistresses under the Church Education Society* (Dublin, 1850).
Falkiner, F. R., *The foundation of the Hospital and Free School of King Charles II* (Dublin, 1906).
The gateway to learning, by a practical K. G. teacher (Dublin, n.d.).
How, F. D., *William Conyngham Plunket* (London, 1900).
Jellett, H., *The Education Question, a letter to the clergy of the united diocese of Cork, Cloyne and Ross* (Dublin, 1860).
Joyce, P. W., *A handbook of school management and methods of teaching* (Dublin, 1863).
"Laicus", *Have we any national Scriptural education in Ireland, or are we likely to have it?* (Dublin, 1860).
Lloyd, H., *The Education Question* (Dublin, 1860).
Mayo, Charles, *Lessons on numbers, as given in a Pestalozzian school, Cheam, Surrey* (London, 1831).
Mayo, Charles & Elizabeth, *Practical remarks on infant education* (London, 1837).
Mayo, Elizabeth, *Lessons on objects* (London, 1831).
Miller G., *The case of the Church Education Society of Ireland argued in reply to Charles Richard Elrington, D.D.* (London, 1847).
Moore, H. Kingsmill, *Fundamental principles of education applied to Sunday school work* (Dublin, 1889).
Moore, H. Kingsmill, *Class teaching for Sunday school teachers* (Dublin, 1888).
Moore, H. Kingsmill. *The training of infants with especial reference to the Sunday school* (London, 1910).
Moore, H. Kingsmill, *The way to teach the Bible, according to the method in use at the Church of Ireland Training College* (Dublin, 1906).
Moore, H. Kingsmill, *An Irish history for young readers* (London, 1914).
Moore, H. Kingsmill, *£200,000 a year for Irish education, how may it best be spent? Written at the request of the Standing Committee of the General*

Synod of the Church of Ireland (Dublin, 1891).
Moore, H. Kingsmill, *An unwritten chapter in the history of education, being the history of the Society for Promoting the Education of the Poor in Ireland generally known as the Kildare Place Society* (London, 1904).
Moore, H. Kingsmill, *Statistics of schools in connection with the Church of Ireland in the Province of Dublin, compiled for the Standing Committee of the General Synod of the Church of Ireland* (Dublin, 1897).
Pestalozzi, J. H. *How Gertrude teaches her children*, trans. L. E. Holland and E. C. Turner (London, 1894).
Plunket, W. C., *A short visit to the Connemara missions* (London, 1863).
Plunket, W. C., *Church and census in Ireland* (Dublin, 1865).
The present state of the controversy between the National Board and the Church Education Society (Dublin, 1860).
Resolution of the conference of Church of Ireland managers of National schools, 1903 (Dublin, 1903).
Robinson, Bessie, *The kindergarten practice for the use of teachers* (Belfast, 1887).
The Schoolmaster's Manual (Dublin, 1825).
Speeches delivered by the Lord Bishop of Ossory and Ferns and the Lord Bishop of Cashel at the annual meeting of the Church Education Society in Ireland (Dublin, 1850).
Starkie, W. J. M., *Recent reforms in Irish education* (Dublin, 1902).
Steele, L. E. (ed.), *Sir Richard Steele, essays: selected and edited* (London, 1902).
Steele, L. E. (ed.), *Sir Richard Steele, selection from the Tatler* (London, 1896).
Taylor, W. Cooke, *Notes on a visit to the model schools in Dublin, and reflections on the state of the education question in Ireland suggested by that visit* (Dublin, 1847).
Tristram, J. W., *'A False Alarm', a brief examination of Dean Dickinson's pamphlet on 'The Present Crisis'* (Dublin, 1896).
Wilkinson, W. T., *The training of teachers, a course of lectures in education* (Dublin, n.d.).
Willock, W. A., *'Truth of both sides' National Education and the Church Education Society, with a proposed solution to the present difficulty* (Dublin, 1859).
Woodward, H., *Thoughts on the points at issue between the established church at the National Board of Education in Ireland* (London, 1884).

IV LATER WORKS

Akenson, D. H., *The Irish Education Experiment* (London, 1970).
Akenson, D. H., *Education and Enmity, the control of schooling in Northern Ireland* (Newton Abbot, 1973).

Akenson, D. H., *A mirror to Kathleen's face: education in independent Ireland, 1922–60* (Montreal and London, 1975).
Akenson, D. H., *The Church of Ireland, ecclesiastical reform and revolution, 1800–1885* (New Haven and London, 1971).
Beattie, J., *Brief history of the Kildare Place Training College, 1811–1921* (n.d.).
Birchenough, C., *History of elementary education* (London, 1932).
Bowen, D., *The Protestant Crusade in Ireland*, 1800–70 (Dublin, 1978).
Brock, W. E., *H. E. Armstrong and the teaching of science, 1880–1930* (London, 1973).
Browne, J. D. & Parkes, S. M., 'Annie Lloyd Evans', *History of Education Society Bulletin*, No. 29 (Spring 1982), pp. 36–40.
Clayton, H., *To school without shoes, a brief history of the Sunday School Society for Ireland* (Dublin, 1979).
Cholmondeley, E., *The story of Charlotte Mason* (London, 1960).
Churchill, W. S., *Lord Randolph Churchill* (London, 1951).
Coolahan, John, *Irish Education, history and structure* (Dublin, 1981).
Coolahan, John, 'The education bill of 1919,—problems of educational reform' *Proceedings of Educational Studies Association of Ireland* (Galway, 1980).
Fynne, R. J., *Montessori and her inspirers* (London, 1924).
Fynne, R. J. (ed.), *Modern teaching: a first book*, 6 vols. (Dublin, 1938–40).
Goldstrom, J. M., *The social content of education* 1808–72: *a study of Irish school text-books* (Shannon, 1972).
Hurley, M. (ed.), *Irish Anglicanism*, 1869–1969 (Dublin, 1969).
Lawrence, E. (ed.), *Friedrich Froebel and English Education* (London, 1952).
McCann, W. P., *Samuel Wilderspin and infant education* (London, 1982).
McCann, W. P. & Stewart, W.A.C., *The Educational Innovators, 1750–1880*, Vol. I (London, 1967).
McDowell, R. B., *The Church of Ireland, 1869–1969* (London, 1975).
McElligott, T. J., *Secondary education in Ireland*, 1810–1921 (Dublin, 1981).
McIvor, J., *The Presbyterian Church and education* (Dublin, 1968).
Marshall, R., *A history of Stranmillis College, Belfast* (Belfast, 1972).
Miller, D. H., *Church, State and Nation in Ireland, 1898–1921* (Dublin, 1973).
Milne, K., 'Irish Charter Schools', *Irish Journal of Education* (1984) viii 1, 3–29.
Moore, H. Kingsmill, *Reminiscences and reflections from some sixty years of life in Ireland* (London, 1930).
Moore, H. Kingsmill, *Ireland and her church, a short history of the Church of Ireland* (Dundalk, 1937).
Moore, H. Kingsmill, *The work of the Incorporated Society for Promoting Protestant Schools in Ireland* (Dundalk, 1938).

Moore, H. Kingsmill, *The teaching of Our Lord with reference to finance* (Dundalk, 1942).

Moore, H. Kingsmill, *Joys of the garden, month by month* (Dublin, 1936).

O'Connell, T. J., *One hundred years of progress, 1868—1968* (Dublin, 1968).

O'Dwyer F., *Lost Dublin* (Dublin, 1980).

O'Heideáin, E., *National school inspection in Ireland: the beginnings* (Dublin, 1967).

Our Lady of Mercy College centenary booklet, 1877—1977 (Dublin, 1977).

Parkes, S. M., *Guide to sources in the history of education, No. 5, Irish education in the British Parliamentary Papers, 1801—1920* (Lancaster and Cork, 1977).

Parkes, S. M., 'The founding of a denominational training college—the Church of Ireland Training College, 1878—1884', *Proceedings of the Educational Studies Association of Ireland* (Limerick, 1980).

Patton, H., *Fifty years of disestablishment* (Dublin, 1922).

Phillips, W. A. (ed.), *History of the Church of Ireland from earliest times to the present day*. 3 vols. (London, 1933).

The Report of the Church of Ireland conference held in Dublin, 11th—14th October, 1932, to which is appended an account of the Commemoration by the Church of Ireland of the 1500th anniversary of the landing of St. Patrick in Ireland (Dublin, 1932).

Rich, R. W., *The training of teachers in England and Wales, during the nineteenth century* (London, 1933).

Sadie, Stanley (ed.), *A new Grove dictionary of music and musicians* (London, 1980).

St. Patrick's College, Drumcondra centenary booklet, 1875—1975 (Dublin, 1975).

Salmon, D. (ed.), *The practical parts of Lancaster's "Improvements" and Bell's "Experiments"* (London, 1922).

Seaver, G., *John Allen Fitzgerald Gregg* (Dublin, 1963).

Selleck, R. J. W., *The new education: the English background, 1870—1914* (Melbourne, 1968).

Silber, K., *Pestalozzi: the man and his work* (London, 1966).

Stewart, W. A. C., *Progressives and radicals in English education, 1750—1970* (London, 1970).

Thom's Irish Who's Who (Dublin, 1923).

Two centenary lectures, Carysfort College, 1877—1977 (Dublin, 1981).

Walsh, P. J., *William J. Walsh, archbishop of Dublin* (Dublin, 1928).

Williams, P. C., 'Pestalozzi and John Synge', *Hermathena* (1968), cvi, 23—39.

Whiteside, L., *A history of the King's Hospital* (Dublin, 1975).

Who was who, 1897—1915 (London, 1967).

INDEX

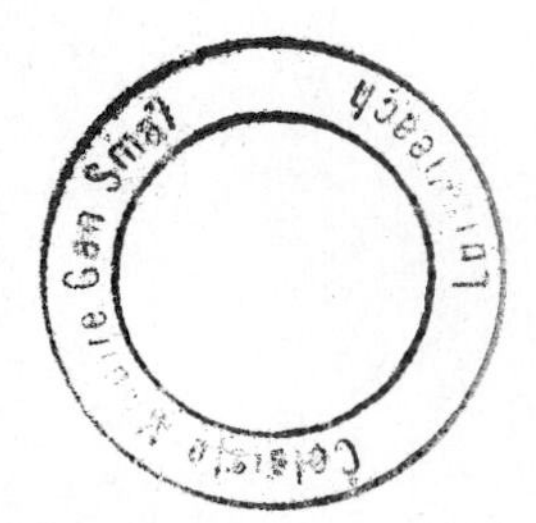